MW01676217

THE POCKET GUIDE TO

WILD FLOWERS OF NORTH AMERICA

THE POCKET GUIDE TO
WILD FLOWERS
OF NORTH AMERICA

PAMELA FOREY

DRAGON'S WORLD

Dragon's World Ltd
Limpsfield
Surrey RH8 0DY
Great Britain

First published by Dragon's World 1990

© Dragon's World 1990
© Text Pamela Forey 1990
© Illustrations Norman Barber, Angela Beard, Richard Bell, Alma Hathaway, Roger Kent, David More, Susanna Stuart-Smith and David Thelwell, all of Bernard Thornton Artists, London 1990

All rights reserved

No part of this book may be reproduced or transmitted in any form or by any means, electronic or mechanical, including photocopying, recording, or any information storage and retrieval system, without permission in writing from Dragon's World Ltd, except by a reviewer who may quote brief passages in a review.

Editor: Trish Burgess
Designer: Ann Doolan
Editorial Director: Pippa Rubinstein

British Library Cataloguing in Publication Data

Forey, Pamela
The pocket guide to wild flowers of North America
1.North America. Flowering plants
I.Title
582'.13'097

ISBN 1 85028 108 4

Typeset by Action Typesetting Ltd, Gloucester

Printed in Singapore

Contents

INTRODUCTION AND KEY 7

Nettle family 12
Smartweed or Buckwheat family 12
Pokeweed family 16
Four-o clock family 16
Goosefoot family 18
Amaranth family 19
Purslane family 20
Pink family 22
Cactus family 26
Buttercup or Crowfoot family 30
Barberry family 38
Lizard's Tail family 39
Water Lily family 40
Sundew family 41
Birthwort family 42
St John's-wort family 42
Fumitory family 44
Poppy family 45
Caper family 47
Mustard family 48
Saxifrage family 54
Rose family 58
Pea and Bean family 64
Geranium family 76
Wood Sorrel family 78
Touch-me-not family 79
Flax family 80
Spurge family 80
Mallow family 82
Violet family 86
Rockrose family 88
Passion Flower family 88
Gourd or Cucumber family 89
Stickleaf family 90
Loosestrife family 91
Evening Primrose family 92
Meadow Beauty family 98
Ginseng family 98
Carrot or Parsley family 100
Wintergreen family 106
Indian Pipe family 107

Heath family 108
Crowberry family 110
Leadwort family 111
Primrose family 112
Gentian family 116
Buckbean family 118
Dogbane family 118
Milkweed family 120
Bedstraw or Madder family 122
Phlox family 124
Morning Glory family 128
Waterleaf family 130
Forget-me-not or Borage family 132
Mint family 136
Nightshade family 142
Snapdragon or Figwort family 144
Broomrape family 152
Plantain family 153
Vervain family 154
Acanthus family 154
Lopseed family 155
Moschatel family 155
Honeysuckle family 156
Valerian family 156
Teasel family 157
Bellflower or Bluebell family 158
Sunflower or Daisy family 160
Water Plantain family 194
Agave family 195
Lily family 196
Amaryllis family 205
Iris family 206
Cattail family 208
Yellow-eyed Grass family 208
Spiderwort family 209
Arum family 210
Orchid family 212

GLOSSARY 219

ACKNOWLEDGMENTS 230

INDEX 231

Introduction

Wild flowers are beautiful, and they form part of our wildlife heritage. Whether they are rare species confined to small areas, or widespread weeds, all have something of interest about them. They can be enjoyed in many ways — in the open on summer vacations, or in the winter by browsing through guides like this one.

This book can be used to identify plants in the field with the help of the Key to the Flower Families. It is also a source of fascinating information. There are far too many species in North America for all to be included in a book of this size, but plants from all parts of the U.S. and Canada, and from the vast majority of plant families are represented.

To identify a plant using the key, you are provided with a series of alternatives, the object being to lead you to one of the flower families. The number at the end of each paragraph refers you to the next paragraph you should read in your search. It is a bit like following a maze with many endings. Once you reach a family name, turn to the relevant page(s) and check there to find your plant.

A floral key can look daunting, especially if the language is unfamiliar. But finding a wild flower and tracking it down through a key is an extremely satisfying experience. All the terms which might be strange are explained in the glossary at the back of the book.

Key to the Flower Families

1 Plants that have their flower parts in 3's, and their leaves have parallel veins. Their name comes from the fact that their seeds contain only 1 seed leaf or cotyledon.
Monocotyledons 2

Plants that have their flower parts in 4's, 5's, or have numerous flower parts, and that have net-like veins, not parallel veins, in their leaves. Their name comes from the fact that their seeds contain 2 seed leaves or cotyledons.
Dicotyledons 6

Monocotyledons

2 Flowers with 3 similar sepals, 2 similar petals (sometimes all 5 are alike), and a central, hanging lip. *Orchid fam.* p. 212.

Flowers not as above. 3

3 Flowers borne in a tight cylindrical spike. *Arum fam.* p. 210, *Cattail fam.* p. 208.

Flowers yellow, borne in a cone-like spike of woody bracts. *Yellow-eyed Grass fam.* p. 208.

Flowers not borne in a tight cylindrical spike or spike of woody bracts. 4

4 Desert plants, usually shrubs, with fleshy or fibrous leaves, and fleshy flowers. *Agave fam.* p. 195.
Aquatic plants, with many carpels in the center of each flower, and fruits formed of many achenes. *Water Plantain fam.* p. 194.
Herbaceous plants, not as above. 5

5 Ovary superior. *Lily fam.* p. 196, *Spiderwort fam.* p. 209.
Ovary inferior. *Amaryllis fam.* p. 205, *Iris fam.* p. 206

Dicotyledons

6 Plants without chlorophyll. *Broomrape fam.* p. 152, *Indian Pipe fam.* p. 107, *Morning Glory fam.* p. 128.
Green plants. 7

7 Petals free from each other, not united into a tube; or petals absent. 8
Petals united into a tube, at least at the base. 32

8 Flowers regular. 9
Flowers bilaterally symmetrical. 31

9 Center of flower often has corona of several rows of filaments, and 3–5 styles, often on a stalk. *Passion Flower fam.* p. 88.
Flowers not as above. 10

10 Flowers small, with tiny calyx and 5 petals, borne in umbels. *Carrot fam.* p. 100, *Ginseng fam.* p. 98.
Flowers not borne in such umbels. 11

11 Sepals and petals both absent. 12
Petals and sepals both present, or petals present, or sepals present. 13

12 Flowers hermaphrodite, borne in spikes. Stamens 6–8. *Lizard's Tail fam.* p. 39.
Flowers hermaphrodite, or male and female flowers on separate plants. Stamens many. *Buttercup fam.* p. 30.
Flowers minute; male and female flowers separate but on same plant, and consisting of 1 stamen and 1 carpel. *Spurge fam.* p. 80.

13 Petals absent. Sepals may be green and sepal-like, or may be colored and resemble petals. In either event, only 1 whorl of perianth segments is present. 14
Petals and sepals present. Petals 4 or 5. 17
Petals and sepals present. Petals more than 5, and may be numerous. 29

14 Leaves with distinctive sheathing stipules at the base. *Smartweed fam.* p. 12.
Leaves without sheathing stipules. 15

15 Flowers green and tiny, borne in spikes, or dangling in leaf axils. Male and female flowers often separate. 16
Flowers are not green and tiny. 17

16 Stipules present. *Nettle fam.* p. 12, *Spurge fam.* p. 80.
Stipules absent. *Goosefoot fam.* p. 18, *Amaranth fam.* p. 19.

17 Stamens numerous, fruit of many achenes or several pods. *Buttercup fam.* p. 30.
Stamens 5–10, fruit a capsule. *Saxifrage fam.* p. 54.
Stamens 5–30, fruit a berry. *Pokeweed fam.* p. 16.
Stamens 2–4, fruit a berry. *Crowberry fam.* p. 110.

18 Flowers with 4 petals. 19
Flowers with 5 petals. 20

19 Flowers with numerous stamens. *Poppy fam.* p. 45, *Caper fam.* p 47.
Flowers with 6 stamens. *Mustard fam.* p. 48.
Flowers with 4 or 8 stamens. *Evening Primrose fam.* p. 92, *Meadow Beauty fam.* p. 98.

20 Male and female flowers separate, stamens 1–5 and united, fruit a fleshy berry. *Gourd fam.* p. 89.
Flowers hermaphrodite, not as above. 21

21 Stamens numerous. 22
Stamens 10 or less. 25

22 Ovary inferior, stamens free or in bundles opposite petals. *Stickleaf fam.* p. 90.
Ovary superior. 23

23 Stamens joined at the base to form a tube, fruit a capsule or formed of many segments, often in a ring. *Mallow fam.* p. 82.
Stamens free or united into bundles. 24

24 Fruit formed of many separate achenes or a cluster of pods. *Buttercup fam.* p. 30.
Fruit a capsule. *St John's-wort fam.* p. 42, *Poppy fam.* p. 45, *Rockrose fam.* p. 88, *Purslane fam.* p. 20.

25 Ovary inferior. *Evening Primrose fam.* p. 92.
Ovary superior. 26

26 Fruits in sections, each section containing a single seed, and with a long "beak" formed from the style. *Geranium fam.* p. 76.
Fruits are capsules, not as above. 27

27 Leaves clover-like, with 3 jointed leaflets which often close downward at night. *Wood Sorrel fam.* p. 78.
Leaves not as above. 28

28 Leaves alternate or in basal rosette. *Saxifrage fam.* p. 54, *Flax fam.* p. 80, *Purslane fam.* p. 20, *Wintergreen fam.* p. 106.
Leaves opposite or in distinct whorls. *Pink fam.* p. 22, *Loosestrife fam.* p. 91, *Purslane fam.* p. 20.

29 Succulent, spiny, desert plants, without leaves. *Cactus fam.* p. 26.
Floating aquatic plants. *Water Lily fam.* p. 40.
Not as either above. 30

30 Stamens numerous. *Buttercup fam.* p. 30, *Poppy fam.* p. 45.

Stamens 4–8. *Barberry fam.* p. 38, *Loosestrife fam.* p. 91, *Purslane fam.* p. 20.

31 Flower with 5 petals, 1 large one at the back, 1 at each side, and 2 forming a keel. Fruit is a pod. *Pea fam.* p. 64.

Flower with 5 petals, 1 large upper one, and 2 on each side fused together. One of the sepals is spurred. Fruit an explosive capsule. *Touch-me-not fam.* p. 79.

Flower with 4 petals, outer 2 spurred, joined at tips, inner 2 often joined. Brittle plants with watery juice. *Fumitory fam.* p. 44.

Flower with 5 petals, the lowermost spurred. Fruit a capsule. *Violet fam.* p. 86.

Flower hooded or spurred. Fruit a cluster of pods. *Buttercup fam.* p. 30.

32 Flowers in distinctive four-sided heads, 1 flower on each side and 1 on the top. *Moschatel*

Flowers not as above. 33

33 Flowers in heads made up of many smaller flowers, each head subtended by an involucre of bracts and resembling a single flower. Fruits are hard, single-seeded achenes. *Sunflower fam.* p. 160.

Flowers in heads of many smaller flowers, each flower subtended by an epicalyx and a bract. Fruits are hard, single-seeded achenes, enclosed in epicalyx. *Teasel fam.* p. 157.

Flowers not in heads as above. 34

34 Flowers without petals, calyx corolla-like (therefore only 1 perianth whorl present). 35

Flowers with both sepals and petals. 36

35 Flowers regular, with long tubular calyx which looks like a corolla. *Four-o'clock fam.*

Flowers bilaterally symmetrical, with three-lobed, corolla-like calyx. *Birthwort fam.* p. 42.

36 Flowers tiny, green and inconspicuous, in spikes. *Plantain fam.* p. 153.

Flowers not as above. 37

37 Flowers regular and tubular. 38

Flowers bilaterally symmetrical, tubular, often two-lipped. 48

38 Flowers with a crown or corona between the petals and stamens. Anthers of stamens joined together in pairs. *Milkweed fam.* p. 120.

Flowers not as above. 39

39 Twining or climbing plants. Stems contain milky juice. *Morning Glory fam.* p. 128.

Plants not as above. 40

40 Inflorescence is a coiled, one-sided cluster, which straightens as it ages. Fruit

consists of 4 nutlets. *Forget-me-not fam.* p. 132.
Not as above. 41

41 Ovary inferior. 42
Ovary superior. 43

42 Fruit dry and one-seeded, or a berry. Leaves opposite. *Honeysuckle fam.* p. 156.
Fruit a capsule. Leaves opposite or in whorls. *Bedstraw fam.* p. 122.
Fruit a capsule. Leaves alternate. Plants have milky juice *Bellflower fam.* p. 158.

43 Small, woody shrubs. Flowers have 5 fused petals and 10 stamens. *Heath fam.* p. 108.
Herbaceous plants. Flowers have as many stamens as petal lobes, or stamens may be numerous. 44

44 Stamens as many as and opposite petal lobes, or numerous. *Purslane fam.* p. 20, *Leadwort fam.* p. 111, *Primrose fam.* p. 112.
Stamens alternating with corolla lobes 45

45 Fruit consists of 2 pods. *Dogbane fam.* p. 118.
Fruit is a capsule or berry. 46

46 Aquatic plants with showy flowers and alternate leaves. *Buckbean fam.* p. 118.
Terrestrial plants, or if marsh plants, then leaves opposite. 47

47 Corolla lobes 4 – 12, leaves entire, opposite, and often connected across the stem; ovary with 1 cell and a single style. *Gentian fam.* p. 116.
Corolla lobes 5, leaves simple, alternate; ovary with 2 cells and single style. *Nightshade fam.* p. 142.
Corolla lobes 5, leaves simple or compound, alternate or opposite; ovary with 3 cells and a single style. *Phlox fam.* p. 124.
Corolla lobes 5, leaves in basal rosette or alternate; ovary with 1 or 2 cells and 2 styles. *Waterleaf fam.* p. 130.

48 At least the terminal branches of the stems four-angled. 49
Stems not four-angled. 50

49 Fruit consists of 4 nutlets. *Mint fam.* p. 136, *Vervain fam.* p. 154.
Fruit dry and indehiscent, hanging downward on stem and enclosed in calyx. *Lopseed fam.* p. 155.

50 Ovary inferior. 51
Ovary superior. *Snapdragon fam.* p. 144, *Acanthus fam.* p. 154.

51 Fruit dry and indehiscent, with single seed. *Valerian fam.* p. 156.
Fruit a capsule or berry *Honeysuckle fam.* p. 156, *Bellflower fam.* p. 158.

Stinging Nettle
Urtica dioica

Nettle family

Urticaceae Herbs and shrubs with about 45 genera and 550 species, mostly in the tropics. Many have stinging hairs. Some are weeds. Some produce useful fibers, others are grown as house-plants.

Family Features Flowers borne in clusters, tiny, unisexual. Petals 0; calyx has 4 or 5 lobes; stamens opposite calyx lobes in male flowers; ovary superior in female flowers. Leaves simple, either opposite or alternate.

Stinging Nettle, *Urtica dioica*, grows in waste places in much of North America. It is a perennial plant, colonizing wide areas. It has erect, four-angled stems and opposite, toothed leaves, all covered with stinging hairs. Tiny greenish flowers are borne in clusters in leaf axils; male and female flowers grow on separate plants.

Sheep Sorrel
Rumex acetosella

Smartweed or Buckwheat family

Polygonaceae Herbs and shrubs with about 40 genera and 800 species, mainly found in temperate regions of the world. Several are good garden plants; others are weeds. A few, like Buckwheat and Rhubarb, are food plants.

Family Features Flowers in conspicuous inflorescences; small. Perianth segments 3–6, may look like petals or sepals; stamens 4–9; ovary superior. Fruits hard, dry, often enclosed in perianth segments. Leaves simple, usually alternate, with distinctive sheathing stipules (ochreae).

There are many **Docks** and **Sorrels**, *Rumex* species, in North America. The most familiar are European plants which have become weeds in waste places, fields and yards. Many native species grow in wet places, on shores and beside streams, in marshes and wet woods.

Curled Dock
Rumex crispus

Sheep Sorrel, *Rumex acetosella*, also called Common or Red Sorrel, is naturalized in acid soils in waste land, fields and yards in most of North America. It is a perennial plant with leaves which resemble spearheads, and leafy flowering stems up to 1ft tall. Male and female flowers are borne on separate plants, in whorls on the branched flowering stems. The fruits are three-sided, golden brown nutlets, conspicuous in their large numbers. The leaves of this plant are acid and eaten in salads.

Curled Dock, *Rumex crispus*, also called Sour Dock, is another perennial weed of roadsides, fields and waste ground throughout the U.S. and southern Canada, often found with Stinging Nettles. Its leaves are recommended as a remedy for nettle stings, and were at one time used to dress burns. Curled Dock leaves grow up to 1ft long, and have curly "crisped" edges. The flowering stems grow up to 3ft tall, with whorls of greenish flowers followed by three-angled green fruits. Each fruit has three red tubercles, one in each angle, and one larger than the others.

Bitter Dock
Rumex obtusifolius

Bitter Dock or Broad-leaved Dock, *Rumex obtusifolius*, is yet another common weed from Europe, growing in moist waste places in many parts of the U.S. and southern Canada. It is similar to Curled Dock, but the edges of its broad leaves are wavy, not curly, and there is only one large red tubercle on each three-angled fruit.

Smartweed or Buckwheat family

Polygonum is a large genus with about 170 species throughout the world; they are known as knotweeds, smartweeds, and bistorts. Many are grown in gardens, others are weeds.

Lady's Thumb
Polygonum persicaria

Lady's Thumb, *Polygonum persicaria*, grows as a weed in moist places, in cultivated and waste ground, and on roadsides in much of North America. It is a hairless annual plant, with branched reddish stems, characteristically swollen above each node. It has small, lance-shaped leaves, each with a single black blotch and a fringed ochrea. Its many pink flowers grow in dense cylindrical spikes on erect leafless, flowering stems.

Knotweed
Polygonum aviculare

Knotweed, *Polygonum aviculare*, grows as a weed throughout the world, absent only from the polar regions, growing in lawns, streets, and waste ground, on beaches and shores. It is a hairless annual plant, often forming prostrate mats, with branched stems up to 6ft long. It has small, linear or lance-shaped leaves with silvery, jagged ochreae and small pinkish flowers in the leaf axils. Dull brown, three-sided fruits are enclosed in persistent perianths.

Mountain Sorrel
Oxyria digyna

Mountain Sorrel, *Oxyria digyna*, grows in rocky places and mountains around the North Pole, south in the Rocky Mountains to Calif. and in the east to N.H. This perennial plant forms clumps of long-stalked leaves with kidney-shaped, rather fleshy blades. In late summer it produces dense clusters of greenish or reddish flowers. The perianth segments turn bright red and persist around the dry winged fruits. The leaves are rich in Vitamin C; they can be used in salads or as a potherb.

There are about 150 **Wild Buckwheats**, *Eriogonum* species, in North America, growing in many dry habitats, mountain ridges, deserts and scrub, hills, plains, and badlands, almost all in the west and midwest. They vary from low-growing, often mat-forming perennial plants to tangled annuals and bushy shrubs.

Sulphur Flower, *Eriogonum umbellatum*, is a perennial, only 1ft tall, with a woody base and a clump of spoon-shaped leaves at the tip of each branch. Bright yellow flowers grow in compound umbels at the tops of long stalks, about 1ft tall. This plant is common on dry slopes and foothills from Calif. to Ore.

Desert Trumpet, *Eriogonum inflatum*, is another perennial, with a rosette of long-stalked, oval leaves and spindly inflorescences of tiny, hairy, yellow flowers. The plant is immediately recognizable from its characteristically swollen and branched flowering stems. This is a conspicuous desert plant in both Mojave and Colorado Deserts, found in scrub, on mesas, and in washes.

Flat-crowned Eriogonum, *Eriogonum deflexum*, is an annual, forming a small basal clump of long-stalked, kidney-shaped, densely woolly leaves, and leafless, widely spreading, branched flowering stems. The small whitish flowers are borne in hanging clusters. This plant grows in desert washes and on their slopes, and in scrub, in Nev. and Ariz.

Sulphur Flower
Eriogonum umbellatum

Desert Trumpet
Eriogonum inflatum

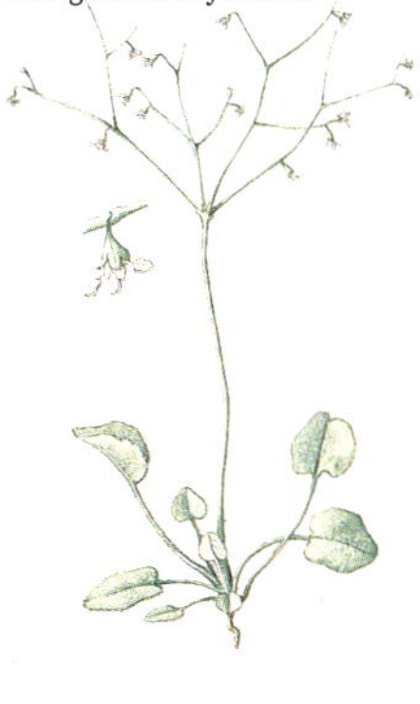

Flat-crowned Eriogonum
Eriogonum deflexum

Pokeweed family

Pokeweed
Phytolacca americana

Phytolaccaceae Herbs, shrubs, and trees with about 15 genera and 100 species, mainly from tropical South America and southern Africa.

Family Features Flowers small, regular; borne in small inflorescences opposite leaves or in leaf axils. Petals 0; sepals 4 or 5; stamens 4 or 5, alternating with sepals, or many stamens; ovary superior, globose with many cells. Fruits fleshy, berry-like. Leaves entire, alternate. Stipules 0.

Pokeweed, *Phytolacca americana*, grows in open areas in damp woods, and on roadsides from Me. to Mich., and south to the Gulf. It is a perennial plant up to 10ft tall, with reddish stems and tapering leaves up to 1ft long. It has a strong, disagreeable scent. Its flowers are borne in vertical clusters; each has greenish-white sepals and a central ovary formed of a ring of about ten sections. The fruits are dark purple berries. Pokeweed is poisonous, but the toxins are not yet present in very young spring shoots, which can be eaten as vegetables.

Four-o'clock family

Desert Sand Verbena
Abronia villosa

Nyctaginaceae A mainly tropical family of herbs, shrubs and trees, with about 30 genera and 300 species, many from America. Some, like bougainvilleas and Marvel of Peru, are spectacular plants for tropical gardens and greenhouses.

Family Features Flowers borne in cymes; hermaphrodite or unisexual; may be surrounded by colored bracts. Petals 0; calyx tubular, corolla-like; stamens 1 to many; ovary superior with 1 cell. Fruits indehiscent. Leaves simple, alternate or opposite.

Desert Sand Verbena, *Abronia villosa*, is a sticky-hairy annual with sprawling stems and opposite trailing leaves. Its fragrant flowers grow in umbels in the leaf axils; each has a long, tubular, rose-purple calyx with a white center. It grows in open sandy places and scrub in Calif., Ariz. and Nev. There are about 18 Sand Verbenas, *Abronia* species, in the west. Many are perennial, often sticky-hairy plants with prostrate stems and white or pink flowers.

Colorado Four o'clock
Mirabilis multiflora

Four-o'clocks, *Mirabilis* species, come mostly from warmer parts of western America, with one species found in the prairies and the east. They are perennial plants of arid and stony places, with opposite leaves and bell-shaped white or pink flowers. The flowers grow in clusters in five-lobed "cups," and open in the evening.

Colorado Four o'clock, *Mirabilis multiflora*, grows in deserts and dry grassland among pinyon and junipers, from Calif. to Tex., and into Mexico. It is a bushy plant, up to 18in tall, with heart-shaped leaves and deep pink flowers. When they open in the evening, the plant can be seen from miles away. This is a medicinal plant, used by the Indians to suppress the appetite.

Windmills
Allionia incarnata

Windmills or Trailing Four o'clock, *Allionia incarnata*, is a desert species of dry stony slopes and scrub, from southern Calif. to Ut. and Tex., south into Mexico. It is a trailing, glandular-hairy plant, with opposite leaves, often one large and one small in each pair. Deep rose-pink flowers are formed in threes, but look like one flower. They open during the day.

Goosefoot family

Chenopodiaceae About 100 genera and over 1400 species of herbs and shrubs, found throughout the world. Many are succulent and grow in arid or salt-rich areas; others are weeds, but some, like beets and spinach, are eaten as vegetables.

Family Features Flowers small or minute, often green; hermaphrodite, or male and female separate; borne in leaf axils or in spikes. Sepals 3–5, fused; petals 0; stamens as many as and opposite the sepals; ovary usually superior. Fruits are tiny nuts. Leaves simple, alternate. Stipules 0.

Lamb's Quarters
Chenopodium album

Oraches, *Atriplex* species, and **Goosefoots,** *Chenopodium* species, are related similar plants. Oraches mostly grow on seashores or in salt marshes, but some grow in waste places, where many of the goosefoots are also found.

Lamb's Quarters, *Chenopodium album*, is an annual weed found in much of the world. It has branched, often reddish stems up to 3ft tall, and diamond-shaped leaves with white bladder-like hairs, especially on the undersides. Dense spikes of tiny greenish flowers grow in the leaf axils in late summer. This plant is edible, and a good substitute for spinach.

Common Orache
Atriplex patula

Common Orache, *Atriplex patula*, is another annual weed, found in waste and saline places in much of the northern hemisphere. It has triangular or arrow-shaped leaves, and tiny, greenish flowers produced in interrupted spikes. It is edible, like spinach.

Russian Tumbleweed or Russian Thistle, *Salsola iberica*, is a tumbleweed, found in the west where it has been introduced from Eurasia. It is a bushy annual plant, with fleshy, spine-tipped leaves and solitary flowers. Each flower has two prickly-pointed bracts. When the fruits form, the calyces become reddish, with membranous wings.

Russian Tumbleweed
Salsola iberica

Amaranth family

Amaranthaceae About 65 genera and 850 species, mostly herbs, mainly from tropical and warm temperate regions. Many are weeds; others, like Love-lies-bleeding, are grown in gardens. The South American Inca Wheat belongs to this family.

Family Features Flowers small, inconspicuous, in dense clusters or spikes, often with membranous bracts; regular, hermaphrodite or unisexual. Sepals 3–5, free or joined at base; petals 0; stamens as many as and opposite sepals; ovary superior with 1 cell. Fruits are membranous, not opening, or opening by a lid. Leaves alternate or opposite, simple and entire. Stipules 0.

Amaranths, genus *Amaranthus*, are a group of about 60 species, found in much of the world. **Pigweed**, *Amaranthus retroflexus*, is an annual weed which grows in gardens and waste places in the U.S. and southern Canada. It has an erect, branched stem up to 6ft tall, with many more or less triangular-ovate leaves, and dense ovoid clusters of green flowers, male and female separate.

Pigweed
Amaranthus retroflexus

Tumbleweed, *Amaranthus albus*, grows in much of North America. When its fruits form, its branched whitish stems dry out, the plant is uprooted and blows in the wind.

Purslane family

Portulacaceae Herbs, often with brightly colored flowers. Many are succulent and grow in hot, dry places. Some are grown as ornamentals, like hybrid forms of *Lewisia*. There are about 19 genera and 350 species in the family, mainly in North and South America. Bitter-root, *Lewisia rediviva*, is the state flower of Montana.

Family Features Flowers solitary or borne in clusters, usually opposite the leaves; regular, hermaphrodite. Sepals 2, free or united; petals 4–6, free or united at base and soon falling; stamens either 4–6 and opposite petals, or numerous; ovary usually superior. Fruits are capsules. Leaves entire, alternate or opposite, with bristly or papery stipules.

Spring Beauty
Claytonia virginica

Miner's Lettuce
Montia perfoliata

Spring Beauty, *Claytonia virginica*, is a delicate, sweetly scented, perennial plant which blooms in the spring. It dies down and disappears by midsummer. It is found in damp woods, fields, and clearings from N.S. to Minn., and south to Ga. and Tex. The plant has a fleshy corm, from which grow several stems up to 1ft tall, with a single pair of linear leaves halfway up each one. At the top of the stem is a cluster of white or pink flowers striped with darker pink. Several other Spring Beauties are found in the Rocky Mountains, as well as Carolina Spring Beauty in the east.

Miner's Lettuce, *Montia perfoliata*, was traditionally eaten by gold miners as a salad and source of Vitamin C. It is a distinctive plant which grows in damp and shady places in the Pacific states from B.C. to Calif. It grows up to 1ft tall, forming small annual clumps of spoon-shaped leaves, and flowering stems which appear to terminate in broad, bowl-like disks. In the center of each disk is a cluster of small, pinkish flowers produced in late spring and early summer. The disk is formed from a pair of leaves which have fused around the flowering stem. Other *Montia* species grow in the west; they have fleshy opposite leaves but their flower clusters are not cupped in disks.

Purslane
Portulaca oleracea

Purslane, *Portulaca oleracea*, is one of the best wild edible plants. Young leafy tips can be used as a vegetable or in salads. It is a common weed of cultivated and waste ground in many of the warm temperate areas of the world, including North America. This is a prostrate, mat-forming plant with reddish stems, and more or less opposite leaves, together with a final leaf rosette beneath the terminal flowers. The leaves are fleshy and shining, ovate and blunt, or spoon-shaped. The flowers are pale yellow, either solitary or in small clusters.

Red Maids
Calandrinia ciliata

Red Maids, *Calandrinia ciliata*, is a western plant, blooming in spring in open grassy places and cultivated fields where there is water early in the year, from B.C. to Calif. and N.M. It is an annual succulent plant, with several spreading stems and linear, rather fleshy leaves. The flowers are bright rose-red, small, and bowl-shaped, and the sepals have hairy margins. The flowers grow in leafy clusters terminating the stems.

Fameflower
Talinum teretifolium

Fameflower, *Talinum teretifolium*, grows on rocky ground, from Penn, south to Ga. and Ala. It is one of several *Talinum* species in the east and midwest. They form clumps of succulent leaves, and have leafless flowering stems about 1ft tall, with pink flowers, in summer.

Pink family

Common Mouse-ear Chickweed
Cerastium fontanum

Caryophyllaceae About 70 genera with 1750 species of herbs. A family with many garden plants, including pinks, carnations, and gypsophilas. They are also used as cut flowers. Some, like chickweeds and Corn Cockle, are weeds.

Family Features Flowers solitary or in cymes; regular, usually hermaphrodite. Sepals 4 or 5, free or united into a tube, often with papery margins; petals 4 or 5, sometimes 0; stamens up to 10, often twice as many as petals; ovary superior. Fruits are dry capsules. Leaves entire, opposite, often connected by a transverse line. Stipules frequently absent but when present are often papery in texture.

Mouse-ear Chickweeds, *Cerastium* species, are so-called because some have short downy hairs on the leaves, resembling fur on the ears of mice. Several are cosmopolitan weeds of short grassy places, lawns, and bare ground, like **Common Mouse-ear Chickweed**, *Cerastium fontanum*. This is a perennial creeping plant, rooting at the nodes, with sticky-glandular stems and opposite, gray-green, hairy leaves. Some of its shoots turn upward, growing 18in tall and producing flowers in terminal, equally branched clusters; each flower has five hairy sepals and five cleft white petals slightly longer than the sepals.

Field Mouse-ear Chickweed
Cerastium arvense

Field Mouse-ear Chickweed, *Cerastium arvense*, is a similar plant and another common weed throughout North America. It can be distinguished from Common Mouse-ear Chickweed by its flowers — the petals are twice as long as the sepals. Many plants in this species are often less obviously hairy, although they are very variable.

The **Chickweeds** or Starworts, *Stellaria* species, can be distinguished from *Cerastium* species because Chickweed flowers have five styles, whereas Mouse-ears have three.

Common Chickweed, *Stellaria media*, is a ubiquitous weed of woods, waste and cultivated land; it is an annual plant which flowers from early spring to late fall. It forms a clump of weak, leafy stems, no more than 15in high, with many tiny white flowers in terminal leafy cymes. Common Chickweed is the plant usually referred to as just "chickweed." It is edible, at its best when boiled briefly and eaten as a vegetable.

Common Chickweed
Stellaria media

Several of the *Stellaria* species are attractive plants with showy white flowers, many found in damp and shady places. Easter-bell, *Stellaria holostea*, is grown in gardens for its satiny white flowers. Lesser Stitchwort, *Stellaria graminea*, has similar flowers and grows in grassy places in the east and midwest.

Long-stalked Starwort, *Stellaria longipes*, is a northern and mountain plant growing in moist grassy places and damp woods. It has weak stems, linear leaves, and a few terminal flowers on long stalks; the flowers have deeply cleft white petals.

Star Chickweed, *Stellaria pubera*, has large white flowers half an inch across, with petals so deeply cleft that it appears to have ten, rather than five petals. It is a perennial plant, with weak stems, opposite elliptical leaves, and flowers in clusters at the tops of the stems. It grows in woods in eastern U.S., from N.J. to Ill., and south to Fla. and Ala.

Star Chickweed
Stellaria pubera

Pink family

Starry Campion
Silene stellata

Fire-pink
Silene virginica

Campions and **Catchflys**, members of the genera *Silene* and *Lychnis*, are similar to Chickweeds and related to them. Many of them are, however, much showier plants, very attractive wild flowers, and some are grown in gardens. There are about 300 *Silene* and 15 *Lychnis* species, the majority of them found in temperate areas of the world.

Starry Campion, *Silene stellata*, is a finely hairy, perennial plant with stems up to 2ft tall, flowering in summer. The stems bear lance-shaped leaves in whorls of four half way up the stem, in opposite pairs near the top. The flowers have deeply fringed petals emerging from bell-shaped calyces; they are borne in loose terminal clusters near the top of the stems. This beautiful plant grows in rich woods from Ont. and Mich., south to Ga. and Tex., and is sometimes grown in wild gardens.

Fire-pink, *Silene virginica*, is one of several *Silene* species with red or pink flowers. It is a short-lived perennial plant, with leaves in twos or fours and clusters of crimson flowers at the tips of weak stems. Each flower has five narrow petals emerging from a long sticky calyx. Fire-pink grows in open woods and rocky places, often in large patches, from southern Ont. to Minn., and south to Ga. and Ark. Wild Pink, *Silene caroliniana*, also provides bright patches of color in similar habitats, from Ont. to Tenn; its flowers have rather spoon-shaped, white to dark pink petals.

By contrast, many members of the pink family are small, insignificant plants, with inconspicuous flowers. **Pearlworts**, *Sagina* species, are tiny mat-forming plants, with green tangled stems and little linear leaves; each plant is only a few inches across and 4in tall.

Procumbent Pearlwort, *Sagina procumbens*, is a perennial species, a weed that grows in damp places, often in lawns and paths in gardens. It produces tiny greenish flowers on long stalks in the leaf axils, each flower with four sepals and often lacking petals. Along with other pearlworts, this plant grows around the North Pole, this one south as far as Del. in the east and Calif. in the west.

Procumbent Pearlwort
Sagina procumbens

Sand Spurrey, *Spergularia rubra*, is a small, usually annual plant, with much branched, often prostrate stems and linear leaves. It bears clusters of small pink flowers at the ends of the stems, the five petals of each flower alternating with the sepals and shorter than them. Sand Spurrey is widespread in southern Canada and much of the U.S., in lime-free sandy or gravelly soils, naturalized from its native Europe. Other sand spurreys are found in salt marshes on the Atlantic and Pacific coasts; these coastal species are similar but have fleshy leaves.

Sand Spurrey
Spergularia rubra

Sea Sandwort, *Honkenya peploides*, is another coastal species from this family, and like coastal sand spurreys, stores water in its fleshy leaves. It forms dense colonies on beaches and sand-dunes, stabilizing the sands with its thick stems which run in and along the sand. Its stems have many fleshy leaves arranged in four overlapping ranks, and it bears small whitish flowers in the axils of the leaves. Male and female flowers grow on separate plants, female flowers with minute petals, male flowers with larger white ones.

Sea Sandwort
Honkenya peploides

Cactus family

Plains Prickly Pear
Opuntia polyacantha

Cactaceae An American family of about 150 genera and over 1500 species, many found in the western deserts. Cactuses are succulent, often spiny plants, mostly leafless and often with ribs or nipples, or with jointed stems. Many are small, others woody and more like shrubs.

Family Features Flowers solitary, regular, hermaphrodite; sepals petal-like; petals in series, largest in the center; stamens many; ovary inferior with 1 cell and many seeds. Fruits are berries, often spiny or bristly.

Tree Cholla
Opuntia imbricata

Prickly Pears and **Chollas** comprise about 300 species in the genus *Opuntia*. They are the only cactuses with leaves – their young sections have small fleshy leaves which soon fall off. The stems have tubercles with two kinds of spines – large, obvious ones and small, easily detached bristles which irritate the skin.

Prickly Pears have flattened stems. **Plains Prickly Pear**, *Opuntia polyacantha*, forms spreading mats of flattened stems, each oval section about 2–4in long. Its tufts of 3-in spines are surrounded by gray woolly areas of bristles. This cactus has yellow or red flowers in early summer. It grows in plains and prairies from B.C. to central southern Canada, and south to Ariz. and Mo. Some prickly pears, like Indian Fig, *O. humifusa*, have pulpy, edible fruits. This plant grows in grasslands, unusually for a cactus in the east, from southern Ont. to Minn., and south to Ga. and Mo.

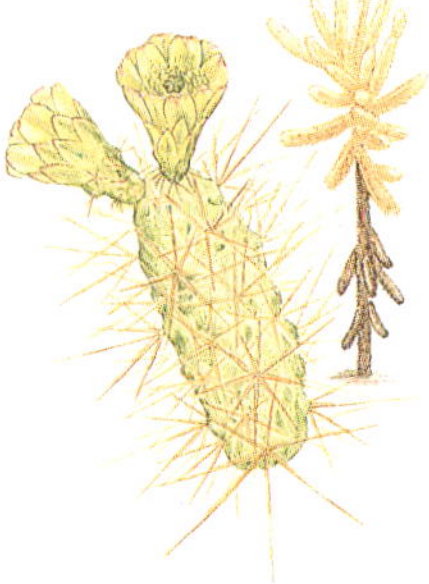

Teddy Bear Cholla
Opuntia bigelovii

Chollas have cylindrical stems. The **Tree Cholla**, *Opuntia imbricata*, grows in plains, foothills, and deserts, from Kan. to Tex., and west to the Rockies. It forms a shrub or small tree, with old dead branches tangled with young green ones. The stems are cylindrical, with long joints and tubercles bearing clusters of 10–30 short, yellowish spines. Dark red or purple flowers appear in summer, toward the ends of the branches.

Teddy Bear Cholla or Jumping Cholla, *Opuntia bigelovii*, has an erect woody stem up to 9ft tall, much branched in the upper half and densely covered with barbed spines, notoriously difficult to remove from the skin. In spring the plant bears yellow or pale greenish flowers, sometimes streaked with lavender. It grows in deserts from southern Calif. to Ariz. and Mexico. It is often common, spreading from detached sections which have formed new plants.

Saguaro Cactus
Carnegiea gigantea

In southeastern Arizona the **Saguaro Cactus**, *Carnegiea gigantea*, the state flower of Arizona, towers up to 50ft tall, with a thick "trunk" and several branches some way up. In the first half of summer it produces clusters of creamy white flowers which open at night near the ends of its branches. The Saguaro Cactus grows on slopes and flats from Ariz. into southern Calif. and Mexico. Its fleshy fruits are eaten by the Indians.

Claret Cup Cactus
Echinocereus triglochidiatus

Many of the *Echinocereus* cactuses are called hedgehog cactuses. They form low mounds of globular or cylindrical, strongly ribbed, very spiny stems. **Claret Cup Cactus**, *Echinocereus triglochidiatus*, grows in dry mountain woods, on rocky slopes, and in desert flats, from Ut. to Calif. and Tex., south into Mexico. It has scarlet flowers growing on the tops of its oblong, ribbed stems in early summer.

Cactus family

Tangled Fishhook
Mammillaria microcarpa

There are about 100 *Mammillaria* species, found in the southwestern area of the U.S. and in central America. Many of them are **Fishhook Cactuses**. They have globular stems with teatlike tubercles (called nipples). On these nipples are clusters of spines, each with a central fishhook-like spine and an outer circle of straight, radial spines. The **Tangled Fishhook**, *Mammillaria microcarpa*, has cylindrical stems, up to 6in tall, many small nipples, and overlapping spines. In early summer it bears deep pink flowers in the spaces between the tubercles, later followed by smooth red fruits. This species grows in grassland and woodland, and in dry gravelly places from southern Calif. to Tex. and into Mexico.

Plains Nipple Cactus
Coryphantha missouriensis

The *Coryphantha* species form another fairly large group of similar cactuses, but their tubercles are grooved and arranged in spiral rows. Their flowers are borne near the top of the plant in the axils of the tubercles. One of the most common is the Foxtail Cactus, *Coryphantha vivipara*, which forms rounded, beehive-like stems up to 2ft tall, with nipples completely hidden by straight spines. The **Plains Nipple Cactus**, *Coryphantha missouriensis*, forms globular stems with large nipples and distinct clusters of grayish spines, 10–20 in a cluster. Its flowers are greenish-yellow, often tinged with pink. It grows in plains and hills from Man. to Tex., and Ariz.

Simpson's Ball Cactus
Pediocactus simpsonii

Simpson's Ball Cactus, *Pediocactus simpsonii*, forms small, more or less spherical stems, at most 8in tall. Each ball has 8–13 ribs with prominent spiny nipples, 8–10 stout central spines, and

20–23 slender radial spines in each cluster. It bears yellow-green, white or purple flowers on the nipples near the top of the stem. This cactus grows among sagebrush, pinyon, and juniper, on tablelands and on the plains from Wash. to S.D., and south through the midwest to Ariz. and N.M.

The **Barrel Cactuses**, about 35 *Ferocactus* species, are often massive cactuses with globular or cylindrical bodies, prominent, often spiral ribs, and heavy, often hooked, spines. **Red Barrel Cactus**, *Ferocactus acanthodes*, is globular at first, later forming a usually unbranched column up to 6ft tall. It has 20–28 ribs, almost hidden by the many spines which are borne in clusters on the ribs. Yellow, funnel-shaped flowers grow near the top of the stem. Red Barrel Cactus grows on rocky slopes and canyon walls, on gravel fans and washes, in deserts from southern Calif. to Ariz. Other species also grow in the southwestern U.S. and in Mexico.

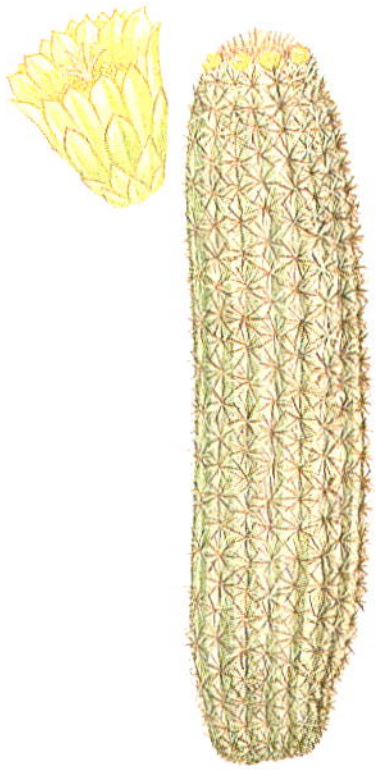

Red Barrel Cactus
Ferocactus acanthodes

Peyote, *Lophophora williamsii*, is a strange cactus, known since Aztec times for its hallucinogenic properties. It is now illegal for anyone except certain Indians to eat it. It looks like a small, gray, knobby stone (sometimes known as a mescal button) sitting half in the soil, but has a very large taproot penetrating deep into the ground. It has no spines, but instead has tufts of woolly hairs on its ribs and bears pink flowers in summer. The "stones" may grow singly or in clumps, and at one time were common, but are now rare from overcollecting. They grow in limestone areas in the deserts of southern Tex. and N.M., and along the Rio Grande into Mexico.

Peyote
Lophophora williamsii

Buttercup or Crowfoot family

Carolina Larkspur
Delphinium carolinianum

Wild Columbine
Aquilegia canadensis

Ranunculaceae About 50 genera and 1900 species of herbs, shrubs, and climbers, mostly from northern temperate and Arctic areas. There are many well-known garden plants in the family, including anemones, columbines delphiniums, and clematis. All members of the family contain acrid alkaloids, and some, like larkspurs and monkshoods, are extremely poisonous.

Family Features Flowers solitary or in terminal inflorescences; regular, hermaphrodite, with all parts free. Sepals 5–8, often overlapping, sometimes petal-like; petals often 5, may be absent or numerous, often overlapping, often with a nectary at the base; stamens numerous and may be petal-like; ovary formed of 1 to many carpels. Fruits are achenes or pods. Leaves usually alternate or basal, often compound or divided.

Larkspurs, *Delphinium* species, are a group of over 50 species spread throughout North America. They are poisonous, particularly dangerous to grazing animals like cattle. These are annual or perennial plants, with clumps of palmately lobed leaves and erect stems bearing showy blue, pink or white flowers. The flowers have five unequal sepals, the upper one spurred. There are four petals, two upper ones with long spurs, and two clawed lower ones, bent backward and often cleft almost in two.

Eastern species include Spring Larkspur, *Delphinium tricorne*, which has blue flowers and grows in rich woods; and **Carolina Larkspur**, *Delphinium carolinianum*, a plant of dry woods and prairies. Plains Delphinium, *Delphinium virescens*, grows in the plains and prairies; it has greenish-white flowers. Western species include *D. nelsonii* with blue flowers, and *D. nudicaule*, with yellow and red flowers, both from the Rocky Mountains.

Columbines, *Aquilegia* species, form a group of over 20 species found in many parts of North America. They are perennial plants, with clumps of delicate compound leaves and erect flowering stems, usually 2–4ft tall, in summer. The spurred flowers are attractive and easily recognizable.

Blue Columbine
Aquilegia coerulea

The **Wild Columbine** of the east, *Aquilegia canadensis*, has nodding red and yellow flowers; it grows in woods and rocky places from N.S. to Sask., south to Fla. and Tex. **Blue Columbine**, *Aquilegia coerulea*, is a Rocky Mountain species and the state flower of Colorado; it has blue sepals and white petals. Garden Columbine, *Aquilegia vulgaris*, has blue, purple or white flowers.

There are about 15 **Monkshoods**, *Aconitum* species, in North America. They are distinctive but not common plants, with perennial clumps of large palmately cleft leaves, and showy blue or white flowers, mostly in late summer. The flowers have five petal-like sepals, the uppermost forming a helmet-shaped hood and concealing two nectaries, remnants of the petals. **Western Monkshood**, *Aconitum columbianum*, grows in mountain woods and meadows from Alas. to Calif. and N.M. *Aconitum uncinatum* grows in mountain woods from Penn. to Ind., and south to Ga. Both species have blue-violet flowers.

Western Monkshood
Aconitum columbianum

Buttercup or Crowfoot family

Early Meadow Rue
Thalictrum dioicum

The **Meadow Rues**, *Thalictrum* species, are beautiful, if inconspicuous, perennial plants, with clumps of compound leaves divided into many lobed leaflets. The flowers grow in branched inflorescences; they have petal-like sepals, which enclose the flowers in bud but fall as they open, and they lack petals. The color of the flowers comes from the many long, fluffy stamens, which may be yellow, white or purplish. Some of the species have male and female flowers on separate plants. Meadow Rues are most often found in wet soils, in woods and meadows, on cliffs and shores, near streams and rivers, throughout North America. **Early Meadow Rue**, *Thalictrum dioicum*, is found in moist woods from Que. to Man., and south to S.C. and Mo.

By far the most widespread of the **Baneberries**, *Actaea* species, is *Actaea rubra*, the **Red Baneberry** which is found in rich woods from Lab. to Alas., and south to Conn. and Ariz. It is a perennial plant with poisonous roots, a few very large pinnate leaves up to 3ft long, and a branched flowering stem. The flowers grow in dense terminal clusters or on long stalks in the leaf axils; the flowers have 3–5 petaloid sepals and 4–10 clawed petals but these soon fall, leaving the many white stamens. The flowers are followed by poisonous red berries. A related species, found infrequently in eastern woods, is White Baneberry, *Actaea alba*, which has poisonous white berries.

Red Baneberry
Actaea rubra

False Bugbane or Tassel Rue, *Trautvetteria caroliniensis*, is a stout perennial plant up to 3ft tall, with large, palmately lobed, toothed leaves and erect flowering stems. Its flowers soon lose the four or five sepals and they have no petals; the nodding bunches of stamens that are left resemble whitish tassels. This plant grows in moist woods and beside streams, in mountains and prairies in much of the U.S., except the arid southwest, but is not common.

False Bugbane
Trautvetteria caroliniensis

Clematises, *Clematis* species, are unusual members of the Buttercup family in that many of them are woody or herbaceous climbers. Others are erect perennial plants. Many species are given the name Leatherflower or Vase flower; these are herbaceous or climbing plants found in the woods and prairies of the east and midwest, and they have characteristic small, purplish, nodding, vase-shaped flowers. Clematises are some of the most popular garden plants. Many hybrids have been developed, some with huge, brilliantly colored flowers.

Virgin's Bower, *Clematis virginiana*, is a climbing plant up to 10ft tall, common in woods and on roadsides, in moist places from N.S. to Man., south to Ga. and La. It has twining stems and compound leaves with twining stalks. In many of the leaf axils grow clusters of white flowers in summer, male and female flowers on separate plants. Each flower has four white, petal-like sepals and no petals. Male flowers have many stamens. Female flowers have several carpels which enlarge in fruit to form globular heads of achenes, each one with a long, plume-like tail. The female plants are especially noticeable in late summer when they may be covered in the conspicuous plumed fruits.

Virgin's Bower
Clematis virginiana

Common Buttercup
Ranunculus acris

Cursed Buttercup
Ranunculus sceleratus

Buttercup or Crowfoot family

The **Buttercups**, crowfoots and spearworts, belonging to the genus *Ranunculus*, are a group of about 300 species, mostly found in the northern hemisphere. They have open, yellow or white flowers, usually with five petals. There is a nectar-secreting depression near the base of each petal. The flowers have numerous stamens and numerous carpels arranged in a head in the center of each flower. These carpels enlarge in fruit to form many single-seeded achenes. All the *Ranunculus* species are acrid and poisonous to a greater or lesser extent, and are dangerous to cattle and other grazing animals, who normally tend to avoid them.

Common Buttercup, *Ranunculus acris*, is a typical buttercup. It is a hairy, perennial plant, with an erect, branched stem up to 3ft tall, compound, palmately cut leaves, and many bright yellow, glossy flowers. It is a European species which has been introduced throughout North America to grow on roadsides, in fields and meadows, and other grassy places.

Cursed Buttercup, *Ranunculus sceleratus*, is so called because it is the most acrid and poisonous of all, and because it grows in lush, swampy meadows, and beside ditches and streams, where cattle graze in summer and may happen to eat them. Cursed Buttercups are annual plants, with hollow, hairless, branched stems up to 2ft tall, and deeply cut, palmate leaves. They bear many small yellow flowers and cylindrical heads of achenes.

Some buttercups are much more unfamiliar. **Seaside Crowfoot**, *Ranunculus cymbalaria*, grows in muddy places and wet, marshy meadows, or along the edges of ponds and streams, usually where the water is brackish or alkaline, in much of North America. Because of its specialized habitat it is often local and confined to small areas. It is a perennial plant which spreads by creeping stems. It forms clumps of rounded, heart-shaped or kidney-shaped, lobed leaves, and leafless flowering stems with a few white flowers.

Seaside Crowfoot
Ranunculus cymbalaria

Many of the *Ranunculus* species are aquatic plants, usually with white flowers. **White Water-crowfoot**, *Ranunculus aquatilis*, is typical, and one of the most common of these species. It grows in slow streams and ponds throughout much of North America. It has finely dissected submerged leaves on very long submerged stems, and rounded, palmately lobed floating leaves. Its small white flowers project above the surface of the water. Rounded heads of achenes follow the flowers and bend downwards, back into the water.

White Water-crowfoot
Ranunculus aquatilis

Marsh Marigold or Cowslip, *Caltha palustris*, grows in marshy meadows and wet woods, along the edges of streams, and in shallow water across Canada and into the northern U.S., south to N.C. in the mountains. This is a hairless, perennial plant up to 2ft tall, which forms a clump of long-stalked, dark green leaves with large, heart-shaped blades. Many showy yellow flowers grow on branched, hollow stems in spring. Each flower may have up to eight petals, as many as 100 stamens, and 5–12 carpels which enlarge into pod-like fruits.

Marsh Marigold
Caltha palustris

Buttercup or Crowfoot family

Canada Anemone
Anemone canadensis

There are about 120 species of **Anemones**, genus *Anemone*, worldwide, mostly in the northern hemisphere. Many are alpine, arctic, and tundra plants. Many anemone species and cultivars are grown in gardens, both in rock gardens and in borders. Anemones are poisonous in the same way as buttercups, and can be a danger to cattle and other grazing animals.

Anemones are usually small perennial plants, with a clump of palmately divided basal leaves and flowers borne on separate stems. Each stem has a whorl of three or more leaves, and one or a few flowers. The flowers lack petals, although this is not immediately evident as the sepals are colored like petals; they may be white, greenish, blue or red. The flowers have numerous stamens and carpels. The latter enlarge in fruit to form many achenes.

Pasque Flower
Anemone patens

About 20 species of *Anemone* grow in North America. The **Canada Anemone**, *Anemone canadensis*, is one of the most widespread, and is typical of many. It has long underground stems, long-stalked, three-lobed, basal leaves, and erect flowering stems with white flowers. It grows in damp meadows and prairies, on shores and in woods, from Lab. to Alta., and south to Md. and N.M. Wood Anemone, *Anemone quinquefolia*, grows in open woods in the east; its spring flowers are white, red-tinged on the undersides. Thimbleweed, *Anemone virginiana*, is another eastern woodlander, with greenish-white flowers and egg-shaped heads of woolly achenes.

Pasque Flower, *Anemone patens*, is a small plant, only 15in tall, and a densely hairy one. In spring it produces several solitary white or blue-purple flowers growing on long stalks from the crown, and then forms a clump of long-stalked, deeply cut leaves. As the flowers die and the fruits ripen, the achenes develop long feathery tips, so that the plant is as noticeable in fruit as it is beautiful in flower. It grows in dry prairies, grasslands, and barrens from Alas. to Ill., and south to Wash. and Tex.; it is the state flower of South Dakota.

Desert Anemone
Anemone tuberosa

Desert Anemone, *Anemone tuberosa*, is one of several western species. It grows among rocks and on dry rocky slopes, from Calif. to Ut. and N.M. It has tuberous roots, a few divided leaves, and flowers in spring, varying in color from white to rose-pink or purple.

There are two **Liverleafs** or liverworts, *Hepatica* species, in North America. Their name comes from the supposed resemblance of their leaves to the lobes of the liver. They are related to the anemones and are small woodland plants, hairy perennials with clumps of lobed leaves and several solitary flowers on long stalks in spring. The flowers lack petals and have 5–12 petal-like sepals.

Round-leaved Hepatica
Hepatica americana

The **Round-leaved Hepatica**, *Hepatica americana*, grows in open woods on acid soils from N.S. to Minn., and south to Ga. It has round-lobed leaves. The Sharp-leaved Hepatica, *Hepatica acutiloba*, has pointed lobes on its leaves and grows in eastern woods but on calcareous soils. The flowers of both species are variable in color, and may be white, pink or blue.

Barberry family

May Apple
Podophyllum peltatum

Blue Cohosh
Caulophyllum thalictroides

Northern Inside-out Flower
Vancouveria hexandra

Berberidaceae A family of mostly shrubs with about 10 genera and nearly 600 species in the world, mainly confined to the northern hemisphere. Some are grown as garden plants; some are poisonous, others edible.

Family Features Flowers solitary or in inflorescences; regular, hermaphrodite. Sepals and petals similar, in 2 or more series, free; stamens 6, opposite petals; ovary superior with 1 cell. Fruits are berries. Leaves alternate, simple or compound.

The **May Apple** or Mandrake, *Podophyllum peltatum*, grows in open woods and on shady roadsides from Que. to Minn., and south to Fla. and Tex., forming carpets of upright, leafy stems. Each stem bears one or two large, deeply lobed, umbrella-like leaves; those with two leaves also bear a single nodding, waxy white flower in May. Its yellow berries are edible when fully ripe. The rest of the plant, including the seeds, is very poisonous.

Blue Cohosh, *Caulophyllum thalictroides*, grows in moist woods from N.B. to Ont. and south to Ala. It forms an erect stem, about 2ft tall, with two leaves, so much divided that they appear to be more than two. In the axil of the upper leaf a cluster of small, yellow-green flowers grows in early summer; each has six petal-like sepals, and six small, hooded petals. Its deep blue, berry-like seeds are poisonous.

Northern Inside-out Flower, *Vancouveria hexandra*, is one of three species found in the Pacific states, this one in coniferous woods of the western Cascades, from Wash. to Calif. It forms slow-spreading carpets of leaves, 15in tall at most. The leaves are divided into three-lobed leaflets. Its white flowers appear in spring on leafless stalks; each appears to be inside out, with swept-back sepals and petals.

Lizard's Tail family

Saururaceae A very small family of herbs with 5 genera and 7 species, found only in North America and eastern Asia. A few are grown in gardens.

Family Features Flowers regular, in dense clusters or spikes with conspicuous colored bracts. Sepals and petals 0; stamens 3, 6 or 8; ovary inferior or superior. Fruits are succulent capsules. Leaves simple and alternate, and stipules are present.

Lizard's Tail
Saururus cernuus

The **Lizard's Tail**, *Saururus cernuus*, grows in shallow water, swamps and marshes from Que. to Minn., and south to Fla. and Tex., most commonly in the south. Its jointed stems grow up to 5ft high and bear large, dark, heart-shaped leaves. In summer the tiny white flowers form long drooping, fragrant spikes, resembling lizards' tails.

Yerba Mansa
Anemopsis californica

In the west **Yerba Mansa**, *Anemopsis californica*, grows in wet, usually saline or alkaline places, from Ore. to Mexico. and into Colo. and Tex., but most commonly in Calif. It forms patches of large elliptical, long-stalked leaves. The flower stalks emerge from among these; each has a few leaves about half way up, and a terminal cone-like spike of flowers above white or red-tinged bracts. The thick creeping rhizomes of this plant have been used in Indian and herbal medicine for a variety of purposes.

Water Lily family

Nymphaeaceae A very small family of aquatic plants, growing in fresh water, with about 6 genera and 70 species found in many parts of the world. They are famous for their beautiful floating leaves and flowers.

Family Features Flowers floating or projecting out of the water; solitary, hermaphrodite, regular, often showy. Sepals 4–6, free; petals numerous, sometimes becoming like stamens near the flower center; stamens numerous; ovary usually superior with 1 to many cells. Fruits are spongy capsules or a group of achenes sunk in the receptacle. Leaves floating, round or heart-shaped, attached by long stalks to roots or rhizomes in the mud. Some species also have thin, translucent, submerged leaves.

Fragrant Water Lily
Nymphaea odorata

The **Fragrant Water Lily**, *Nymphaea odorata*, is the most widespread American species, growing wild in quiet waters and ponds from Nf. to Man., and south to Fla. and Tex. along the coastal plain. It is also planted in ponds in many other areas. Its floating leaves have rounded blades, purple on the underside; they are attached to the rhizome in the mud at the bottom by long stalks. The floating flowers are fragrant, with many white petals and yellow stamens.

Yellow Water Lily
Nuphar polysepalum

The **Yellow Water Lily**, *Nuphar polysepalum*, is also called Indian Pond Lily and Spatterdock. It is a western species of ponds and slow-moving streams, found from Alas. to Calif., and east to S.D. and Colo. It has floating heart-shaped leaves and thin, delicate submerged leaves. The flowers project above the water; they are bowl-shaped, with 5–12 thick, yellow sepals, many petals and stamens, and a broad disk-like stigma. The egg-shaped fruit ripens above water, bursting to release the edible seeds, which can be roasted like popcorn or ground into meal.

The **Lotus Lily** or American Lotus, *Nelumbo lutea*, is another plant of quiet waters, growing in ponds and slow-moving streams from southern Ont. to Minn., south to Fla. and Tex. Its large rounded leaves often project above the water, like the pale yellow flowers. These have many sepals and petals, many stamens, and a flat-topped receptacle with ovaries sunk into cavities in it. The receptacle enlarges as the embedded fruits ripen to become hard and nut-like. Roots, shoots, and seeds are all edible.

Lotus Lily
Nelumbo lutea

Sundew family

Droseraceae These are insectivorous plants, with rosettes of sticky, glandular leaves which function as insect traps. They have regular flowers, usually with 5 separate sepals and petals, 5 stamens and a single ovary. There are 4 genera and about 100 species, found throughout the world in acid soils, in sandy and boggy places.

The **Round-leaved Sundew**, *Drosera rotundifolia*, is a typical sundew. It grows in bogs and swamps in the temperate regions of the northern hemisphere, south as far as Ga., Ill. and Calif. in North America. This tiny plant has a rosette of long-stalked leaves, their blades covered in red-tipped glands which secrete a sticky fluid. This traps and digests flies, which are then absorbed by the leaves. In summer it forms 8-in tall, leafless flowering stems, with one-sided clusters of small white or pink flowers.

Round-leaved Sundew
Drosera rotundifolia

Dutchman's Pipe
Aristolochia durior

Birthwort family

Aristolochiaceae About 7 genera and 400 species of twining vines and herbs, found in the tropics and temperate areas of the world.

Family Features Flowers solitary or in clusters in leaf axils; usually bilaterally symmetrical, hermaphrodite, often fetid. Calyx 3-lobed, often tubular and often corolla-like; petals minute or 0; stamens 6 or 12; ovary usually inferior with 4–6 cells. Fruit usually a capsule. Leaves alternate, simple. Stipules 0.

Dutchman's Pipe, *Aristolochia durior*, is a climbing vine which grows in mountain woods, in moist places, and beside streams, from Penn. to Ky. and Ga. In the northeast it is often planted around porches. It has long-stalked, broadly heart-shaped leaves, up to 8in long, and unique pipe-like flowers in the leaf axils.

Wild Ginger
Asarum canadense

Wild Ginger, *Asarum canadense*, forms spreading patches of leaves. The 6–10-in tall leaves grow in pairs, with long stalks and broad, heart-shaped blades. At ground level, in the axil between each pair of leaves, a single brownish flower appears in spring. It is cup-shaped with three lobes at the opening. Wild Ginger grows in rich woods from N.B. to Ont., and south to N.C. and Ark. The plant has a scent of ginger when bruised, and the more strongly scented roots can be used as a spicy substitute for true ginger.

St John's-wort family

Hypericaceae There are 8 genera and about 400 species of herbs, shrubs, and trees in this family, mainly in temperate regions and in mountain areas in the tropics. Several shrubs are highly ornamental plants for the garden.

Family Features Flowers distinctive, showy, regular, hermaphrodite, yellow or white. Sepals 5; petals 5; stamens numerous, often united into bundles and appearing to fill the center of the flower in *Hypericum*, by far the largest genus; ovary superior with 1, 3 or 5 cells. Fruit usually a capsule. Leaves opposite or in whorls, simple and often dotted with glands. Stipules 0.

Common St John's-wort
Hypericum perforatum

Common St John's-wort, *Hypericum perfoliatum*, is one of many species which grow in North America; several are similar to this one, others are creeping plants and shrubs. Common St John's-wort is a weed of roadsides, waste places, and meadows in much of North America. It is a perennial plant, with a branched stem, about 2ft tall, and opposite, linear leaves, covered by translucent dots (glands) which show up when the leaves are held to the light. The flowers are borne in a large compound inflorescence and are typical of the genus, with five yellow petals and many stamens. In this species the petals have black dots around their margins.

Marsh St John's-wort
Triadenum virginicum

Marsh St John's-wort, *Triadenum virginicum*, is one of several related marsh plants found most commonly on the coastal plain in the east. It is a perennial, with erect stems up to 2ft tall, and opposite, oblong, gland-dotted leaves. Clusters of flesh-colored flowers terminate the stems and grow in the upper leaf axils. Each flower has three groups of three stamens alternating with three orange glands.

Fumitory family

Fumariaceae About 16 genera and 450 species, all herbs, in the northern temperate regions and north Africa. Several, such as Bleeding Hearts and Dutchman's Breeches, are garden plants.

Family Features Flowers bilaterally symmetrical, hermaphrodite. Sepals 2, soon falling; petals 4 (2 inner petals often joined together over the stigma, and 2 outer, spurred or pouched petals, separate at the base but joined at their tips); stamens 6, in 2 groups of 3, with joined filaments, opposite the outer petals; ovary has 1 cell. Fruit a capsule or nutlet. These are smooth, brittle plants with watery juice and they have alternate divided leaves.

Dutchman's Breeches
Dicentra cucullaria

There are nine species of *Dicentra* in North America, some of them (like Bleeding Hearts) grown in gardens. **Dutchman's Breeches**, *Dicentra cucullaria*, is the most widespread, growing in rich woods from Que. to Minn., and south to Ga. and Kan. It is a perennial plant, with feathery, gray-green basal leaves, about 6in tall. Its name describes perfectly the shape of the flowers, which resemble white breeches hanging upside down from the flower stalks. They appear in spring. Squirrel-corn, *D. canadensis*, has similar flowers with shorter "legs" on the "breeches." Other species include *D. eximia* from the east and *D. formosa* from the west.

Common Fumitory
Fumaria officinalis

Common Fumitory, *Fumaria officinalis*, is a European plant which is found scattered in waste places throughout much of North America. It is a small straggling plant with much-divided blue-gray leaves and curious flowers, growing in loose spikes. They are tubular, pink with red-tipped spurs.

Poppy family

Papaveraceae About 26 genera and 200 species, mostly herbs, with a very few shrubs and trees, found mainly in subtropical and temperate regions of the northern hemisphere. Probably the most famous member of the family is the Opium Poppy, whose seed heads provide opium, source of morphine or heroin. Poppy seeds are rich in oil which is used in soaps, paints, salad oils and cattle cake. They are cultivated in many parts of the world. Some members of the family are grown in gardens.

Family Features Flowers usually solitary, regular, hermaphrodite. Sepals 2–3, soon falling; petals 4–6 or 8–12, often crumpled, free; stamens numerous; ovary superior with 2 or more united cells. Fruits are capsules. Leaves alternate, often much divided. Stipules 0. The plants contain colored sap.

Celandine
Chelidonium majus

Celandine, *Chelidonium majus*, is a Eurasian perennial, a former herbal plant with a caustic orange sap once used to treat warts. It may be found in moist or shady places, usually near dwellings or on roadsides, in eastern U.S. and Canada. It has almost hairless divided leaves on erect brittle stems and grows up to 3ft tall. The small, pale yellow flowers grow in terminal clusters and are followed by slender capsules.

Bloodroot
Sanguinaria canadensis

Bloodroot, *Sanguinaria canadensis*, is a perennial plant with stout rhizomes containing caustic red sap. It has many individual round, lobed, blue-green leaves on long stalks, about 10in tall. The solitary white flowers appear before the leaves in spring. Bloodroot is found in rich woods from N.S. to Man., and south to Fla. and Okla. A very beautiful double form is grown in gardens.

Poppy family

California Poppy
Eschscholtzia californica

Western North America is a good place to find a diversity of poppies, including Prickly Poppies, which are the *Argemone* species, Matilija Poppies, the *Romneya* species, and Tree Poppies, the *Dendromecon* species.

One of the best known western poppies is the **California Poppy**, *Eschscholtzia californica*, a showy plant often grown in gardens. It is only 2ft tall, with a clump of smooth, blue-green, dissected leaves and solitary, orange-yellow flowers. This is the state flower of California, growing from southern Calif. to Wash. It is common in grassy places and on hillsides. The flowers open in sunlight, closing at night and remaining closed on cloudy days.

Cream Cups
Platystemon californicus

Cream Cups, *Platystemon californicus*, is found in grassy places from Calif. to Ut. and Ariz. It forms a clump of softly hairy linear leaves and has several similarly hairy stems, each with a single white or yellow flower.

Wind Poppy
Stylomecon heterophylla

The **Wind Poppy**, *Stylomecon heterophylla*, is found only in grassy places in the foothills of the Sierra Nevada and Coast Ranges, in Calif. and Baja Calif. It is not a common plant, but is a brightly colored one with orange-red petals, purplish at the base. Fire Poppy, *Papaver californicum*, is similar, with brick-red flowers. It appears only after a fire in the Californian chaparral, its seeds remaining dormant in the ground from fire to fire.

The **Corn Poppy** or Red Poppy, *Papaver rhoeas*, is most familiar as the symbol of Remembrance Day. It is a Eurasian plant grown in gardens, a stiffly hairy annual plant with an erect stem, up to 2ft tall, and divided leaves. Its red, bowl-shaped flowers have black stamens in the center. The capsules, which follow the flowers, are like pepper shakers, with a ring of holes beneath the lid through which the seeds are scattered as the capsules sway in the wind.

Corn Poppy
Papaver rhoeas

Caper family

Capparidaceae About 30 genera and 650 species, found in the tropical and warm temperate regions of the world. This is mostly a family of trees and shrubs, but in the U.S. the members are usually herbs. A few are grown as ornamental plants.

Family Features Flowers solitary or in terminal racemes, regular or irregular, hermaphrodite. Sepals and petals usually 4, free; stamens many; ovary superior with 2 cells. Fruit a capsule or berry. Leaves alternate, simple or palmately compound. Stipules 0, minute or in the form of thorns.

Yellow Bee Plant, *Cleome lutea*, is one of several western species. It grows in sandy flats and scrub, often near water, from Wash. to Calif., and east to Mont. and N.M. This is a branched annual plant, up to 5ft tall, with many palmately compound leaves. At the tops of the stems are clusters of yellow flowers, very attractive to bees, dense at first but opening up as time goes on, the lower flowers die and the slender arched pods form. The Rocky Mountain Bee Plant, *Cleome serrulata*, has pink flowers; it is found in waste places and rangeland, from the prairies to the Pacific states. All *Cleome* species have an unpleasant scent, supposedly like goats.

Yellow Bee Plant
Cleome lutea

Shepherd's Purse
Capsella bursa-pastoris

Watercress
Nasturtium officinale

Yellow Cress
Rorippa islandica

Mustard family

Cruciferae or Brassicaceae
An important family with 375 genera and 3200 species of herbs, found mainly in north temperate regions. It contains many crop plants, including cabbages and broccoli, kale, turnip, watercress, mustards, and rape, together with ornamental garden plants and weeds.

Family Features Flowers in racemes, regular, hermaphrodite. Sepals 4, free; petals 4, free, in the form of a cross; stamens 6; ovary superior. Fruits are capsules called siliquas, with 2 valves opening from below, and a central septum to which seeds are attached. Leaves alternate. Stipules 0.

Shepherd's Purse, *Capsella bursa-pastoris*, is a familiar garden weed throughout the world. It is a small annual or biennial plant, with a rosette of simple lobed leaves and a flowering stem up to 15in tall. Its tiny white flowers are followed by heart-shaped capsules. As in all members of the family, the inflorescence starts as a dense cluster of buds, gradually lengthening as the flowers open, wither, and die, and the capsules gradually form.

Watercress, *Nasturtium officinale*, is a popular salad plant, rich in Vitamins A and C. It is cultivated and has become naturalized in many parts of the U.S. and southern Canada, in the quiet waters of streams. This is a dark green plant with hollow stems which root in the mud, and then grow up toward the light to float on the surface. It has compound leaves with 5–9 leaflets. The racemes of white flowers appear in summer and are followed by erect, curving cylindrical seedpods in which the seeds can be seen quite clearly.

Yellow Cress or Marsh Cress, *Rorippa islandica*, is one of several species related to Watercress, but inedible; they are often placed in the same genus. However, the yellow cresses have yellow flowers. They grow in wet places, on sandy shores and swamps, in many parts of North America. Some are annual plants, others are perennials, and they vary in the shape of their leaves and fruits, and in the size of their flowers.

Spring Cress
Cardamine bulbosa

Bittercresses, belonging to the genus *Cardamine*, consist of a group of about 25 species, found throughout North America. They are mostly smooth, hairless plants, often growing in wet places, and flowering in spring and early summer; they are edible and may be used in salads, Pennsylvania Bittercress, *Cardamine pensylvanica*, being the native equivalent of watercress.

Spring Cress, *Cardamine bulbosa*, is a slender plant, with a crisp white tuber, and an erect stem about 20in tall, with white flowers in spring. Its tuber can be grated like horseradish, whereas its young spring leaves can be added to salads. It can be found in shallow water and wet woods, from Que. to Minn., and south to Fla. and Tex.

Jointed Charlock
Raphanus raphanistrum

Jointed Charlock, *Raphanus raphanistrum*, is a European plant established as a weed of fields, waste places and roadsides in North America. It is an annual plant, with rough hairy stems and lobed leaves. It has yellowish, mauve-veined flowers, becoming whiter with age. Its cylindrical pods become ribbed and constricted between each seed as they dry, breaking up into one-seeded sections.

Mustard family

Hedge Mustard
Sisymbrium officinale

Hedge Mustard, *Sisymbrium officinale*, is a European species naturalized as a weed in grain fields and waste land in much of the U.S. and southern Canada. This is an annual, much branched, bristly plant, growing about 2ft tall, with deeply cut basal leaves and narrow, toothed stem leaves. The flowering stems jut out from the main branches, almost at right angles, and the pale yellow flowers open over a long period in summer. When the plant is in fruit, its stems become very elongated, with the long pods overlapping each other and pressed closely to the stems.

Tumbling Mustard, *Sisymbrium altissimum*, is a similar plant, a weed found in western grain fields. When their seeds are ripe, the plants die, their roots can then be dislodged from the soil by the wind, and they become tumbleweeds, shedding their seeds as they are blown about the landscape.

Wintercress
Barbarea vulgaris

Wintercress, *Barbarea vulgaris*, is also a European species found in North America, growing in damp places, on roadsides, in wet meadows and fields. It may be a weed, but its winter leaf rosettes are rich in Vitamin C and excellent in salads. In summer the rosettes produce several erect, branched leafy stems with terminal inflorescences of bright yellow flowers.

The genus *Brassica* has produced many of the most important crop members of the family, including cabbages, turnips, rape, and black mustard.

Black Mustard, *Brassica nigra*, has been cultivated in Europe for centuries for its seeds, which are used to make mustard. In North America the plant grows as a weed of waste places and fields. It is an annual, with a much branched stem growing up to 3ft tall, with bristly lobed leaves. The flowers are bright yellow and are followed by upright, quadrangular pods, constricted around the seeds and pressed closely against the stems.

Charlock, *Sinapis arvensis*, is a European plant also known as Wild Mustard, at one time a serious weed of vegetable and grain crops, until the advent of modern farming techniques. In North America it is a local weed of fields and gardens, waste ground and roadsides. It is an annual plant, with an erect, often branched, stiffly hairy stem, and roughly hairy leaves. The bright yellow flowers produce long beaked pods, held upright and away from the stem. The seeds can be used as a substitute for those of Black Mustard.

Peppergrass, *Lepidium virginicum*, is a small weed which grows on roadsides and in waste places, in fields and gardens, across North America. It is an annual or biennial plant with lobed basal leaves and an erect flowering stem. The flowers are tiny, white and inconspicuous, and are followed by round flattened fruits, notched at the top. This is one of many species known as peppergrass, small weeds with tiny white or yellow flowers. The leaves can be eaten in salads. Western Peppergrass, *Lepidium montanum*, is showier, one of several species found in western deserts and rangeland. Its many stems end in dense racemes of white flowers. Garden Cress, cultivated all over the world for salads, is *Lepidium sativum*.

Black Mustard
Brassica nigra

Charlock
Sinapis arvensis

Peppergrass
Lepidium virginicum

Mustard family

Western Wallflower
Erysimum asperum

Hairy Rock Cress
Arabis hirsuta

Whitlow Grass
Draba verna

Many members of this family are grown in flower gardens. Garden Wallflower, *Erysimum cheiri* or *Cheiranthus cheiri*, is a popular plant in spring displays, grown in many gardens in North America, occasionally escaping to grow wild.

In the west it has several wild, showy relatives, like the **Western Wallflower** or Plains Wallflower, *Erysimum asperum*. This is a variable biennial plant, with a clump of lance-shaped basal leaves in the first year, and an inflorescence of yellow, burnt-orange or brick-red flowers in the second. It develops slender, quadrangular pods held erect or at an oblique angle as time goes on. The plant grows in dry places, on open hillsides and flats, throughout western North America.

Rock Cresses are a large group of North American and Eurasian plants belonging to the genus *Arabis*; some are grown in rock gardens. There are over 50 species in North America, many growing in the Rocky Mountains and Pacific Coast Ranges. **Hairy Rock Cress**, *Arabis hirsuta*, is a biennial plant with a rosette of simple leaves and an erect flowering stem with white flowers. Its cylindrical pods are held erect close to the stem. Hairy Rock Cress grows around the North Pole, on hillsides, in woods and meadows, south in North America to Calif. and N.M. in the west, and to La. and Ark. in the east.

Spreading Rock Cress, *Arabis divaricarpa*, has lance-shaped leaves, purple flowers, and erect spreading pods. It grows on dry mountain slopes beneath pine trees from Alas. to Que., and south in the Rocky Mountains to Calif.

The genus *Draba* has about 300 arctic and alpine species from North America and Eurasia. They are mostly low-growing plants with tufts of simple, often lance-shaped leaves, and little, erect flowering stems. **Whitlow Grass**, *Draba verna*, is an annual plant with a small clump of hairy, spoon-shaped leaves, and a flowering stem only 8in tall at most. Its minute flowers are white, each one with a deep notch, and they are followed by little elliptical pods. Whitlow Grass grows on roadsides, in fields and gardens, often in bare poor soil, throughout much of North America.

Tansy Mustard
Descurainia pinnata

Tansy Mustard, *Descurainia pinnata*, grows in many dry open places and open woods across North America. It is an annual plant, with a basal tuft of divided leaves which wither as the flowering stem develops. The inflorescences are typical cruciferous ones, dense early in the season, elongating and opening out as the flowers die and the pods form. The pods are narrowly club-shaped, with two rows of seeds.

Golden Prince's Plume
Stanleya pinnata

Prince's Plumes, *Stanleya* species, are a group of six western species with plume-like spikes of flowers, all but one of them bright yellow in color. **Golden Prince's Plume**, *Stanleya pinnata*, is a perennial, almost shrubby, bluish-green plant, with branched leafy stems up to 5ft tall. The flowers are rather different to those of most members of this family: the yellow sepals enclose the buds but bend backward as the flowers open, and the four petals are densely hairy on the inside, and have spreading, yellow linear blades. The stamens are long and project out of the flowers. The pods are long and spreading, often curved.

Spotted Saxifrage
Saxifraga bronchialis

Purple Saxifrage
Saxifraga oppositifolia

Early Saxifrage
Saxifraga virginiensis

Saxifrage family

Saxifragaceae About 30 genera and 580 species of herbs, mainly in temperate regions of the northern hemisphere. Many are grown in rock gardens and flower borders.

Family Features Flowers usually regular, hermaphrodite. Sepals and petals 5, alternating; in some species petals 0; stamens 5–10; ovary has 1–3 cells, often joined at the base but with free styles and stigmas. The flowers are distinctive, with a flat ring around the ovary, often glistening with nectar, on which the stamens, petals, and sepals are inserted. Fruits are capsules. Leaves alternate. Stipules 0.

The **Saxifrages**, belonging to the genus *Saxifraga*, are the largest group in the family, with over 300 species. Many of them grow in the rocky crevices and cracks of the high mountains, but others grow at lower altitudes in mountain woods and meadows.

Spotted Saxifrage, *Saxifraga bronchialis*, is a northwestern and Rocky Mountain species, growing among rocks. It is like many alpine saxifrages in form, with rosettes of spine-tipped, rigid leaves forming moss-like mats; each rosette is less than half an inch across (in some saxifrages they are much smaller). The white, purple-spotted, star-like flowers are produced by a few of the rosettes each year. The rosettes die after flowering.

Purple Saxifrage, *Saxifraga oppositifolia*, forms loose mats of stems with opposite fleshy leaves, so close together at the tips that they look like rosettes. This is a very small plant, only 3–4in high, but its solitary purple flowers measure half an inch across.

They are borne at the tips of the stems in late summer. Purple Saxifrage grows in limestone soils, among rocks and on slopes in the Arctic mountains, south in the U.S. into Wyo.

Early Saxifrage, *Saxifraga virginiensis*, is a different kind of saxifrage, a much bigger plant with clumps of toothed, ovate, 3-in long leaves. Its white flowers appear in spring, on leafless flower stalks. At first the inflorescences are dense but they become looser as the flowers open, growing up to 15in tall. It grows in thin woodland, on hillsides and among rocks, from N.B. to Man., and south to Ga. and Okla. It is one of several similar saxifrages in North America.

Miterwort
Mitella diphylla

Miterwort or Bishop's Cap, *Mitella diphylla* is one of many woodland plants belonging to the saxifrage family. This plant forms spreading clumps of shallowly lobed and rather hairy leaves. In early summer its slender flowering stems bear white flowers with elaborately fringed petals. The flowers are followed by capsules shaped like bishops' hats. This plant grows in rich woods from Que. to Minn., and south to Ga. and Mo., in uplands in the south. A related smaller species, *Mitella nuda*, has yellow-green flowers, and other species grow in the west.

Foamflower
Tiarella cordifolia

Foamflower, *Tiarella cordifolia*, is another plant of rich woods. It is native from N.S. to Ont., south to Ga. and Ala. It makes spreading colonies of lobed, rather hairy leaves. In late spring and early summer its many flowering stems bear flowers with white petals and white protruding stamens — resembling the foam of its name.

Saxifrage family

Alumroot
Heuchera americana

Jack-o'-the-rocks
Heuchera rubescens

False Goatsbeard
Astilbe biternata

Coral Bells, *Heuchera sanguinea*, is often grown in gardens for its attractive leaves and wiry stems with small, but bright pink flowers in early summer. The species grows wild in the mountains of Ariz. and Mexico. There are nearly 40 species of *Heuchera* in North America, most with much less brightly colored flowers than Coral Bells, and some plain dull. Their petals are small, and the sepals form the most conspicuous part of the bell-shaped or urn-shaped flowers.

One of the most common is **Alumroot**, *Heuchera americana*. It forms clumps of somewhat floppy, maple-like leaves, and flowers in spring or early summer, sending up slender stalks with drooping, bell-shaped, yellow-green flowers. Alumroot grows in dry woods and shaded slopes, from Ont. to Mich., and south to Ga. and Okla. Midland Alumroot, *H. richardsonii*, is a similar midwestern species, growing in dry woods and prairies.

Several *Heuchera* species grow in the west, mostly with white or greenish flowers. **Jack-o'-the-rocks**, *Heuchera rubescens*, is a mountain plant, growing on rocky slopes in the Sierra Nevada. It forms clumps of leathery, maple-like leaves, and flowers in early summer. The flowers are white or pale pink, narrowly bell-shaped, with tiny petals emerging from the calyces. The Poker Heuchera, *H. cylindrica*, forms dense spikes of creamy flowers, which grow on erect stalks above leathery, maple-like leaves.

The **Astilbes**, genus *Astilbe*, are well known to gardeners for the color they bring to damp flower borders during summer. One species grows wild in

North America. This is the **False Goatsbeard**, *Astilbe biternata*, a plant of moist mountain woods, found from Va. to Ga., and west to Tenn. It forms a loose clump of stems up to 6ft tall, with large compound, much divided leaves. Individually the flowers are small, but they are gathered into large, branched, often drooping, terminal clusters, very impressive when in full bloom.

Prairie Star or Starflower, *Lithophragma parviflora*, is one of about a dozen western and midwestern species, known as Woodland Stars. Prairie Star grows in the lower areas of the Rocky Mountains and on the prairies, on open slopes, in dry woods, and among sagebrush, from B.C. to Alta., and south to Calif. and Neb. Its early spring flowers have white or pinkish petals cleft into three or five lobes. They open before the leaves are fully emerged. The leaves are lobed and hairy, growing in clumps.

Prairie Star
Lithophragma parviflora

Grass of Parnassus is a name given to a group of about 50 *Parnassia* species found in the northern hemisphere. They grow in wet meadows and bogs, on shores and by streams, usually on calcareous soils. These are perennial plants, with rosettes of leaves, and solitary white flowers. The flowers have five fertile stamens between the petals and five three-pronged, sterile ones opposite the petals. *Parnassia glauca* is an eastern species with ovate blades on its leaves and heavily veined petals. The species *P. fimbriata* is a western one, with kidney-shaped leaf blades and fringed edges to its petals. *P. palustris* is a circumboreal species, with heart-shaped leaves, conspicuously veined petals, and fringed sterile stamens.

Grass of Parnassus
Parnassia glauca

Prairie Smoke
Geum triflorum

Water Avens
Geum rivale

Goatsbeard
Aruncus dioicus

Rose family

Rosaceae A large and important family, with about 100 genera and 2000 species, found throughout the world, but especially in the temperate regions. It includes many fruit trees, like apples and pears, together with ornamental trees, shrubs, and herbs for the garden.

Family Features Flowers regular, hermaphrodite. Sepals and petals 5, free, often overlapping; stamens numerous; ovary usually superior, with sepals, petals, and stamens in rings around its base, or inferior; ovary has 1 to many cells, free or united, styles usually free. Fruits are achenes, drupes or pomes. Leaves usually alternate, simple or compound, usually with 2 stipules.

There are over 15 species of **Avens**, *Geum* species, in North America, out of a total of about 40 in the northern hemisphere. One of the most eye-catching is **Prairie Smoke**, *Geum triflorum*, not when it is in flower but when it is in fruit. This plant grows in dry prairies and woods across southern Canada and northern U.S., south in the mountains to Ut. and Calif. It is a hairy perennial plant, with a clump of pinnate leaves in which small leaflets alternate with larger ones. Its flowering stems bear terminal clusters of reddish, nodding, urn-shaped flowers. The fruits consist of a cluster of achenes with enormously long feathery styles, the whole effect being of a purple "feather duster."

Water Avens, *Geum rivale*, is another mainly northern plant, growing in wet meadows and marshes from Nf. to Alta., south to Penn. and Ind. in the east, and to N.M. in the west. It forms a clump of pinnate leaves, each with a very broad terminal leaflet. Nodding flowers grow on leafy flowering stems in loose terminal clusters; they have purplish sepals and pale yellowish petals, suffused with purple. The fruit consists of numerous hooked achenes, which catch in fur or clothes; they form a highly effective dispersal mechanism.

Goatsbeard, *Aruncus dioicus*, is a perennial plant, with several erect leafy stems up to 6ft tall, topped in early to mid summer with plumes of white fluffy flowers. It has large compound leaves up to 20in long, with long stalks and pointed-oblong, doubly serrated leaflets. The plant grows in rich woods from Penn. to Io., and south to Ala. and Ark.

Queen of the Prairie
Filipendula rubra

Queen of the Prairie, *Filipendula rubra*, grows in wet meadows and prairies, and in low-lying woods, from Ver. to Minn., and south to Ky. and Ga., but it is less common in the east and south. It is a showy species, with a large clump of leafy erect stems up to 6ft tall. The leaves are dark green and pinnate with many toothed, deeply lobed leaflets. From midsummer onwards the plant produces terminal sprays of fluffy, tiny pink, sweetly scented flowers. A related European species, *Filipendula ulmaria*, with white flowers, has escaped from gardens in the northeast, to grow wild in similar habitats.

Canadian Burnet
Sanguisorba canadensis

Canadian Burnet, *Sanguisorba canadensis*, is another wetland plant, growing in swamps and bogs, marshes, wet meadows, and prairies, from Nf. to Man., south to Del. and Ind., and in the mountains to Ga. It is a perennial plant, forming a handsome clump of pinnate leaves with poker-like spikes of fluffy white, petal-less flowers.

Rose family

Rough-fruited Cinquefoil
Potentilla recta

Silverweed
Potentilla anserina

Sticky Cinquefoil
Potentilla glandulosa

Cinquefoils, members of the genus *Potentilla*, are a large group of over 300 mostly northern temperate species, with over 70 in North America. Their flowers have five petals, cupped not only in a calyx of green sepals, but also in an epicalyx — this looks like a second set of sepals beneath the true sepals. Most have yellow flowers. Their fruits are clusters of dry achenes, often partly enclosed by the persistent calyx. They are often confused with buttercups. But buttercups have simple or divided leaves, not compound ones with separate leaflets; buttercup leaves lack stipules and their flowers have no epicalyx.

Rough-fruited Cinquefoil, *Potentilla recta*, has leaves typical of Five-finger Cinquefoils; there are several species of these, all with leaves that are palmately compound, with several toothed leaflets (often five, hence five-finger). This one grows in waste ground, on roadsides, and in fields, from N.S. to Ont., south through much of eastern US, and west into the prairies of Neb. and Kan. It is a hairy plant, with flowering stems up to 2ft tall, and large pale yellow flowers. Common Cinquefoil, *P. simplex*, and the dwarfer Canadian Cinquefoil, *P. canadensis*, are similar eastern species that grow in dry woods and fields.

Silverweed, *Potentilla anserina*, is a lover of damp places, growing in moist meadows, on wet banks and roadsides. This plant, like several other cinquefoils, grows across the northern hemisphere. And like many other cinquefoils, it has pinnate leaves. In the leaves of this plant, pairs of small toothed leaflets alternate with pairs of larger ones. It is a hairy, creeping plant with leaves that are silvery-hairy beneath. The flowers are the usual cinquefoil ones, with yellow petals. A similar species, Pacific Silverweed, *P. egedei*, is found along the coastal strand of the Pacific.

Sticky Cinquefoil, *Potentilla glandulosa*, is a western species, growing in open places from B.C. to Calif., and at lower elevations through the mountains to Mont. and Ariz. It is a perennial plant, with a sticky texture due to the many glands that cover its stems. It forms a clump of pinnate leaves and several erect, reddish, leafy flowering stems. The flowers vary in color from creamy white to pale yellow; they are borne in loose terminal clusters.

Tall Cinquefoil
Potentilla arguta

Tall Cinquefoil, *Potentilla arguta*, has white flowers. It is a perennial plant, growing in dry woods and prairies from Que. to Mack., south to D.C. in the east, and to Ariz. in the west. The plant forms a clump of pinnate leaves, rather like those of Silverweed in shape, but covered in sticky brown hairs, like the whole plant. It has stout, erect flowering stems up to 3ft tall, topped with dense clusters of flowers.

Wild Strawberries are much smaller, but sweeter than cultivated ones. There are two widespread species in North America: the native *Fragaria virginiana*, and the introduced European Wild Strawberry, *Fragaria vesca*. They are both perennial plants, with small clumps of compound leaves. The plants spread by runners — long stems which grow out all around the mother plant to form new plants. The white flowers, and then the strawberries, grow in small clusters on leafless stalks.

Wild Strawberry
Fragaria virginiana

Rose family

Agrimony
Agrimonia gryposepala

Honey Dew
Horkelia cuneata

Gordon's Ivesia
Ivesia gordonii

Agrimony is a name given to a group of 15 similar species found throughout the northern hemisphere and in South America. One of the most widespread in North America is *Agrimonia gryposepala*. It grows in open woods and disturbed areas from N.S. to Ont., south to S.C. and Tenn., in the mountains in the south. It is also found in Calif. and N.M. It forms an erect leafy stem, with compound leaves in which large leaflets are interspersed with small ones. Sparse spikes of small yellow flowers are produced in the latter half of summer. The fruits are distinctive, being top-shaped with several rows of hooked bristles on the top surface.

The **Horkelias**, *Horkelia* species, are perennial plants with clumps of pinnate leaves, the upper leaflets joined together. The flowers are usually white, saucer-shaped or cup-shaped, borne in clusters on erect stems, separate from the leaves. Each flower has ten stamens and many carpels. There are about 17 species in western North America. **Honeydew**, *Horkelia cuneata*, is a Californian species with hairy glandular leaves and deeply saucer-shaped flowers. It grows in open sandy fields and woods.

Gordon's Ivesia, *Ivesia gordonii*, is one of about 20 species from western North America. Many grow in the Rocky Mountains and the Great Basin. These are perennial plants with clumps of pinnate leaves and dense clusters of yellow, white or purple flowers on separate stalks. Gordon's Ivesia grows among rocks above the timberline. It forms dense, 8-in tall clumps of almost fern-like leaves. The open yellow flowers are borne in tight heads on almost leafless stalks in the latter half of summer. Each flower has five sepals and five shorter petals.

There are many native **Roses**, *Rosa* species, in North America, as well as European ones which, introduced into gardens, have escaped to grow wild. The **Pasture Rose**, *Rosa carolina*, is one of the smaller native ones, rarely more than 3ft tall. It is found in prairies and pastures, in dry woods, fields and rocky areas, from Me. to Minn., and south to Fla. and Tex. It forms slender, arching branches armed with stiff hairs and prickles. It has compound leaves, each with 3–7 oval leaflets, and is deciduous, losing its leaves in winter. The solitary pink flowers appear in spring or early summer; each flower has five petals and numerous stamens. The fruits (or hips) which follow are formed from the ovary which becomes fleshy and brightly colored. They are red, globular and edible, rich in Vitamin C and minerals.

Pasture Rose
Rosa carolina

The **Sweetbriar** or Eglantine, *Rosa eglanteria*, is a European rose which grows wild in many parts of North America. It may be found in disturbed areas, along roadsides and woodland edges, in old fields and pastures. It is a shrub, with stout arching stems 6–9ft tall, armed with flattened, broad-based thorns. The leaves have 7–9 elliptical leaflets and are covered with stalked glands; they smell of green apples when crushed. The pink flowers appear in early summer, and are followed by red, elongated hips. This is a useful plant: the flesh of the hips can be eaten raw or used to make syrups; the leaves can be steeped in boiling water to make tea; and the petals can be added to salads or candied.

Sweetbriar
Rosa eglanteria

Pea and Bean family

Mottled Milkvetch
Astragalus lentiginosus

Canada Milkvetch
Astragalus canadensis

Leguminosae The third largest family of flowering plants in the world, with about 600 genera and 12,000 species. It includes herbs, shrubs, trees, climbers, water and desert plants, many economically important crops and timber plants, garden plants, poisonous species, and weeds.

There are three sub-families in the Leguminosae, by far the biggest in the temperate regions of the world being the **Papilionoideae**. The features of this group are: flowers bilaterally symmetrical, hermaphrodite; sepals usually 5, fused into a tube; petals 5, unequal — 1 standard petal, 2 wing petals, and 2 lower petals often joined together to form a keel which encloses stamens and ovary; stamens 10, usually with 9 fused and 1 free; ovary superior. Fruit a legume, a pod which splits open along one or both seams. Leaves simple or compound, the latter often with tendrils. Stipules large and leaf-like, small, or forming spines. Nodules on the roots contain bacteria which fix nitrogen and supply the plant with nitrates.

The **Milkvetches** (sometimes called locoweeds), have about 400 species in the genus *Astragalus*, most of them found in the west. A few are excellent forage plants, but many are toxic to cattle and horses. Milkvetches are herbaceous plants, with pinnate leaves formed of an odd number of leaflets. The typical pea flowers grow in racemes in the leaf axils. Their ovoid or oblong pods are often two-celled, and woody or leathery.

Many of the *Astragalus* species have inflated pods, like **Mottled Milkvetch**, *Astragalus lentiginosus*, a highly variable perennial plant found in dry habitats throughout the west from Canada to Mexico. It may be erect or prostrate, hairless or silky-hairy. Its flowers may be purple, pink, yellow or white. The pods are inflated. They always have upturned beaks, but vary in texture from membranous to leathery.

Canada Milkvetch, *Astragalus canadensis*, grows across the U.S. and most of southern Canada in many moist habitats. It is a perennial plant, with strong, erect, and leafy stems. Each leaf has 15–29 elliptical leaflets. The pea-like flowers are pale yellow or white, borne in dense racemes in summer. They are followed by crowded, pointed-oblong pods held erect.

Purple Locoweed
Oxytropis lambertii

The *Oxytropis* species, the **Locoweeds** or Crazyweeds, comprise about 20 species, mostly from the midwest and Rocky Mountain areas. Several are notoriously poisonous to stock, including the common **Purple Locoweed**, *Oxytropis lambertii*, which grows on plains and prairies from Man. to Tex., and west to Mont. and Ariz. This plant forms tufts of silvery, silky leaves and stems, only about 15in tall, with elongated racemes of bright reddish-purple, pea-like flowers held above the leaves in spring and summer.

Late Yellow Locoweed
Oxytropis campestris

Late Yellow Locoweed, *Oxytropis campestris*, grows in prairies and open woods in northern midwestern states and southern Canada. It is a perennial, silky-hairy plant, 6–24in tall with 19–31 lance-shaped leaflets on its leaves. Its yellow-white flowers are borne in stiff racemes and followed by semi-membranous, oblong pods, often with black and white hairs.

Pea and Bean family

The vetches and tares, *Vicia* species, and the wild peas or vetchlings, *Lathyrus* species, are both groups of climbing or scrambling plants. They cling to anything within reach, using the tendrils on their leaves.

Cow Vetch
Vicia cracca

There are about 130 species of **Vetches**, *Vicia* species, in the world, in northern temperate regions and South America. Some are important crop plants, like *Vicia faba*, which is the Horse Bean, and Common Vetch, *Vicia sativa*, which is cultivated for fodder. Others are weeds, often natives of Europe and introduced with seed lots.

Cow Vetch, *Vicia cracca*, grows in meadows and fields, along roadsides, and in woods throughout much of North America, where it has been introduced from Europe. It is a small scrambling plant, up to 3ft tall, twining through other plants with its forked tendrils. It has showy racemes of bright bluish-purple, pea-like flowers growing on long stalks in the leaf axils. They are followed by squarish pods holding several seeds.

American Vetch
Vicia americana

American Vetch, *Vicia americana*, is a native species growing in much of North America, widespread in many different habitats in the west but less so in the east, and mostly found in moist woods in the mountains. It is a climbing perennial plant, with tendrils which cling to surrounding vegetation, and showy blue-purple flowers in early summer. Each leaf has 8–14 oblong leaflets, as well as tendrils. The pea-like flowers are borne in loose racemes of 2–9 flowers, growing on stalks in the axils of the leaves; the racemes are shorter than the leaves.

Sweet Peas and the Everlasting Pea of gardens both belong to the genus *Lathyrus*. There are about 100 wild species in this genus in North America, known as **Wild Peas** or vetchlings. They are similar in appearance to the vetches.

Most of them are poisonous, but the **Beach Pea**, *Lathyrus japonicus*, is an exception, and its young seeds are edible, like peas. This plant grows on sandy beaches and shores on the Atlantic and Pacific coasts, and around the Great Lakes.It has slightly fleshy, often bluish foliage on prostrate, angled stems. The pinnate leaves have 3–6 pairs of leaflets and a terminal coiled tendril. In the latter part of summer racemes of flowers grow in the leaf axils; eastern plants have purple flowers, but western ones often have flowers with a purple standard, and a whitish keel and wings.

Beach Pea
Lathyrus japonicus

Vetchling, *Lathyrus palustris*, grows in marshes and swamps, wet meadows and shores across northern North America, south to Penn. in the east, and in the west to Calif., in the mountains and along the coast. Coastal plants on both sides of the continent tend to be hairier than inland plants. This slender climbing plant has winged stems. Its compound leaves have 4–6 leaflets and a terminal branched tendril; small racemes of red-purple, pea-like flowers grow on long stalks in the leaf axils in midsummer.

Vetchling
Lathyrus palustris

The **Crown Vetch**, *Coronilla varia*, is alien to North America, where it has escaped after introduction as a garden plant from Europe and Asia. It is a small straggling perennial up to 20in tall, with umbels of pink, pea-like flowers growing on long stalks in the leaf axils in summer.

Crown Vetch
Coronilla varia

Pea and Bean family

Slender Bush Clover
Lespedeza virginica

Slender Bush Clover, *Lespedeza virginica*, is one of about 20 bush clovers in eastern North America, all small herbaceous plants. This is one of the tallest, with erect branched stems growing up to 3ft high. It is found in dry upland woods and thickets, from Mass. to Wis., and south to Ga. and Tex. It also extends into southern Ont. and west into Kan. This is a very leafy, downy plant; each compound leaf is divided into three narrow leaflets. Like some of the other bush clovers, the plant has two kinds of flowers: small clusters of petal-less ones in the middle of the stems, and showy clusters of purple petalous flowers growing from the upper leaf axils.

Showy Tick-trefoil
Desmodium canadense

The **Tick-trefoils**, *Desmodium* species, are another group of herbaceous leguminous plants, with nearly 50 species in North America. **Showy Tick-trefoil**, *Desmodium canadense*, is one of the most common, growing in thickets, on riverbanks, and in moist soil, from Que. to Alta., south to S.C. and Ark. This is a bushy, finely hairy plant, up to 6ft tall, with many clover-like leaves, each with three long-oval leaflets. It has many terminal racemes of pink or purple, pea-like flowers in late summer. The pods which follow the flowers are characteristic of tick-trefoils. They do not split open like those of most of the pea family species; instead they become transversely segmented, each segment containing one seed, and eventually split into one-seeded sections. The pods are covered in hooked hairs which become attached to clothes or animals.

Groundnut, *Apios americana*, is a perennial, twining, vine-like plant, with a string of small white tubers forming along the length of its roots. Its stems grow up to 10ft long, and bear pinnate leaves, each with 5–7 ovate leaflets. In the axils of the leaves grow dense clusters of curious brownish-purple flowers; each flower has a reflexed standard petal, two turned-back wing petals, and a horseshoe-shaped, upturned keel. The pods which follow contain several seeds, edible when they are young. The tubers are also edible, with a turnip-like flavor. Groundnut can be found in moist woods and thickets from N.S. to S.D., and south to Fla. and Tex.

Groundnut
Apios americana

The **Hog-peanut,** *Amphicarpa bracteata*, is another useful plant, with edible seeds. However, the pods which contain these seeds are usually underground, the seeds produced by the "normal" pods which grow on the aerial parts of the plant are inedible! This is a perennial plant with twining, vine-like stems and compound leaves, each with three pointed-ovate leaflets. Flowers grow in clusters on long stalks from the axils of the leaves; they are followed by curved pods, usually with three inedible seeds. In contrast to these "normal" flowers and pods, the plant also produces petal-less flowers on thin runners growing from the base of the stem, from which develop small, one-seeded, often subterranean pods. The seeds are edible when boiled. Hog-peanut vines are very common in thickets and moist woods from N.S. to Man. and Mont., south to Fla. and Tex.

Hog Peanut
Amphicarpa bracteata

Butterfly Pea, *Clitória mariana*, grows in dry upland woods from N.Y. to Io., south to Fla. and Tex. It is a twining plant, its compound leaves have three ovate leaflets, and solitary, blue, pea-like flowers grow in its leaf axils.

Butterfly Pea
Clitoria mariana

Pea and Bean family

Wild Licorice
Glycyrrhiza lepidota

Leadplant
Amorpha canescens

Silver Scurf Pea
Psoralea argophylla

Wild Licorice, *Glycyrrhiza lepidota*, is related to European Licorice, *Glycyrrhiza glabra*, from which licorice is extracted. The wild species can also be used as a source of licorice. The wild plant grows in patches in moist ground in waste places, river bottoms, meadows, and prairies, from western Ont. to B.C., and south to Calif. and Tex. Further east it is naturalized and grows wild along railroads and in waste places.

Wild Licorice is a perennial plant with erect, often rather viscid stems, up to 3ft tall, with many compound leaves. These have 11–19 lance-shaped leaflets. The flowers are yellowish or greenish-white, and borne in dense racemes (like bottle-brushes) on long stalks in the leaf axils. The flowers are followed by characteristic brown, oblong pods which are covered by hooked prickly hairs.

Leadplant, *Amorpha canescens*, is unusual among members of the Pea family because its flowers have only one petal — the standard. Its gray leaves and dense racemes of blue flowers make it a conspicuous plant of the dry plains and prairies. It grows from Mich. to Sask., and south to Ark. and N.M. It is a perennial plant, with shrubby stems, up to 3ft tall, and many leaves, each with between 15 and 45 crowded leaflets covered with dense white hairs. The inflorescences are conspicuous but each individual flower is small, with a single blue petal and 10 bright orange stamens. The pods which follow are hairy.

Silver Scurf Pea, *Psoralea argophylla*, is one of about 30 *Psoralea* species, found mostly in the western and midwest regions of the U.S. It grows in plains and prairies from Wis. to southern Alta., and south to Mo. and N.M. The plant has erect, branched stems up to 2ft tall, with compound leaves, each with 3–5 oval leaflets. The leaflets are densely covered with silky white hairs, at least on the undersides and frequently on both sides. The very dark blue flowers grow in small interrupted spikes on long stalks in the upper leaf axils. The pods which follow the flowers are silky, and contain one seed each. This plant is reported to be poisonous, although the related Indian Breadroot, *Psoralea esculenta*, has edible taproots eaten by the Indians.

Bird's-foot Trefoil
Lotus corniculatus

Bird's-foot Trefoil, *Lotus corniculatus*, is a European plant widely naturalized in North America. It is a small trailing, perennial plant with a clump of slender leafy stems which only grow erect if supported by surrounding vegetation. The leaves are compound, each with three leaflets. In summer the plant bears heads of bright yellow, often red-tinged, pea-like flowers, growing on long stalks from the leaf axils. These are followed by elongated pods.

Spanish Lotus
Lotus purshianus

Spanish Lotus, *Lotus purshianus*, is one of about 45 *Lotus* species found in North America, many of them confined to the west and southwest. It is an annual, much branched plant, with only three leaflets on each leaf, and solitary pale pink flowers in the leaf axils. It grows in disturbed dry places and fields from B.C. to Calif. The Hill Lotus, *Lotus humistratus*, is an annual, sprawling, matted plant, with solitary, tiny yellow flowers in the axils of gray-haired leaves; it is common in the foothills of the southern Rockies. Deerweed, *L. scoparius*, is more like a bushy shrub with erect green stems.

Pea and Bean family

White Clover
Trifolium repens

There are nearly 300 species of *Trifolium*, mostly found in north temperate regions, with about 90 species in North America. The majority are **Clovers**. They have compound leaves with three leaflets, and heads or dense head-like spikes of flowers. The flowers are rich in nectar and much sought out by bees. The petals, and often the sepals, persist on the flower heads when pods are formed, so that the head looks withered and brown.

Red Clover
Trifolium pratense

The seed of **White Clover**, *Trifolium repens*, is often added to lawn seed mixes, since the presence of its roots with their nodules improves the soil. It is common throughout North America, in lawns and on roadsides, naturalized from Europe. It is a small plant with creeping stems and leaves with three rounded leaflets; a white band partly encircles the base of each leaflet. The globular heads of white or pink flowers grow in the leaf axils in summer; each head has many flowers and, as in all clovers, the petals are more or less united into a tube with the standard folded around the wings.

Bighead Clover
Trifolium macrocephalum

Many varieties of **Red Clover**, *Trifolium pratense*, are grown as field crops. Red Clover is also found wild in fields and roadsides throughout temperate North America. It is a perennial plant, with thin leafy stems, up to 2ft tall. The leaves have narrow pointed leaflets, each with a whitish, crescent-shaped mark toward the base. The pink-purple, ovoid heads of flowers appear in summer.

Bighead Clover, *Trifolium macrocephalum*, is a native species. It is a low-growing plant with a spreading rosette of stems, only 12in tall at most, palmately compound leaves and large terminal reddish heads; it grows in sage brush and pine woods in the west. Cow Clover, *T. wormskjoldii*, another western species, grows in damp meadows and beside mountain streams; it forms a prostrate mat with large, red-mauve flower heads.

The **Hop-clovers**, also *Trifolium* species, are small, straggling, annual, much branched plants, with clover-like leaves and tiny heads of yellow flowers in summer. There are three similar species in North America, all weeds from Europe, like *Trifolium agrarium*, the species illustrated, growing in lawns, on roadsides, and in waste places. They have one-seeded pods enfolded in the dried remains of the petals.

Hop Clover
Trifolium agrarium

Black Medick, *Medicago lupulina*, resembles the Hop-clovers, but is easy to distinguish in fruit because the petals fall off once flowering is over, and the pods are like tiny, black, coiled, kidney-shaped shells. This is another Eurasian plant found as a weed in North America. It is an annual, with prostrate stems, clover-like leaves, and tiny heads of yellow flowers. It is related to Alfalfa.

Black Medick
Medicago lupulina

Yellow Sweet Clover, *Melilotus officinalis*, although closely related to the medicks, is a taller biennial plant, up to 5ft high, with slender racemes of yellow, pea-like flowers in late summer. It has clover-like leaves with toothed, elliptical leaflets, and a scent of new-mown grass, especially when drying. It comes from Eurasia and is naturalized in waste places and fields in much of North America. White Sweet Clover, *Melilotus alba*, with white flowers, grows in similar places.

Yellow Sweet Clover
Melilotus officinalis

Pea and Bean family

Wild Indigo
Baptisia tinctoria

Wild Indigo, *Baptisia tinctoria*, is one of several related plants, mainly from the east and midwest. It is a smooth, bushy perennial plant about 3ft tall. It has many clover-like leaves, each with three ovate, rounded leaflets, and numerous loose clusters of yellow, pea-like flowers in midsummer, followed by short round pods. Wild Indigo grows in dry or sandy soils, in open woods or burned fields, from southern Ont. to Mich., south to Fla. and Tenn.

There are over 100 species of **Lupins** in North America, belonging to the genus *Lupinus*. Most grow in poor soils, enriching it in the process, for they trap nitrogen with their root nodules. They are annual or perennial plants, with erect stems, palmately compound leaves, and terminal racemes of showy flowers. Most have blue flowers, but some have yellow, white or reddish flowers. The flowers are pea-like, the standard petal with its sides bent backward.

Blue-pod Lupin
Lupinus polyphyllos

Blue-pod Lupin, *Lupinus polyphyllos*, is one of the largest. It has stout, erect stems up to 5ft tall, large palmate leaves, and long, dense terminal racemes of blue flowers. This lupin is unusual in growing, not in poor soils, but in lush damp meadows, beside streams, and in moist woods. It is found from B.C. to Colo. and Alta., south to Calif. This has been one of the most important species in the development of garden lupins.

Tree Lupin
Lupinus arboreus

The **Tree Lupin**, *Lupinus arboreus*, is a semi-shrubby plant, with many erect branched stems up to 6ft tall, and more or less silky palmate leaves. Each one has 5–12 leaflets. The flowers grow in loose racemes, they are usually yellow but may be lilac or a mixture. Tree Lupins grow in sandy places on the coast of Calif, and are also planted on old industrial waste land and spoil heaps elsewhere in North America.

The **Rattleboxes**, *Crotalaria* species, have inflated pods in which the dry seeds rattle as they mature. There are about 10 species, mostly from the east and midwest. They are poisonous annual or perennial plants, with simple leaves, and racemes of yellow, pea-like flowers. **Showy Rattlebox**, *Crotalaria spectabilis*, is an Old World plant naturalized in fields, roadsides, and waste places in the southeast. It has erect stems up to 3ft tall, with ovate leaves and large showy flowers.

Showy Rattlebox
Crotalaria spectabilis

The **Caesalpinioideae** is the subfamily which contains sennas, Judas trees, Honey Locust, etc. Its members have pinnate leaves, and flowers in the leaf axils. The flowers have 5 petals, the upper one (the standard) and the lowermost one larger than the others, and 10 free stamens.

There are about 35 species of **Sennas**, *Cassia* species, in North America; some are herbs, others shrubs, most with yellow flowers and nearly equal petals. **Wild Senna** is a name given to two similar species: *C. hebecarpa* and *C. marilandica*, both perennial plants about 6ft tall, with large pinnate leaves and racemes of yellow flowers. They grow in moist woods and along roadsides in the east. The pods of the first are densely hairy, those of the latter species almost hairless. *Cassia marilandica* is used in herb medicine as a laxative, like commercial senna.

Wild Senna
Cassia hebecarpa

Geranium family

Geraniaceae There are about 5 genera and 750 species, mostly herbs, in this small but familiar family. Some are grown in gardens and greenhouses.

Family Features Flowers more or less regular, hermaphrodite, with parts in 5's. Sepals and petals 5, free and overlapping; stamens 10–15, often joined at the base; ovary superior, with 3–5 cells. Fruits are lobed capsules, with 1 seed in each lobe, and with stigmas elongated into long beaks. Leaves alternate, simple or compound, often palmately lobed. Stipules present.

Spotted Cranesbill
Geranium maculatum

Wild Cranesbills belong to the genus *Geranium*, with about 300 species of mainly temperate region, annual or perennial plants. **Spotted Cranesbill**, *Geranium maculatum*, grows in woods and meadows from Me. to Man., south to Ga., and west to Tenn. and Kan. It is a perennial plant, with a clump of long-stalked palmate leaves. It has rose-pink flowers in loose terminal clusters on separate flowering stalks. Each flowering stalk has a pair of leaves about half way up the stem. Within each flower cluster the flowers grow in pairs. This arrangement of leaves and flowers is characteristic of cranesbills.

Carolina Cranesbill
Geranium carolinianum

The fruits of the cranesbills are highly distinctive. Each fruit consists of five spoon-shaped sections, the bowl of each spoon containing one seed. When the seeds are ripe, they are ejected suddenly as the spoon-handles contract and pull the bowls upward, flinging out the seeds. Afterward the spoons are left curled about the central axis of the fruit.

Carolina Cranesbill, *Geranium carolinianum*, is a small hairy annual plant about 1ft tall, with many branched stems and small pink flowers with very separate, notched petals. It grows in dry and sandy soils, in barren open places and waste ground across southern Canada and in much of the U.S.

Richardson's Cranesbill
Geranium richardsonii

Richardson's Cranesbill, *Geranium richardsonii*, is a perennial western species, growing in damp woods and meadows from B.C. to Sask., and south to Calif. and N.M. It grows about 2–3ft tall, has a clump of deeply cleft basal leaves and several flowering stems with small clusters of white or pinkish, purple-veined flowers.

Herb Robert
Geranium robertianum

Herb Robert, *Geranium robertianum*, is a European plant naturalized in the northeast. It has palmate, almost ferny leaves, with a disagreeable scent. This is an annual, often hairy plant, with branched straggling stems growing up to about 1ft tall, and bright pink flowers. In the fruits each spoon-shaped section comes away whole with the seed, leaving the central axis naked.

Filaree
Erodium cicutarium

The **Storksbills**, from the genus *Erodium*, come mostly from the Mediterranean, and one or two have become weeds in North America. The **Filaree** or Common Storksbill, *Erodium cicutarium*, grows in disturbed and open areas, in fields and on roadsides in much of North America. It is an annual plant, with prostrate branched stems, pinnate ferny leaves, and terminal umbels of pink flowers. The fruits are similar in form to those of the cranesbills, but with much longer "handles" to the "spoons." They split into single-seeded sections, the beaks remaining attached to the seeds and becoming coiled like corkscrews.

Wood Sorrel family

Violet Wood Sorrel
Oxalis violacea

Oxalidaceae There are 3 genera and nearly 900 species in this family, mainly tropical in their distribution, but also found in temperate regions. They are mostly herbs; several are grown in gardens and rock gardens, others are weeds. These are often small, fragile-looking plants, but may be extremely difficult to eradicate because they spread by underground bulbils as well as by abundant seeds.

Family Features Flowers solitary or in cymes; regular, hermaphrodite. Sepals 5; petals 5; stamens 10; ovary superior with 5 cells. Fruits are usually capsules. Leaves clover-like, with 3 rounded leaflets jointed to the leaf stalk, and often folding downward at night.

About 800 of the species in this family belong to the genus *Oxalis*. **Violet Wood Sorrel**, *Oxalis violacea*, is a small native plant of dry woods and prairies, found from Me. to S.D., and south to Fla. and Tex. It has clover-like leaves, and leafless flower stalks about 1ft tall, with umbel-like clusters of rose-violet flowers in early summer. The leaves of this plant, like those of other wood sorrels, are edible in small quantities; they give a sour flavor to salads.

Yellow Wood Sorrel
Oxalis europaea

Yellow Wood Sorrel, *Oxalis europaea*, grows in woods and fields, in gardens and waste land, in much of southern Canada and the U.S. It is a perennial plant with more or less upright, leafy stems, clover-like leaves that fold down at night, and small clusters of yellow flowers in the leaf axils. The very similar Upright Yellow Sorrel, *Oxalis corniculata*, is a common weed in the south, where it grows in gardens and greenhouses.

Touch-me-not family

Balsaminaceae This family has 4 genera and 600 species, 500 of them in the genus *Impatiens*. They are mostly from tropical Asia and Africa, but a few species are native to temperate North America and Europe. Some are grown as ornamentals in gardens and greenhouses.

Family Features Flowers often drooping, solitary or in racemes in leaf axils; bilaterally symmetrical, hermaphrodite. Sepals 3–5, often petal-like, 1 larger than the others and forming a spur; petals 5, the largest uppermost, and 2 on each side usually fused together; stamens 5, alternating with petals; ovary superior with 5 cells. Fruits are capsules; when they are ripe a light touch will trigger them into sudden opening. Leaves simple, alternate, opposite or in whorls. Many are rather succulent herbs with watery translucent stems.

Spotted Touch-me-not
Impatiens capensis

Spotted Touch-me-not, *Impatiens capensis*, grows in wet shady places, along streams, by springs, and in moist woods, from Nf. to Sask., and south to S.C. and Okla. It is an annual plant up to 5ft tall, with succulent translucent stems, and thin, elliptical leaves with wavy margins. The flowers are large and helmet-shaped, hanging in small clusters in the leaf axils in summer; they are orange-yellow with red-brown spots. The capsules burst open at the slightest touch.

Pale Touch-me-not
Impatiens pallida

Pale Touch-me-not, *Impatiens pallida*, is similar but has pale yellow flowers with few red-brown spots. It grows in wet, shady places in meadows and woods, from Que. to Sask., and south to N.C. and Mo., but is less common than Spotted Touch-me-not.

Flax family

Wild Flax
Linum perenne

Linaceae There are about 12 genera and nearly 300 species in this family of herbs and shrubs, growing in tropical and temperate regions. Linen and linseed oil come from Cultivated Flax.

Family Features Flowers usually borne in cymes or racemes, regular, hermaphrodite. Sepals 5; petals 5; stamens 5 or 10, often joined in a ring at the base of the filaments; ovary superior with 2–6 cells. Fruits are usually capsules. Leaves usually alternate, simple, entire, with or without stipules.

Wild Flax, *Linum perenne*, is a perennial, 2–3ft tall plant, which grows in the plains from Man. and Wis. to Alas., and south to Tex. and Calif. It has erect stems, many linear leaves, and loose clusters of sky blue flowers in midsummer. This is one of over 30 *Linum* species found in North America.

Spurge family

Cypress Spurge
Euphorbia cyparissias

Euphorbiaceae A very large family of trees, shrubs, and herbs, most from the tropics, some from the temperate regions. It contains 300 genera and 5000 species, some of them, like rubber and castor oil, of economic importance.

Family Features Flowers regular. Male and female flowers separate, usually on the same plant. Sepals usually present, petals usually absent, but both may be missing. Stamens 1 to many. Ovary superior with 3 cells. Fruits are capsules or drupes. Leaves usually simple, alternate, usually with stipules.

The **Spurges**, *Euphorbia* species, are a vast group of 2000 herbs, shrubs, and trees. Their flowers are very reduced, males consisting of a single stamen, females of a single pistil. Several male flowers are arranged around one female in a bract, the whole arrangement resembling a single flower. These are grouped together in clusters with special, often colored leaves beneath. Spurges have white milky sap, often caustic, sometimes very poisonous.

Some spurges, like **Cypress Spurge**, *Euphorbia cyparissias*, are weeds. It grows in much of the U.S. in waste places, roadsides, and cemeteries. This plant has many erect, branched stems up to 1ft tall, with dense linear leaves. Flower umbels grow at the top of many of the stems, with special round, yellow-green leaves turning red in the sun or with age.

Fire-on-the-mountain
Euphorbia heterophylla

Fire-on-the-mountain or Wild Poinsettia, *Euphorbia heterophylla*, is an annual with an erect branched stem up to 3ft tall, and simple or lobed leaves. Those beneath the flowers are blotched with red or white. Flowers appear in late summer, male flowers in cups, while the female flowers hang outside like little balls. This plant grows in sandy soil, in open places, from Wis. to S.D., and south to Fla. and Ariz. It is also grown in gardens, and may escape from cultivation to grow in disturbed places.

Tread-softly
Cnidoscolus stimulosus

Tread-softly or Spurge Nettle, *Cnidoscolus stimulosus*, is a perennial plant, with erect or sprawling stems, up to 3ft tall, large palmately lobed leaves, and fragrant, trumpet-like flowers. It has many stinging hairs which inflict a painful rash, like that of a stinging nettle. This plant grows in sandy woods and fields from Va. to Fla. and Tex., most commonly in the coastal plain.

Mallow family

Velvet-leaf
Abutilon theophrastii

Flower-of-an-hour
Hibiscus trionum

Common Mallow
Malva neglecta

Malvaceae About 40 genera and 900 species of herbs, shrubs, and trees, in tropical and temperate regions of the world, many in tropical areas of America. The family contains plants grown for ornament, and some, like cotton, are important fiber plants.

Family Features Flowers solitary or in branched clusters in leaf axils; regular, hermaphrodite. Sepals 5, often united; petals 5, usually free; stamens numerous, joined at the base to form a tube; ovary superior with 5 to many cells. Fruit may be a capsule or split into many one-seeded sections. Leaves alternate, entire or palmately lobed. Stipules present. Plants are often velvety, with star-shaped hairs, or scaly.

Abutilon is a mainly tropical genus of shrubs and herbs, with about 100 species. **Velvet-leaf**, *Abutilon theophrastii*, is an Asian plant which has escaped from cultivation to become naturalized in disturbed places in many parts of North America, mostly in the south. This velvety annual plant has a branched stem up to 6ft tall, large, heart-shaped leaves up to 8in across, and solitary yellow flowers in the leaf axils. Its fruits consist of 10–15 hairy, one-seeded sections with horizontal beaks.

There are about 200 species of *Hibiscus* in the warmer regions of the world. **Flower-of-an-hour**, *Hibiscus trionum*, comes from southeastern Europe, but grows in disturbed places in North America. It is a branched annual plant, with an erect stem up to 2ft tall, and three-lobed, wavy-margined leaves. Solitary flowers grow in the leaf axils in summer; the flowers are pale yellow with purple centers and last for only a few hours. The fruits are capsules enclosed in bristly, five-angled calyces, which become inflated and papery.

Mallows are a group of about 30 species belonging to the genus *Malva*. They come from Europe and Asia, and several have become familiar weeds in North America. Mallow fruits resemble round cheeses cut into segments. The base of the fruit is formed from the receptacle cupped in the calyx, and the segments are formed from a flat ring of one-seeded nutlets.

Musk Mallow
Malva moschata

Common Mallow, *Malva neglecta*, is a common weed in gardens and waste places. It is a downy annual plant, with sprawling stems up to 2ft tall, and long-stalked, palmate leaves. The flowers are white, veined or tinged with pink or purple, with notched petals.

Musk Mallow, *Malva moschata*, grows in waste places and on roadsides from Que. to B.C., south in the east to Va. and Neb. This is a perennial plant up to 4ft tall, with branched hairy stems. Its lower leaves are kidney-shaped, upper ones divided into linear segments. The rose pink or purple flowers grow in dense terminal clusters and are followed by densely hairy, dark fruits.

Wheel Mallow
Modiola caroliniana

Wheel Mallow, *Modiola caroliniana*, is native as far north as S.C., but is naturalized further north and in Calif. It is an annual or biennial weed found in lawns and waste places. This is a prostrate plant, with stems up to 2ft long, maple-like leaves, and small, solitary, reddish-purple flowers in the leaf axils. Like the mallows, the plant has a cheese-like fruit.

Mallow family

In the Mallow family, there are several genera and many species native to western North America. Many of them are mountain plants, growing in lush mountain meadows and by springs, while others are from arid areas and deserts.

Winecups
Callirhoë involucrata

The **Poppy Mallows**, *Callirhoë* species, are a small group of southern and midwestern species. **Winecups**, *Callirhoë involucrata*, is the most widely distributed, growing in prairies and plains from Minn. to Wyo., and south to Tex. It is a perennial plant, with trailing hairy stems, palmately cleft leaves, and a few large, bowl-shaped, crimson flowers on long stalks in the leaf axils. The flowers have broadly truncated petals and three bracts beneath the calyx, two features characteristic of poppy mallows. The fruits resemble those of mallows, in a ring with 10–20 nutlets.

Scarlet Globemallow
Sphaeralcea coccinea

The **Globemallows**, belonging to the genus *Sphaeralcea*, are a group of about 20 western species. They are perennial plants with palmate leaves and erect stems with spikes of reddish flowers. Many of them are covered with soft, velvety hairs, and the backs of their fruits are also densely hairy.

Scarlet Globemallow, *Sphaeralcea coccinea*, grows in plains and dry prairies from Man. to Alta., south to Tex., and N.M. It is a spreading, perennial plant, with weakly erect stems and rounded, lobed leaves. Its clusters of brick-red flowers form patches of color on roadsides in early summer.

Mountain Globemallow
Iliamna rivularis

The *Iliamna* species are also known as globemallows. **Mountain Globe-mallow**, *Iliamna rivularis*, grows in moist soil, beside springs, and along the sides of rivers and streams in the Rocky Mountains from B.C. to Ore., and east to Mont. and Colo. It is a perennial plant with clumps of large, maple-like leaves, less deeply dissected than the leaves of many mallows, and erect leafy spikes of pink, hollyhock-like flowers, 3–6ft tall, in summer. The fruits of *Iliamna* species are formed in a ring, like those of many mallows, but they have more than one seed in each segment.

Checkermallow
Sidalcea neomexicana

The **Checkermallows**, *Sidalcea* species, are another group of mostly western mallows, most with pink flowers. Some are grown as garden plants. *Sidalcea neomexicana* is a typical Checkermallow and one of the most widespread, growing in wet, often alkaline, places in the Rocky Mountains, and beside streams and springs. It is a perennial plant, with a clump of shallowly lobed leaves and narrow flowering spikes up to 3ft tall, crowded with pink flowers. White Checkermallow, *Sidalcea candida*, is one of the few mallows with white flowers; it grows in wet places in the Rocky Mountains.

Alkali Mallow
Sida hederacea

The **Alkali Mallow**, *Sida hederacea*, is a rather different plant, with prostrate stems and small, whitish-yellow flowers in the axils of the leaves. It is velvety in texture, with whitish, star-shaped hairs, and it has rounded, kidney-shaped leaves. This plant grows in many wet and alkaline places in the southwestern U.S. and Pacific states. It is one of about 20 *Sida* species in North America, many of them with yellow flowers. Some of them are tropical weeds, extending north as far as Va., and growing in waste places and on roadsides.

Violet family

Common Blue Violet
Viola papilionacea

Violaceae There are 22 genera and 900 species in the family, mostly herbs of temperate and tropical regions, some 500 in the genus *Viola*. Pansies and violets are popular garden plants.

Family Features Flowers solitary or in racemes; regular or bilaterally symmetrical. Sepals 5; petals 5, usually unequal and the lowermost spurred; stamens 5, with anthers joined in a ring, lowermost stamen often spurred; ovary superior with 1 cell. Fruits are capsules or berries. Leaves simple and alternate; stipules leafy.

Western Dog Violet
Viola adunca

There are over 80 **Violets**, *Viola* species, in North America, found especially in damp or shady places. They are small plants, either with rosettes of leaves and flowers on separate stalks, or with long leafy stems with flowers in the leaf axils. Leaves may be long and narrow, round and toothed, or dissected. Violets have spurred, bilaterally symmetrical flowers with five petals in spring. In summer they produce flowers which are hidden beneath the foliage, do not open, and are self-pollinated.

Downy Yellow Violet
Viola pubescens

Common Blue Violet or Meadow Violet, *Viola papilionacea*, has rosettes of pointed, heart-shaped, long-stalked leaves. The blue-violet flowers have white beards on the two lateral petals. This plant grows in damp woods and meadows from Mass. to Minn., and south to Ga. and Okla.

Western Dog Violet, *Viola adunca*, has long erect stems with rounded, scallop-edged leaves, and pale to dark violet flowers in the leaf axils. The plant grows in open woods, meadows and hillsides from Canada to Calif., and on the Great Plains. Eastern Dog Violet, *V. conspersa*, grows in damp mountain meadows and woods from Que. to Ga.

The majority of the yellow violets have leafy stems. **Downy Yellow Violet**, *Viola pubescens*, grows in woods from Que. to N.D., and south to Ga. and Okla. It is a softly hairy plant, with stems reaching 16in long, and leaves 5in wide. Its flowers are clear yellow with purple-brown veins.

Yellow Prairie Violet, *Viola nuttallii*, has more or less upright stems, and lance-shaped or ovate leaves. Its yellow flowers are brown-veined, often tinged with purple on the outside. This violet grows in prairies and woods from Minn. to Mo., and west to B.C. and Calif.

Many white violets are small rosette-forming plants of northern woods. **Kidney-leaved Violet**, *V. renifolia*, grows in swamps and woods in Canada and northern U.S., and in mountains in the east and west. **Canada Violet**, *V. canadensis*, has leafy stems up to 15in long, and pointed, heart-shaped leaves. Its white flowers have a central yellow blotch. It grows in moist woods in southern Canada, northern U.S., and in the mountains.

The **Green Violet**, *Hybanthus concolor*, is very different. It is a coarse plant, with erect leafy stems up to 3ft tall. In the axils of the broad leaves grow little drooping flowers with greenish-white petals. The lowermost petal is wider than the others and is spurred. This plant grows in rich woods and ravines from Ont. to Mich., south to Ga., Ark., and Kan.

Yellow Prairie Violet
Viola nuttallii

Kidney-leaved Violet
Viola renifolia

Green Violet
Hybanthus concolor

Frostweed
Helianthemum canadense

Passion Flower
Passiflora incarnata

Wild Pumpkin
Cucurbita foetidissima

Rockrose family

Cistaceae There are about 8 genera and 200 species in this family of herbs and shrubs, most from the Mediterranean region. Some are grown in gardens.

Family Features Flowers regular, hermaphrodite. Sepals 3–5, free, contorted; petals 5, often contorted, soon falling; stamens many, free; ovary superior. Fruits are capsules. Leaves usually opposite, entire. Stipules present.

Frostweed, *Helianthemum canadense*, grows in dry, sandy soil in open places or woods from Me. to Minn., and south to N.C. and Tenn. It has thin wiry stems, linear leaves, and yellow flowers.

Passion Flower family

Passifloraceae There are about 12 genera and 600 species in this mainly tropical family of trees, shrubs, and vines. Several are grown in gardens.

Family Features Flowers regular, hermaphrodite or unisexual. Sepals 5; petals 5, often joined at base; stamens 5 or more; ovary superior, with 3–5 styles, frequently on a stalk. Flowers often have a corona — 1 or more rows of filaments at base of petals. Fruits are capsules or berries. Leaves alternate, entire or lobed. Stipules small, soon falling.

Passion Flowers are climbers, often with bizarre flowers. *Passiflora incarnata* from the eastern U.S. has solitary, wheel-like flowers, with white sepals and petals, a purple and pink corona, creamy anthers and stigma. Its edible yellow berries are known as maypops. It grows in woods and fields, and on roadsides.

Gourd or Cucumber family

Cucurbitaceae A family of about 100 genera and 900 species, mainly from the tropics, mostly trailing herbs or vines. Important food plants in the family include melons and squashes.

Family Features Flowers regular, male and female separate. Sepals 4–6, more or less united into a tube; petals 5; stamens 1–5, usually more or less united; ovary inferior, with 1–3 cells. Fruit usually a fleshy berry with leathery rind. Leaves alternate, often palmately lobed. Plants often stiffly hairy, with watery juice. Many have tendrils.

Wild Cucumber
Echinocystis lobata

Wild Pumpkin, *Cucurbita foetidissima*, has rough, trailing stems up to 20ft long, large, gray-green, lobed leaves, and funnel-shaped, yellow flowers. The fruits are inedible — hard, spherical pumpkins, green-striped when young, lemon-yellow when ripe. This monstrous plant grows in dry and sandy places, in plains and deserts, from Mo. to Calif., and into Mexico. Further east it grows along the railroads.

Bur-cucumber
Sicyos angulatus

Wild Cucumber, *Echinocystis lobata*, is found in moist woods and meadows, from N.B. to Sask., south to Fla. and Tex. This annual vine has maple-like leaves and sprays of white flowers in the leaf axils. Its solitary prickly berries become dry as they ripen.

Bur-cucumber, *Sicyos angulatus*, is a similar plant, also a climbing vine with palmate leaves, but its bristly, single-seeded fruits grow in clusters. It is found in moist places from Que. to Minn., and south to Fla. and Ariz.

Stickleaf family

White-stemmed Stickleaf
Mentzelia albicaulis

Desert Rock Nettle
Eucnide urens

Purple Loosestrife
Lythrum salicaria

Loasaceae A small family of herbs, with about 15 genera and 250 species, mostly from warm, dry temperate and tropical regions of America.

Family Features Flowers solitary or in clusters; regular, hermaphrodite. Sepals 4–5, fused into a tube, often ribbed, often persistent; petals 4–5, sometimes with claws; stamens usually numerous, free or in bundles opposite petals; ovary inferior with 1–3 cells. Fruit a capsule. Leaves opposite or alternate, simple or divided. Stipules 0. Hairy plants clothed with rough bristly, barbed or stinging hairs.

About 50 *Mentzelia* species grow in the west, many in dry sandy or gravelly places. Many are annual plants, with branched, often white stems, and rigid leaves. Some are called Blazing Stars for their yellow star-like flowers, others are named stickleafs because their barbed hairs cling to clothes or animal hair.

White-stemmed Stickleaf, *Mentzelia albicaulis*, has slender white stems with narrow leaves and small, tubular flowers. This annual plant is common in dry sandy places east of the Sierra Nevada from Calif. to B.C., and across to N.M. and Neb. Giant Blazing Star, *M. laevicaulis*, is a larger plant up to 5ft tall, with lemon-yellow flowers. It grows in dry gravelly places from Calif. to B.C., east to Ut. and Mont.

Desert Rock Nettle, *Eucnide urens*, is a bushy plant with stinging hairs. It has 2-ft tall, sprawling, yellowish stems, and ovate toothed leaves. In early summer it bears many pale yellow flowers. This plant grows in rocky places in deserts from southern Calif. to Ut. and Ariz.

Loosestrife family

Lythraceae There are about 25 genera and 550 species of herbs and shrubs in this family, which come from all over the world, except the cold regions. Some are grown as garden ornamentals. Some species yield dyes, including henna.

Family Features Flowers solitary or in clusters; regular, hermaphrodite. Sepals 4–8, joined to form a tube; petals 4–8, free, often crumpled; stamens 4–8, as many as or twice as many as petals, inserted below the petals on the calyx-tube; ovary superior with 2–6 cells. Fruits are usually capsules. Leaves usually opposite or whorled. Stipules minute or 0.

Winged Loosestrife
Lythrum alatum

Lythrum is a genus of about 30 herbs and small shrubs found throughout the world. **Purple Loosestrife**, *Lythrum salicaria*, grows in most of the northern hemisphere, beside water and in marshes. It is a perennial plant, with tall, leafy stems and terminal spikes of reddish-purple flowers. The flower spikes are made up of whorls of flowers, each with six crumpled petals.

Winged Loosestrife, *Lythrum alatum*, has erect, branched, four-angled stems with thick, pointed leaves, and solitary flowers in the upper leaf axils. It grows in moist soil on the prairies from southern Ont. to Ky. and Tex.

Water Willow
Decodon verticillatus

Water Willow, *Decodon verticillatus*, grows in arching tangles of slender stems, often leaning over the shallow water of bogs and swamps, from Que. to Ill., and south to Fla. and La. It has lance-shaped leaves and clusters of pinkish- purple flowers in the axils of the upper leaves; each flower has a cup-like calyx and five narrow petals.

Evening Primrose family

Fireweed
Chamaenerion angustifolium

Onagraceae There are about 20 genera and 650 species in this family of herbs and shrubs, found throughout the world, but most commonly in temperate regions. Ornamental garden plants in the family include fuchsias, evening primroses and godetias.

Family Features Flowers regular, hermaphrodite. Calyx of 4–5 sepals, fused together and to the ovary; petals 4–5, free, often contorted or overlapping; stamens as many as or twice as many as calyx-lobes; ovary usually inferior, with 2–6 cells and few to many seeds. Fruits are usually capsules. Leaves simple, opposite or alternate. Stipules usually 0.

River Beauty
Epilobium latifolium

Fireweed, *Chamaenerion angustifolium*, forms drifts of purple-red flowers in late summer, especially after fires when it rapidly colonizes burned-over areas. It spreads into wide colonies by means of creeping underground rhizomes, forming many erect leafy stems up to 6ft tall, topped by long spikes of showy red-purple flowers in mid and late summer. The ovaries of the flowers are below the petals and develop into 3-in long capsules, which split open to reveal silky-haired seeds. These are blown by the wind to invade new areas.

Most of the **Willowherbs** belong to the genus *Epilobium*, a large group with over 100 species, found throughout the world except in the tropics. They are annual or perennial plants with pink or purple flowers. **River-beauty**, *Epilobium latifolium*, is a northern willowherb, which grows on river banks and in streams, from Que. to Alas., and in the Rocky Mountains. It has short, often arching stems up to 20in tall, forming tangled masses with fleshy, often whitish leaves, and clusters of magenta flowers in the upper leaf axils. Its flowers have the typical willowherb form, with elongated ovaries beneath the petals. Young shoots can be cooked and eaten like asparagus.

Parched Willowherb
Epilobium paniculatum

Parched Willowherb, *Epilobium paniculatum*, is an annual hairless plant, growing up to 6ft tall. Its stem is simple and has shredding skin near the base, and is very much branched above, with alternate linear leaves and flowers on all the branches. The small flowers have four pink, notched petals above an elongated ovary, which elongates even more in fruit to form a four-angled, linear capsule. This is a common plant of dry places in the west, from B.C. to Calif., through the mountains to S.D. and N.M. Other similar willowherbs grow in the west.

Seedbox
Ludwigia alternifolia

There are about 30 species of *Ludwigia*, mostly from the eastern U.S. They are perennial aquatic or marsh plants, with erect, creeping or floating stems, their flowers like those of evening primroses. **Seedbox**, *Ludwigia alternifolia*, is an erect plant, with branched stems and lance-shaped leaves. Solitary yellow flowers grow in the axils of the upper leaves; each flower has four petals alternating with four broad sepals which are longer than the petals. The flowers are followed by squarish capsules, opening by a pore at the top — the seedboxes. This plant grows in swamps and wet places from southern Ont. to Fla. and Tex.

Evening Primrose family

Enchanter's Nightshade
Circaea alpina

Enchanter's Nightshade, *Circaea alpina*, is a little woodland plant, growing in cool damp woods across Canada, south as far as N.Y. and S.D., further south in the mountains to Tenn. in the east, and N.M. in the west. It has weak stems, 1ft tall at most, and toothed, pointed heart-shaped leaves with winged stalks. In late summer this plant forms sparse racemes of tiny white flowers; each flower has two sepals, two notched petals, and two stamens, and grows on a downward-pointing stalk. The fruits that follow are bristly capsules.

California Fuchsia
Zauschneria californica

California Fuchsia, *Zauschneria californica*, is a native plant which is also grown in gardens. It is rather shrubby, with many branches and linear leaves, often covered with short, matted, grayish hairs. In late summer and fall it covers itself with brilliant red, trumpet-shaped flowers, growing in the axils of the upper leaves. The flowers are followed by erect, linear, four-angled capsules. In the wild the plant grows on dry lower slopes, in chaparral, and in the coastal sage brush from southern Ore. to Baja Calif., and east to N.M.

There are about 33 *Clarkia* species in western North America and Chile, all of them annuals, most with showy flowers, and some of them grown in gardens. **Farewell-to-spring** or Herald-of-summer, *Clarkia amoena*, has erect or sprawling stems, up to 3ft tall, with lance-shaped leaves, like many other clarkias, and terminal flowers opening from erect buds. The sepals are joined at the tips and are pushed out to one side when the flowers open. The flowers are bowl-shaped, with four petal-lobes, pink or lavender with bright red blotches in the center of each petal. Farewell-to-spring grows on slopes and bluffs near the sea, in coastal scrub and grasslands from southern B.C. to central Calif.

Tongue Clarkia, *Clarkia rhomboidea*, grows on open slopes and in chaparral from Calif. and Ariz. to Wash. and Mont. It has a simple or somewhat branched stem, up to 3ft tall, with a few ovate leaves and flowers near the top. The stem is curved while the flower buds are forming, and the buds droop, the stem straightening up as the flowers open. The flowers have lobed petals; they are pink or lavender with darker flecks, and the petals have a red base. Some of the clarkias have truly elaborate flowers, like Lovely Clarkia, *C. concinna*, with four petals arranged in a cross, each petal trilobed.

Scarlet Beeblossom, *Gaura coccinea*, does not have scarlet flowers, at least not at first. The flowers open white in the evening, gradually becoming darker pink during the next day but falling before evening. This is a perennial bushy plant, with branched stems and more or less toothed, linear or lance-shaped leaves. The flowers grow in terminal spikes; each one has four unequal clawed petals, all spreading upward, and eight stamens with long filaments. The fruits which follow are erect, four-angled, club-shaped capsules. This plant grows on dry slopes, usually near limestone, among pinyon and junipers, in the plains and prairies, and in the mountains from Man. to Tex. and into Mexico, west in the U.S. to Calif. and to Mont.

Farewell-to-spring
Clarkia amoena

Tongue Clarkia
Clarkia rhomboidea

Scarlet Beeblossom
Gaura coccinea

Evening Primrose family

The **Evening Primroses**, members of the genus *Oenothera*, are a large group of New World species, mostly found in the temperate regions, many in the west. They often have fragrant white or yellow flowers, which open in the evening.

Common Evening Primrose
Oenothera biennis

One of the most widespread is **Common Evening Primrose**, *Oenothera biennis*, which grows in much of the U.S. and southern Canada. It is a biennial plant, with a rosette of lance-shaped, often wavy leaves in the first year, and a leafy flowering spike up to 5ft tall in the second. The large, yellow, four-petalled flowers open in the evening. The fruits are large capsules, held more or less upright. Evening primrose oil is extracted from this plant.

Showy Evening Primrose
Oenothera speciosa

One of the most attractive evening primroses, a plant often grown in gardens, is **Showy Evening Primrose**, *Oenothera speciosa*, with white or pink flowers. This is a perennial plant, with erect, branched stems up to 2ft tall, and many lobed, lance-shaped leaves. It bears showy flowers in the axils of the upper leaves in early summer; they open in the evening from nodding buds. In its native state this plant grows in dry open places, in the prairies and plains from Mo. and Kan. to Tex., and into Mexico, but it has also become naturalized further east, growing in waste places and roadsides.

In the west, evening primroses and suncups, as some of them are called, grow in all kinds of habitats from deserts to coastal dunes, in the mountains, in chaparral and sage scrub, in washes, dry flats, and grasslands. They vary from small rosette-forming plants which hug the ground to plants with erect stems, like Common Evening Primrose.

Yellow Cups, *Oenothera brevipes*, grows in the Mojave and Colorado deserts, in Nev. and Ariz., in Creosote Bush scrub, on dry slopes, and in washes. Like many desert plants, it is an annual. It forms a reddish, erect stem up to 15in tall, growing from a rosette of deeply toothed basal leaves. Its flowers are bright yellow, borne in a terminal cluster on the stem, and followed by linear capsules.

The **Birdcage Evening Primrose**, *Oenothera deltoides*, is given this name because its dead stems look like a birdcage. This desert plant grows as a winter or spring annual in sandy places and in Creosote Bush scrub, in the Mojave and Colorado deserts, and into Ariz. It has sprawling, pale stems, 1ft tall at most, with peeling skin, and long-stalked ovate leaves on the stems and in a basal rosette. In the axils of the upper leaves are large white flowers which turn pink as they age. The fruits that follow are cylindrical, woody capsules, also with peeling skin, light brown in color with purple spots.

Brown-eyes, *Oenothera clavaeformis*, gets its name from the brown spot at the base of each petal. It is an annual plant with a rosette of irregularly toothed leaves and a single stem, only 15in tall, topped by a raceme of white flowers. The flowers darken to reddish as they age. Brown Eyes grows in sandy soils from the Great Basin to Calif., in the Mojave and Colorado deserts.

Yellow Cups
Oenothera brevipes

Birdcage Evening Primrose
Oenothera deltoides

Brown-eyes
Oenothera clavaeformis

Meadow Beauty family

Common Meadow Beauty
Rhexia virginica

Melastomataceae A large family of tropical and subtropical plants, with about 240 genera and 3000 species of trees, shrubs and herbs. It is represented in North America by 1 genus and about 10 species.

Meadow Beauties, *Rhexia* species, are found in eastern and southern North America. They are perennial plants with branched stems, opposite, almost stalkless leaves, and large, usually pink or purple flowers. The flowers are regular, hermaphrodite, with four sepals fused into a tube, four petals and eight stamens. The fruit is a capsule enclosed by the calyx, which becomes distended and develops a flaring neck, so that the whole thing resembles an urn.

One of the most widespread is **Common Meadow Beauty**, *Rhexia virginica*, also known as Virginia Meadow Beauty. It grows in moist meadows, beside bogs and ditches, in wet sandy pinelands, from N.S. to Wis., and south to Fla. and Tex.

Wild Sarsaparilla
Aralia nudicaulis

Ginseng family

Araliaceae A mostly tropical family of 55 genera and about 700 species, chiefly trees and shrubs. Some, like ivy, are grown in gardens. One of the most famous family members is Ginseng.

Family Features Flowers small, regular, hermaphrodite. Calyx toothed; petals 3 – many, often 5, free or united; stamens free, alternating with petals; ovary inferior, usually with as many cells as petals. Fruit is a drupe or berry.

Leaves simple or compound, usually alternate, often covered with star-shaped hairs. Stipules minute.

Spikenard
Aralia racemosa

Several species of *Aralia* are found in North America, most being perennial herbs. The long rhizomes of **Wild Sarsaparilla**, *Aralia nudicaulis*, were used by many tribes of Indians for their tonic and stimulant properties, to make tea and root beer. The plant grows in upland woods from Nf. to B.C., and south to Ga. and Colo. From its rhizomes grow stems bearing umbrella-like leaves. Each leaf has three long-stalked, pinnately divided sections. The greenish-white flowers appear in early summer, borne in rounded umbels on separate long stalks. The fruits are dark blue-black berries.

Spikenard, *Aralia racemosa*, is also used by American Indians in their herbal medicine, for making tea and root beer. It has erect stems which grow up to 6ft tall, each stem bearing a few large spreading leaves and compound terminal umbels of tiny green flowers. The flowers are followed by purple berries.

American Ginseng
Panax quinquefolius

American Ginseng, *Panax quinquefolius*, is a popular herbal remedy, although it is far from clear what its effects are. At one time this plant grew in rich woods from N.S. to Minn., south to Ind. and in the mountains to Ga., but it is extinct in many regions. It is a perennial, with a fleshy, slow-growing, spindle-shaped root, and an erect stem up to 2ft tall, with a circle of three compound leaves at the top. At the center of this circle is the single umbel of small greenish flowers, appearing in mid summer and followed by red berries.

Carrot or Parsley family

Water Pennywort
Hydrocotyle americana

Wild Carrot
Daucus carota

Umbelliferae or Apiaceae A large family of herbs, with about 270 genera and 2800 species, mostly from northern temperate regions. Many kitchen herbs come from this family, like parsley, fennel and dill, and vegetables like carrots and parsnips. Some species, like the hemlocks, are very poisonous.

Family Features Flowers tiny, regular and hermaphrodite, borne in umbels. Calyx 5-lobed, fused to ovary; petals 5, free; stamens 5, alternating with petals; ovary inferior with 2 cells. The fruit consists of two sections, one each side of the central axis of the fruit, and often joined together and suspended across the top of the central axis. When the fruit is ripe it splits from the bottom, each section swinging from the top and exposing the seeds. Leaves alternate, usually compound, often divided, with sheathing bases. Many species have furrowed stems, either with soft pith or hollow in the center. Many are aromatic.

Water Pennyworts, *Hydrocotyle* species, are small perennial plants associated with wet places and water. They have creeping or floating stems, and rounded leaves, like "pennies." *Hydrocotyle americana* has very slender, creeping stems, long-stalked, shallowly lobed, rounded leaves, and small clusters of greenish-white flowers in the leaf axils. The plant grows in wet woods, bogs and meadows, from Nf. to Wis., south to N.C. and Tenn.

Wild Carrot, *Daucus carota*, is a common weed of waste places, roadsides and fallow fields nearly throughout the continent. It is a biennial plant, with ferny leaves in the first year and leafy flowering stems in the second. These have dense umbels of creamy white flowers, usually with one central purplish or red flower in each umbel. The fruiting umbels close up and resemble birds' nests, with spiky fruits.

Venus' Comb, *Scandix pecten-veneris*, grows as a weed in fields and on roadsides in the northeastern US but has become rarer as a result of modern farming techniques. It is an annual, with a branched stem up to 2ft tall, and dissected leaves. The small white flowers are borne in simple umbels in early summer. The plant becomes distinctive when the fruits form, for they are 2–3in long with very long beaks.

Venus' Comb
Scandix pecten-veneris

Sweet Cicely, *Osmorhiza claytoni*, is one of several similar species found in North America. This one grows in moist woods from N.S. to Sask., and south to N.C. and Ark. It is a hairy perennial plant, with a root smelling of anise, branched erect stems, and spreading, bluntly divided leaves. The small white flowers grow in sparse, flat-topped, compound umbels, and are followed by dark, hairy, narrowly elliptical fruits.

Sweet Cicely
Osmorhiza claytoni

Black Snakeroot or American Sanicle, *Sanicula marilandica*, was used in Indian herb medicine to treat fevers and St Vitus' Dance; more recently it has been used as a remedy for sore throats and mouth ulcers. It is a perennial plant with a clump of palmately cleft leaves with five toothed leaflets. The flower stalks bear dense compound umbels of greenish-white flowers. The fruits which follow are ovoid, with hooked bristles.

Black Snakeroot
Sanicula marilandica

Carrot or Parsley family

Hemlock
Conium maculatum

Several of the umbellifers are deadly poisonous. **Hemlock**, *Conium maculatum*, is originally a Eurasian plant, but is now widely naturalized as a weed in waste places and on roadsides, usually in damp places, throughout many parts of the U.S. and southern Canada. It is one of the most poisonous, and can cause paralysis and death. In appearance it is like many other umbellifers, with upright stems, fern-like leaves, and umbels of white flowers in summer. Its distinguishing features are its smooth, furrowed, grayish, hollow stems with purplish spots, and its unpleasant scent, often likened to cat's urine. It is a biennial plant, with only a clump of leaves in the first year, flowering stems up to 6ft tall in the second. Its dark brown fruits are globular, with wavy, pale brown ridges.

Water Hemlock
Cicuta maculata

An equally poisonous native species is **Water Hemlock**, *Cicuta maculata*, which grows in swamps and wet meadows, in ditches and wet thickets, from Que. to Wyo., and south to Fla. and Mexico. This is a perennial plant, with a branched stem up to 6ft tall, with compound pinnate leaves and domed compound umbels of white flowers. It can be recognized by its hollow, purple-streaked stems, and yellow, oily sap which smells of parsnips. There are other species of *Cicuta* in North America, all poisonous, all growing in wet places, and all with thickened roots and the parsnip scent. However, the others do not have spotted stems. The roots are the most poisonous part, and even a small quantity may prove lethal.

In contrast to this poisonous lookalike, **Water Parsnip**, *Sium suave*, has edible roots but is so similar in appearance to Water Hemlock, that it is better not to take any risks in eating its wild roots. It is a perennial plant, with a tall branched, angular stem, and once-pinnate leaves with lance-shaped leaflets. Its umbels of white flowers appear in late summer. The plant grows in wet meadows and swamps across much of North America.

Cow Parsnip, *Heracleum lanatum*, is a large, hairy perennial plant, one of the largest umbellifers and up to 9ft tall. It has an erect stem, hollow inside, ridged and woolly in texture. The leaves are huge, each divided into three often deeply toothed leaflets, measuring up to 2ft across. The white flowers are borne in compound umbels, 6–12in across. The flowers in each umbel vary — those near the rim with enlarged, notched petals pointing toward the outside. The fruits are oval with broad, winged ridges. The plant grows in wet places, in meadows, and beside streams throughout much of North America. Its young stems and roots can be used as a vegetable.

The true **Parsnip**, *Pastinaca sativa*, has yellow flowers and a strong parsnip smell. It is a biennial plant, with a clump of pinnately divided leaves and an edible taproot in the first year. In the second year it forms hollow, furrowed stems up to 5ft tall, and bright green leaves with serrated leaflets. They bear dense compound umbels of tiny yellow flowers in late summer. Each flower has five inrolled petals. Wild Parsnips are native to Eurasia but have become naturalized over most of North America, growing in waste places, on roadsides, and in fields.

Water Parsnip
Sium suave

Cow Parsnip
Heracleum lanatum

Parsnip
Pastinaca sativa

Fennel
Foeniculum vulgare

Dill
Anethum graveolens

Golden Alexanders
Zizia aurea

Carrot or Parsley family

Fennel, *Foeniculum vulgare*, is a familiar salad plant and vegetable, with an anise-like scent and taste. It is native to the Mediterranean but is naturalized over much of the U.S., especially in the warmer south, growing in waste places, on roadsides, in fields and grasslands. It is a short-lived, perennial plant, with an erect, solid stem up to 6ft tall, and many extremely finely divided, ferny leaves. Growing opposite the upper leaves are compound umbels of yellow flowers. The fruits are egg-shaped and ribbed.

Dill, *Anethum graveolens*, is one of several aromatic umbellifers cultivated for their seeds, which are used to flavor food. Dill is native to the Mediterranean, but has escaped from cultivation in many parts of the U.S. to grow in waste places and on roadsides. It is an erect, branched, annual plant, up to 5ft tall, hairless and blue-green in color, with compound leaves so finely divided that their segments appear threadlike. The greenish-yellow flowers are borne in large compound umbels, with 30–40 small umbels in each compound one. The fruits are flattened and elliptical, and strongly ridged.

There are three species of **Golden Alexanders** in the genus *Zizia*, all found in wet woods and meadows. They are hairless perennial plants, with branched stems up to 3ft tall, and loose compound umbels of golden yellow flowers. *Zizia aurea* is found from Que. to Sask., and south to Fla. and Tex. Its leaves are compound, with lance-shaped, serrated leaflets, and it has 10–18 little umbels in each compound umbel. *Zizia aptera* grows in southern Canada, south to Ga., and to Colo. in the west. It has simple, heart-shaped basal leaves. The third species, *Z. trifoliata*, is found in mountain woods of the southeastern U.S.; it has compound leaves and 4–10 little umbels in each compound umbel.

About 80 **Prairie Parsleys**, *Lomatium* species, grow in western North America. They are perennial plants, with compound, often ferny leaves, and yellow or purple flowers in compound umbels. Many have very short stems, and some have edible roots, known as cous and eaten by Indians. Their leaves often smell like parsley.

Biscuitroot
Lomatium macrocarpum

Biscuitroot, *Lomatium macrocarpum*, grows in dry open places from B.C. to Alta., and south to Calif. It may be quite densely hairy and purplish in color at the base. Its tiny, white or yellow flowers grow in dense compound umbels, 5–25 small umbels in each compound one. The fruits are flattened oblongs with narrow wings.

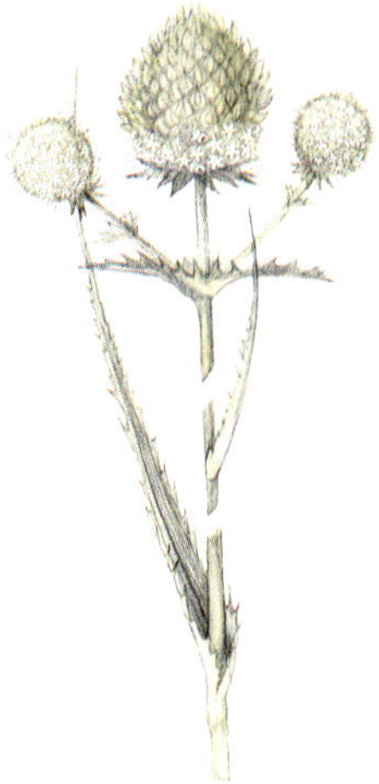

Rattlesnake Master
Eryngium yuccifolium

Rattlesnake Master, *Eryngium yuccifolium*, is not immediately recognizable as an umbellifer; its flowers are in heads rather than umbels, and its leaves are like those of a yucca. It is a perennial plant, with a clump of linear, spine-edged leaves, and a single flowering stem up to 5ft tall and branched near the top to bear the flower heads. These heads consist of about 30 densely packed flowers with white or greenish petals, each one cupped in a green bract. The plant grows in woods and prairies, from New England to Minn., and south to Fla. and Tex.

Pipsissewa
Chimaphila umbellata

White Wintergreen
Pyrola elliptica

Shortleaf Wintergreen
Pyrola virens

Wintergreen family

Pyrolaceae A small family with 4 genera and about 40 species of evergreen herbs, mostly from Arctic and northern temperate regions. They are sometimes included in the Heath family or combined with the Indian Pipe family.

Family Features Flowers solitary or in clusters, often nodding, regular, hermaphrodite. Calyx of 4 or 5 fused sepals; petals usually 5, free or joined at the base; stamens usually 10; ovary usually superior, with 4–5 cells. Fruit is a globular capsule with many small seeds. Leaves simple, in basal rosette or, if on the stems, alternate or in whorls. Stipules 0.

About 12 **Wintergreens**, *Pyrola* species, grow in North America, usually in coniferous woods. They have rosettes of evergreen leaves and leafless stems, with terminal clusters of nodding white or pink flowers. **White Wintergreen** or Shinleaf, *Pyrola elliptica*, is typical, growing in woods from Nf. to B.C., south to W.Va., into Mont. and Ida. in the west. It has a rosette of broadly ovate leaves and a raceme of nodding white flowers in summer.

Shortleaf Wintergreen, *Pyrola virens*, is a smaller plant, with white, green-veined flowers. It grows in dry woods in Canada and the northern U.S.

Pipsissewa or Prince's Pine, *Chimaphila umbellata*, is a small subshrubby plant with creeping rhizomes and whorls of leathery, toothed leaves. Its 1-ft tall stems bear 4–8 nodding, fragrant, waxy flowers in summer; each flower has five white or purplish petals, and ten radiating stamens. The plant is usually found in coniferous woods across southern Canada and much of the U.S. It is used in the herbal medicine of many Indian tribes to treat kidney infections.

Indian Pipe family

Monotropaceae Specialized plants, lacking chlorophyll and growing in soils rich in raw humus, often in coniferous woodland. They are white, pink or brownish in color, with a mass of roots covered in fungi. The fungi presumably enable them to absorb nutrients from the humus in the soil. There are about 12 genera and 30 species in the north temperate regions.

Family Features Flowers regular, hermaphrodite, dull in color, solitary or in racemes on erect stems. Sepals 2–6, free; petals usually 4–5, free or forming a lobed corolla; stamens twice as many as petals; ovary superior, with 1–6 cells. Fruits are capsules. Leaves are scales.

Indian Pipe
Monotropa uniflora

Indian Pipe, *Monotropa uniflora*, forms white, fleshy stems up to 9in tall in the leaf litter of woods in summer. Each stem has transparent scale-like leaves and bends over at the top, where the single little, bell-like flower hangs. Pinesap, *M. hypopitys*, is similar but has brownish stems and several flowers. Both are found throughout North America.

Pinedrops
Pterospora andromedea

Pinedrops, *Pterospora andromedea*, forms a clump of reddish-brown, erect stems up to 3ft tall, with drooping, yellowish, bell-like flowers that glisten translucently. The stems persist for several years after flowering, becoming dried and dark brown in color. The plant grows in northern coniferous woods.

Heath family

Ericaceae This is a large family, with about 70 genera and 1500 species, growing throughout the world. Many grow in acid soils. All members of the family are woody to a greater or lesser extent, and some are large shrubs or trees. Others are creeping, subshrubby plants. Fine garden plants include azaleas, rhododendrons, and heathers. Cranberries and blueberries are grown for their fruits.

Family Features Flowers often showy, solitary or in clusters, usually regular and hermaphrodite. Calyx tubular, formed of 4 or 5 sepals; corolla tubular or bell-like, formed of 4 or 5 joined petals; stamens twice as many as petal-lobes; ovary superior with several cells. Fruits are capsules, berries or drupes. Leaves usually evergreen, mostly simple, usually alternate. Stipules 0.

Kinnikinnick
Arctostaphylos uva-ursi

Known to Indians as **Kinnikinnick**, and to Europeans as Bearberry, *Arctostaphylos uva-ursi* grows right around the North Pole, south in North America to Va., N.M., and Calif. It is found in exposed sandy and rocky ground, like pine barrens, where it may cover large areas. This is a prostrate, shrubby plant with woody stems and spoon-shaped, evergreen leaves. It bears pink-tinged, white, bell-like flowers in early summer, and red, mealy berries in winter. The berries are edible if cooked, and said to be palatable with cream and sugar. The Indians dried and smoked the leaves as a tobacco substitute. The leaves are rich in tannins and were also used for tanning leather. There are many other *Arctostaphylos* species in Central America and Calif., where they are known as Manzanitas. They are woody plants, shrubs or crooked trees.

Wintergreen
Gaultheria procumbens

Wintergreen, *Gaultheria procumbens*, is another northern creeping plant, also known as Checkerberry. It is the source of Oil of Wintergreen, used to flavor cough drops, candy, and toothpaste. In the wild, Wintergreen grows in woodlands in acid soil, from Nf. to Man., south to Va. and Ky., and in the mountains to Ga. It has creeping rhizomes from which grow many erect green stems. These have evergreen leaves crowded near the tops, and white, bell-shaped flowers drooping from the leaf axils. The berries ripen to red by late summer and often remain on the plants through the winter.

Mountain Heather
Cassiope mertensiana

Mountain Heather, *Cassiope mertensiana*, is one of several **Moss Heathers**, *Cassiope* species, found in the north and northwest. The name moss heather is descriptive of these small matted, creeping shrubs, with their flat, linear, evergreen leaves, crowded close to the stems. Mountain Heather grows in the northwest on slopes near the timber line in the mountains from Alas. to Calif. and Nev. In late summer it bears small, white, bell-like flowers in leaf axils near the ends of the branches.

Pink Mountain Heather
Phyllodoce empetriformis

Pink Mountain Heather, *Phyllodoce empetriformis*, is another low creeping shrublet, with needle-like, evergreen leaves. In the latter half of summer it bears pink, urn-shaped flowers in the leaf axils near the ends of the branches. This plant grows in alpine meadows and slopes in the Rocky Mountains from Alas. to Calif. and Colo. Cream Mountain Heather, *P. glandulifera*, grows in the mountains from Ore. and Wyo. northward; it has yellowish or greenish-white flowers.

Heath family

Alpine Azalea
Loiseleuria procumbens

Alpine azalea, *Loiseleuria procumbens*, is an attractive, far northern plant, growing in exposed rocky or peaty areas all around the North Pole, from northern Canada south to the mountains of N.Y. It forms bushy mats of branched, woody stems, with opposite, evergreen leaves. Small clusters of white or pink, bell-shaped flowers in summer are followed by ovoid capsules.

Over 30 *Vaccinium* species grow in North America, including cranberries, bilberries, and huckleberries. **Cranberry**, *Vaccinium macrocarpon*, is a trailing shrub with slender stems and small, evergreen, elliptical leaves. It bears clusters of nodding, pinkish-white flowers in the axils of the lower leaves, recognizable from their four backward-pointing petals and cone of fused stamens. They are followed by dark red fruits. Plants grow in bogs and along lake shores from Nf. to Man., south to Va., and in the mountains to Tenn.

Cranberry
Vaccinium macrocarpon

Cowberry or Mountain Cranberry, *Vaccinium vitis-idaea*, grows in bogs and among rocks throughout boreal North America, south to the mountains of New England, Minn., and B.C. This is another low-growing, creeping shrub with many arching branches and leathery leaves. It bears drooping clusters of bell-shaped, pink-tinged, white flowers terminating the stems in mid summer, then red, edible berries in fall.

Crowberry family

Empetraceae A very small family, with 3 genera and 9 species, from temperate and Arctic regions, South America, and Tristan da Cunha.

Crowberry, *Empetrum nigrum*, is the only widespread or common member of the family in North America, growing in acid peaty soils in the boreal north, south to the mountains of New England and Minn. It is a low-growing, evergreen shrub, with slender stems, and small, leathery, needle-like leaves. Tiny pink flowers grow in the axils of the leaves, male and female flowers on separate plants, and the female plants produce juicy black berries.

Cowberry
Vaccinium vitis-idaea

Leadwort family

Plumbaginaceae A relatively small family of herbs and shrubs, with 10 genera and 300 species. They are especially numerous in the Mediterranean area and in Asia.

Family Features Flowers regular, hermaphrodite, borne in one-sided inflorescences or in heads, with sheathing, often dry, papery bracts. Calyx ribbed, often papery, formed from 5 fused sepals; corolla of 5 fused petals which often persist around the fruits; stamens 5, opposite the petals; ovary superior with 1 cell and 5 styles. Fruits are nuts or capsules opening by lids. Leaves simple, often in basal rosette. Stipules 0.

Crowberry
Empetrum nigrum

Thrift, *Armeria maritima*, grows in salt-marshes, on coastal bluffs, and in sandy places around the northern coasts of North America, from Nf. to Calif. It is a little, cushion-forming plant, with tufts of narrow, rather fleshy leaves, growing from the branches of a woody rootstock. Red-purple flowers with papery bracts grow in heads, on long separate stalks. The plant is often grown in gardens, forming carpets as it grows older.

Thrift
Armeria maritima

Primrose family

Primulaceae There are about 28 genera and 800 species of herbs in this family, mostly found in the northern hemisphere, and many restricted to the mountains. They include some choice garden plants, including primulas and cyclamens.

Family Features Flowers regular, hermaphrodite, solitary or borne in branched clusters or umbels. Calyx toothed, formed of 5 fused sepals; corolla lobed, formed of 5 fused petals; stamens usually 5, opposite the petal-lobes; ovary superior with 1 cell. Fruits are capsules with many seeds. The majority have their leaves in basal rosettes. Others have leafy stems with simple or lobed leaves.

Fairy Candelabra
Androsace septentrionalis

There are about 60 species of *Androsace* in the northern hemisphere, many confined to the mountains, and some grown in rock gardens. They are small plants which form a basal rosette of leaves, and several leafless flowering stems with umbels of small flowers.

Fairy Candelabra, *Androsace septentrionalis*, is more widely distributed than many, growing in rocky places in the Rocky Mountains, and in sandy places on the northern prairies and plains. It is an annual plant, no more than 10in tall at most, with a rosette of lance-shaped leaves, and umbels of pale pink or white flowers.

Western Shooting Star
Dodecatheon pulchellum

Shooting Stars are a group of about 14 species, many from western North America and belonging to the genus *Dodecatheon*. They have distinctive dart-like flowers, with swept-back corolla lobes, and fused stamens forming a beak. They are perennial plants, with rosettes of smooth, lance-shaped or ovate leaves, and leafless stalks with umbels of drooping flowers. The flowers of most species are pink or magenta, banded with white or yellow. **Western Shooting Star**, *D. pulchellum*, is one of the most widely distributed, growing in grassland, on the coast, and in the mountains, from Alas. to Mexico, and east to Wis. The similar *D. meadia* is an eastern species, found from Md. to Wis., south to Ga. and Tex. Both species may be grown in damp places in the garden.

Scarlet Pimpernel
Anagallis arvensis

Scarlet Pimpernel, *Anagallis arvensis*, is an attractive little European plant grown in gardens in North America, and now growing wild in back yards, roadsides, and waste places throughout much of the continent. It has sprawling stems with opposite, pointed-ovate leaves, and many solitary red flowers on long stalks in the leaf axils. These flowers open in the morning, closing at about 3 o'clock in the afternoon, and remaining closed in dull weather. Its many flowers produce capsules, which open by hinged lids to release the seeds.

Sea Milkwort
Glaux maritima

Sea Milkwort, *Glaux maritima*, is another creeping plant, but found in very different conditions. It grows around the coasts of the north temperate regions, in grassy salt-marshes, on rocks and cliffs, and in estuaries, also in alkaline places inland. It is a small perennial, succulent plant, with prostrate stems rooting at the nodes, and bearing many pairs of pointed-ovate, blue-green leaves. The solitary flowers grow in the leaf axils in summer; they have no petals but the bell-shaped calyx is white or pink. The fruits are globular capsules which split into five valves to release the seeds.

Bird's-eye Primrose
Primula mistassinica

Swamp Candles
Lysimachia terrestris

Moneywort
Lysimachia nummularia

Primrose family

The **Primulas**, genus *Primula*, are a large group of species centered in Asia, and beloved of gardeners throughout the temperate world.

In North America, there are relatively few native *Primula* species. They follow the pattern of the genus in being perennial plants with rosettes of basal leaves, and separate leafless flower stalks carrying the flowers. Parry's Primrose, *Primula parryi*, is a western species, growing in mountain crevices and on wet screes. It has large, rather fleshy leaves, and an umbel of bright pink or purple, yellow-eyed flowers.

Bird's-eye Primrose, *Primula mistassinica*, is a northern and eastern plant of cliffs, rocks, and shores, found from Lab. to Alas., and south to N.Y. and Minn. It has a rosette of toothed leaves, dusted on the undersides with white or yellow powder, a character seen in many primroses. It has umbels of pink or white flowers with yellow eyes and notched petals.

The **Loosestrifes**, the *Lysimachia* species, are mostly erect plants with leafy stems, and flowers in the axils of the upper leaves. There are nearly 100 species in the temperate regions of the world, with several in the U.S. and Canada. Fringed Loosestrife, *Lysimachia ciliata*, grows in marshes and beside streams from N.S. to B.C., and south to Fla. and N.M. It has clusters of yellow flowers in the axils of the upper leaves.

By contrast, the flowers of **Swamp Candles**, *Lysimachia terrestris*, grow in showy terminal racemes on erect stems up to 3ft tall. They are bright yellow, marked with red lines and spots. The plant grows in open swamps and wet places, where it spreads by means of special buds produced in the leaf axils. This species is found from Nf. to Minn., and south to S.C. and Tenn.

Moneywort, *Lysimachia nummularia*, is a rather different plant, with prostrate, creeping stems, opposite, rounded leaves, and the typical yellow loosestrife flowers in the leaf axils. It was introduced into North America from Europe as a garden plant, and now grows more or less wild in wet pastures and woods in many parts of the continent, more commonly in the east where it may become a weed.

Starflower
Trientalis borealis

The **Starflower**, *Trientalis borealis*, is a flower found in the peaty or humus-rich soils of the cool northern woods. It is found from N.S. and Lab. to Alta., as far south as Penn. and Minn. This is a perennial plant, with erect stems in spring. Each stem has a whorl of shiny, dark green leaves at the top, with two white, star-like flowers on long stalks growing from the center of the whorl.

Featherfoil
Hottonia inflata

Featherfoil, *Hottonia inflata*, grows in the water of ponds and ditches, in swamps and slow-moving rivers in the east, from Me. to Fla. in the coastal plain, and up the Mississippi River valley. It may be abundant one year and disappear the next. It has a submerged stem with many feathery leaves, and an umbel of flowering stalks which emerge from the water. These flowering stalks are hollow and inflated, constricted at the nodes where the whorls of flowers grow with leafy bracts. The flowers are tubular, with white petals emerging from large green sepals.

Gentian family

Fringed Gentian
Gentiana crinita

Downy Gentian
Gentiana puberula

Autumn Gentian
Gentianella amarella

Gentianaceae A family of herbaceous plants, with about 80 genera and 900 species, found mainly in the temperate regions of the world. Some of the gentians are grown in rock gardens.

Family Features Flowers solitary or in clusters, regular, hermaphrodite, usually showy. Calyx formed of 4–12 fused sepals; corolla tubular or wheel-shaped, formed of 4–12 fused petals; stamens as many as petal-lobes and alternating with them; ovary superior, usually with 1 cell. Fruits are capsules with many seeds. Leaves entire, opposite and often connected to each other in pairs across the stem.

Gentians form a group of about 400 *Gentiana* species, mainly from the mountains and cool regions of the northern hemisphere, with over 30 in North America. Most are perennial plants with erect stems, opposite leaves and showy flowers in the upper leaf axils. The flower parts are usually in fives.

All gentians have attractive flowers, but those of **Fringed Gentian**, *Gentiana crinita*, are special. This is a 3-ft tall plant that grows in wet meadows and seepage areas, in woods and prairies, from Me. to Man. and south in the mountains to Ga. It is an annual or biennial plant that is becoming rare, and its flowers should not be picked. Unusually among gentians, its flowers have only four petal-lobes.

Downy Gentian, *Gentiana puberula*, is more typical in having funnel-shaped flowers with five corolla-lobes. Its blue flowers are borne in dense terminal clusters on 2-ft tall, unbranched, leafy stems in late summer and fall. The plant grows in upland woods and prairies from

O. to Man., south and west to Ky. and Kan. Some of the gentians have flowers that never open, like the Closed Gentian, *G. andrewsii*, found in wet woods and meadows in the east.

Autumn Gentian or Northern Gentian, *Gentianella amarella*, grows in moist places throughout the north, south into Vt. in the east, and down through the Rockies to Mexico in the west. It is an annual or biennial plant, like most *Gentianella* species, with erect, 2-ft tall, branched and leafy stems, and bluish or purple flowers in the leaf axils. The flowers are smaller and duller than those of the gentians, trumpet-shaped with a fringe of long hairs in the throat.

Rosita
Centaurium calycosum

Rosita, *Centaurium calycosum*, grows in moist places in prairies and meadows, and along streams, from Tex. to Calif., north into Colo. and Ut. It is an annual plant, with branched stems and opposite lance-shaped leaves; trumpet-shaped, pink flowers grow on long stalks in the leaf axils in early summer. Several other species grow in North America.

Rose Pink
Sabatia angularis

The **Rose Pink**, *Sabatia angularis*, sometimes called the Rose Gentian and grown in wet places in gardens, is one of several *Sabatia* species found in the eastern US, many in brackish marshes or in wet places in the coastal plain. Rose Pink, however, has a wider distribution, growing in wet places from Conn. to Fla. and Tex., but also west to Mich. and Kan. It is an annual or biennial plant, with stout stems, sharply four-angled at the base. Further up the plant the stems fork. It has many ovate, opposite leaves, and pink flowers grow in the axils of the upper leaves.

Buckbean
Menyanthes trifoliata

Floating Hearts
Nymphoides aquatica

Dogbane
Apocynum androsaemifolium

Buckbean family

Menyanthaceae A small family of aquatic herbs, with 5 genera and 33 species, found in many parts of the world.

Family Features Flowers showy, regular, hermaphrodite. Calyx lobed, with 5 fused sepals; corolla with 5 fused petals; stamens 5; ovary superior with 1 cell. Fruits are capsules.

Buckbean, *Menyanthes trifoliata*, grows on the edges of lakes and ponds, in marshes and bogs, throughout boreal North America and around the North Pole. It forms colonies of creeping stems with erect compound leaves, each with three leaflets. The pink-tinged white flowers grow in clusters on leafless stalks in early summer; their petals have delicate fringed margins.

There are two species of *Nymphoides* or **Floating Hearts** in North America. They have floating heart-shaped leaves, and floating white, five-petalled flowers. *N. aquatica* grows in ponds and slow-moving streams in the coastal plain in the east. *N. cordata* grows in similar places across southern Canada and in the eastern U.S. Its leaves are variegated with purple.

Dogbane family

Apocynaceae About 180 genera and over 1500 species of herbs, shrubs and climbing plants occur in this family, mostly in the tropics and subtropics. Ornamental garden plants include oleander and frangipani. Many are extremely poisonous, like the African Bushman's Poison Tree.

Family Features Flowers regular, hermaphrodite. Calyx lobed, formed of 5 fused sepals; corolla funnel-shaped, formed of 5 fused petals; stamens 5; ovary superior, with 2 cells. Fruits are often 2 pods. Leaves usually opposite or in whorls.

The several species of *Apocynum* found in North America are perennial herbs, with erect stems and fibrous bark. **Dogbane**, *Apocynum androsaemifolium*, grows in woods, fields, and on roadsides in much of North America. Its bushy stems bear opposite drooping, ovate leaves, and clusters of bell-like flowers. The flowers are pink, striped darker pink inside. The fruit is a pair of drooping, narrow seed pods. Its stems contain poisonous milky sap.

Indian Hemp, *Apocynum cannabinum*, is much more poisonous. The plant is abundant on woodland edges, roadsides, fields, and waste places throughout much of the U.S. and Canada, more commonly in the south. It is similar to Dogbane but has cylindrical, greenish-white flowers, and its seedpods grow up to 8in long.

Blue Star, *Amsonia tabernaemontana*, is a perennial plant, with little-branched, erect stems filled with milky sap, and alternate ovate leaves. The blue flowers are followed by erect cylindrical pods. It grows in rich deciduous woods and bottomlands, from N.J. south in the coastal plain, and west to Kan.

The two **Periwinkles**, *Vinca minor* and *Vinca major*, are little and large versions of a creeping plant with bright blue, wheel-like flowers. They are European plants which have escaped to grow on roadsides, in waste places, and woods in many parts of North America.

Indian Hemp
Apocynum cannabinum

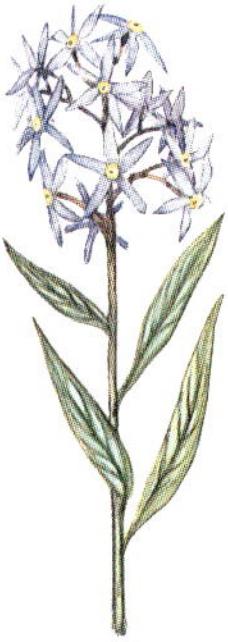

Blue Star
Amsonia tabernaemontana

Lesser Periwinkle
Vinca minor

Milkweed family

Butterfly-weed
Asclepias tuberosa

Common Milkweed
Asclepias syriaca

Showy Milkweed
Asclepias speciosa

Asclepiadaceae About 200 genera and 2000 species are in this family of herbs, shrubs, and climbing vines, most from the warmer regions of the world. They contain a milky juice that is poisonous in many species.

Family Features Flowers regular, hermaphrodite. Calyx formed of 5 fused sepals; corolla formed of 5 fused petals, often with a corona; stamens 5, with anthers fused to stigma, and pollen grains united in pollinia, these joined together in pairs by horny bands; ovary superior, with 2 cells. Fruits are pairs of follicles, with many seeds. Because pollination is complex, not many fruits are formed. Leaves simple, opposite.

Milkweeds are a large group of New World species, belonging to the genus *Asclepias*, with about 60 in North America. Their distinctive flowers are borne in large showy umbels. Each flower has five large, brightly colored and reflexed petals. On the stamen tube is the crown or corona, a structure made up of five hoods which contain nectar. Milkweed fruits are large, erect pods containing hairy seeds.

Butterfly-weed, *Asclepias tuberosa*, has orange or red, sometimes yellow, flowers, which attract butterflies. They are borne in large umbels at the tops of the stems and in the upper leaf axils in summer. It is a perennial plant, with erect leafy stems up to 2ft tall. It grows in dry upland woods and prairies, and in open fields, from N.H. to S.D., south to Fla. and Mexico, most commonly in the south. The plant is also called Pleurisy Root, from its use in Indian and herb medicine as a remedy for pleurisy, bronchitis and other chest complaints.

Common Milkweed, *Asclepias syriaca*, is a much stouter, quite downy plant, with leafy stems up to 6ft tall. Its purplish flowers are borne in compact umbels in the leaf axils. The plant grows in fields and meadows, on roadsides, and in waste places, from N.B. to Sask., south to Ga. and Kan. Its young shoots are edible if cooked in several changes of water to remove the sap.

Showy Milkweed, *Asclepias speciosa*, is a western species, a velvety, gray-white perennial plant up to 6ft tall, with large opposite leaves on erect stems, and umbels of pink flowers. It grows in dry soils and grassland, in valleys and along waterways, from B.C. to Calif., and east to the Mississippi Valley. Like those of Common Milkweed, its young shoots can be eaten if boiled in several changes of water to remove the milky juice.

Whorled Milkweed
Asclepias verticillata

Whorled Milkweed, *Asclepias verticillata*, has whorls of 3–6 narrow leaves on slender stems, and umbels of greenish-white flowers in the upper leaf axils. This mainly midwestern species grows in prairies and fields, on roadsides and in upland woods, from Mass. to Sask., south to Fla. and Ariz.

Fringed Milkvine, *Sarcostemma cynanchoides*, is a climbing vine which twines in and around other bushes in the deserts, plains, and brush of southwestern U.S. and Mexico. It has opposite, lance-shaped or narrowly triangular leaves, like arrow-heads, and umbels of purplish flowers in the leaf axils. Each flower is star-like, with five furry-edged petals. A similar desert species, *S. hirtellum*, has greenish-white flowers with smooth edges to the petals.

Fringed Milkvine
Sarcostemma cynanchoides

Bedstraw or Madder family

Lady's Bedstraw
Galium verum

Northern Bedstraw
Galium boreale

Rubiaceae One of the largest families of flowering plants, with about 500 genera and 6000 species, mostly found in the tropics. Coffee and quinine both come from plants in this family. Gardenias are grown for their flowers.

Family Features Flowers regular, hermaphrodite. Calyx with 4 or 5 fused sepals; corolla with 4 or 5 fused petals; stamens inserted in corolla-tube, as many as and alternating with corolla-lobes; ovary inferior, with 2 or more cells. Fruits are berries, drupes or capsules. Leaves usually entire, opposite or in whorls. Stipules may resemble leaves.

There are not that many family members in temperate regions — about 140 in North America, the majority small herbaceous plants in the genus *Galium*, the **Bedstraws**. They are slender plants, with four-angled stems, and leaves in whorls. The flowers are small and either borne in dense clusters terminating the stems, or in leaf axils.

Lady's Bedstraw, *Galium verum*, was at one time used to stuff mattresses, to curdle milk in cheese-making, and in herb medicine. It also yields a red dye. It is a low-growing, perennial plant, with wiry creeping stems and upright leafy stems, forming dense patches on roadsides and in fields across Canada and into the northern U.S. Its stems bear whorls of 8–12 leaves, and dense clusters of yellow flowers in late summer.

Many bedstraws are similar to Lady's Bedstraw, but have white flowers. Several are boreal plants, like **Northern**

Bedstraw, *Galium boreale*. It usually grows in damp places, among rocks, and beside streams, south to Ky. in the east and Calif. in the west. It has many stems, with whorls of four lance-shaped leaves, and dense clusters of white flowers in mid summer.

Cleavers
Galium aparine

Cleavers, *Galium aparine*, grows in shady places throughout the northern hemisphere. This annual plant has weak, scrambling stems, which cling to vegetation by hooks on the angles of the stems. The narrow leaves grow in whorls of 6–8, and small clusters of tiny, greenish-white flowers grow in the leaf axils. They are followed by paired globular fruits, covered in tiny hooks. The fruits can be roasted to make coffee, and the young shoots used as a vegetable.

Bluets
Houstonia caerulea

Bluets is a name given to several dainty, eastern plants, species of *Houstonia*. *Houstonia caerulea* is a hairless perennial plant with slender rhizomes from which grow little branched stems, 8in tall at most, with opposite, ovate leaves. In early summer they produce blue, yellow-eyed flowers, growing on stalks in the axils of the upper leaves. This plant is found in moist soil in woods and fields, from N.S. to Wis., and south to Ga. and Ark.

Partridge-berry
Mitchella repens

Partridge-berry, *Mitchella repens*, has trailing stems that root at the nodes, and opposite, shiny evergreen leaves. It bears twinned, pink or white tubular flowers in the axils of the uppermost leaves in early summer, followed by red berries. The berries persist into winter and are edible, but rather tasteless and dry. The plant grows in woods from N.S. to Ont., south to Fla. and Tex.

Phlox family

Polemoniaceae A small family with about 15 genera and 300 species, most from North America, especially from the west. The majority are herbs. Many varieties of phlox are grown in gardens.

Family Features Flowers usually in terminal clusters or solitary, regular, hermaphrodite. Calyx lobed, with 5 fused sepals, often with membranous sections between the lobes; corolla funnel-shaped or bell-shaped, with 5 fused petals; stamens 5, inserted on the corolla and alternating with the corolla lobes; ovary superior, usually with 3 cells. Fruit usually a capsule. Leaves alternate or opposite; they may be simple, dissected or compound.

Garden Phlox
Phlox paniculata

Desert Mountain Phlox
Phlox austromontana

Showy Jacob's Ladder
Polemonium pulcherrimum

Phloxes, *Phlox* species, come in several kinds: herbaceous plants with tall leafy stems and terminal clusters of showy flowers; trailing woodland or mountain plants, with linear leaves; or cushion-forming alpine plants.

Garden Phlox, *Phlox paniculata*, is a large herbaceous perennial plant with many garden varieties. Wild plants are native from N.Y. to Ill., south to Ga. and Ark., and found in moist places, woods and thickets; elsewhere they are likely to have escaped from gardens. This is a handsome plant, with leafy stems up to 6ft tall, and a cluster of showy pink flowers in the latter half of summer. Annual Phlox, *Phlox drummondii*, is a much smaller annual species, only 18in tall, and used for summer bedding. It grows wild in Tex., in open sandy places.

Desert Mountain Phlox, *Phlox austromontana*, is a little tufted plant that grows in dry rocky places in the mountains from Calif. to Ariz., and north to Ore. and Ida. It is a perennial, with a woody base and many short, branched stems, only 4in long, covered with linear, gray-green, pungent leaves. Its white or pink flowers grow at the stem tips in early summer.

Jacob's Ladder is a name given to *Polemonium* species because of their ladder-like leaves. Several are grown in gardens. **Showy Jacob's Ladder**, *Polemonium pulcherrimum*, is common in dry rocky places throughout the Rocky Mountains, forming clumps of skunk-scented leaves growing from a woody, branched base. Its flowering stems bear terminal clusters of blue, yellow-throated, funnel-shaped flowers. The similar *P. reptans* is found in the east.

Skunkweed
Navarretia squarrosa

Another plant with a skunky odor is **Skunkweed**, *Navarretia squarrosa*. It is one of about 30 species in the western genus *Navarretia*, all spiny annual plants with rigid, usually branched stems, needle-shaped or prickly leaves, and flowers borne in dense heads with spiny bracts. Skunkweed grows in dry flats and woods in the foothills from B.C. to Calif. It grows up to 2ft tall, has shiny, prickly-lobed, rigid leaves, and spiny-bracted clusters of tubular, blue-purple flowers.

Wool Stars, *Eriastrum* species, are a small group of western plants with star-like flowers; some of them have woolly flower clusters. **Sapphire Wool Star**, *Eriastrum sapphiricum*, is a sticky annual plant up to 1ft tall, with branched stems and linear or narrowly three-lobed leaves. Its tubular, blue flowers grow with bracts in clusters tipping each branch. It is found in Calif., in coastal sage scrub, chaparral, pine woods and desert.

Sapphire Wool Star
Eriastrum sapphiricum

Banded Gilia
Gilia cana

Blue-headed Gilia
Gilia capitata

Sky Rocket
Ipomopsis aggregata

Phlox family

There are about 50 species of *Gilia* found in western North America and in South America. Some of them are grown in gardens. Most are annuals, many with dissected leaves, often concentrated in a basal rosette or on the lower stems. Their flowers range in color from pink to white, blue, lavender or even yellow; they are often tubular or funnel-shaped, with partly membranous calyces. The flowers may be solitary, in loose clusters or dense heads.

Banded Gilia, *Gilia cana*, is an annual plant with a rosette of lobed or toothed leaves, more or less densely covered with cobweb-like hairs. Its flowers are tubular, with broad, spreading corolla-lobes, pinkish-purple in color, with a band of yellow around the tube. They are borne in loose clusters on branched flowering stems up to 1ft tall, in the latter half of summer. Plants grow in a variety of habitats in Calif., in canyons and washes, in Creosote Bush, Joshua Tree and Pinyon scrub, in the deserts, and in dry places in the mountains.

Blue-headed Gilia, *Gilia capitata*, is another annual with a rosette of dissected leaves and branched flowering stalks. But the tubular, blue-violet flowers are gathered into dense balls of 50–100 flowers. This plant is found on grassy slopes and in pine forests, in the western Cascades and Coast Ranges from B.C. to Calif. It is one of several *Gilia* species with ball-like heads of flowers.

Sky Rocket, *Ipomopsis aggregata*, is grown in gardens, in spite of its slight odor of skunk. It is a biennial to perennial plant with simple or branched stems up to 4ft tall, and dissected leaves mostly near the base of the stems. The many tubular flowers are usually red mottled with yellow, but may be pink, and they have pointed petal-lobes, often bent backward. Skyrocket grows in open dry and rocky places, in scrub and pine woods, and in chaparral, often forming patches of bright color in early summer. It is found from B.C. to Calif., through the mountains and in the western plains to N.D. and Tex., south into Mexico.

Tiny Trumpet
Collomia linearis

Tiny Trumpet, *Collomia linearis*, is one of several western *Collomia* species. It is common in the Rocky Mountains, where it grows in dry places above 3000ft, but is also found from B.C. to Ont. and Neb., growing as a weed in waste places and on roadsides. It is a small annual plant, with a leafy stem up to 1ft tall, and head-like clusters of pink-purple, tubular flowers terminating the stem and on branches growing from the leaf axils. Its leaves are alternate and linear or lance-shaped.

There are about 40 *Linanthus* species, mostly found in western North America and Chile. Many have characteristic opposite leaves divided into linear segments, giving the stems a bottlebrush appearance. Their flowers are usually white, blue or pink, often with spots or bands of other colors.

Desert Gold
Linanthus aureus

Desert Gold, *Linanthus aureus*, however, has yellow flowers, pale to deep yellow with a brown-purple throat. It is a tiny annual plant, 4in tall at most, with slender stems and segmented leaves. This is a plant which favors dry places; it is found in the Mojave and Colorado deserts, and scattered through other parts of Calif., into Nev. and N.M.

Field Bindweed
Convolvulus arvensis

Hedge Bindweed
Calystegia sepium

Morning Glory family

Convolvulaceae A mostly tropical family, with about 55 genera and 1650 species of herbs and shrubs, many of them climbers with twining stems. The ornamental Morning Glories, the bindweeds which are pernicious weeds, and the useful sweet potatoes all come from this family.

Family Features Flowers regular, hermaphrodite. Sepals 5, free, overlapping; corolla formed of 5 fused petals; stamens 5, inserted at base of corolla and alternating with petal-lobes; ovary superior with 1–4 cells. Fruits are usually capsules. Leaves simple, alternate. Stipules 0. Stems contain milky juice.

Field Bindweed, *Convolvulus arvensis*, is a weed that grows in waste places and on roadsides in many parts of the U.S. and southern Canada. It has underground rhizomes which penetrate to a depth of 6ft or more, so that they are difficult to eradicate, and small fragments can grow into new plants. Its stems festoon fences and twist around other plants, strangling them if left alone. The stems twist in a counter-clockwise direction. They bear arrow-shaped leaves and funnel-shaped flowers, usually pink but sometimes white.

Hedge Bindweed, *Calystegia sepium*, is a similar but larger plant, with arrow-shaped leaves 2–5in long, and funnel-shaped flowers about 2in long. Its flowers tend to be white but may be pink. This is another strangler, with twining stems twisting counterclockwise, but because it is bigger and more vigorous it can damage surrounding plants much more quickly. It grows in waste and disturbed places throughout much of the northern hemisphere.

Many of the *Ipomoea* species are called morning glories. **Common Morning Glory**, *Ipomoea purpurea*, is grown as an ornamental plant in gardens, and has escaped into the wild in many eastern regions to grow on roadsides and in waste places. It is an annual plant which forms a twining vine, with hairy stems, broad heart-shaped leaves, and clusters of funnel-shaped flowers in shades of white, pink, purple, and blue. Wild Potato-vine, also called Manroot, *Ipomoea pandurata*, is a perennial plant of the east and midwest which produces enormous edible tubers on its roots. It has heart-shaped leaves, and its flowers are white with purple centers.

Common Morning Glory
Ipomoea purpurea

The **Dodders**, members of the genus *Cuscuta*, are sometimes included in a separate family because they are parasitic plants, quite unlike any others. They lack roots but have yellow or brown twining stems, with leaves reduced to tiny scales, and clusters of small white or yellow flowers in late summer. There are many dodder species in North America, parasitizing a wide variety of other plants. One of the most harmful is *Cuscuta epithymum*, introduced from Europe, which parasitizes clover and alfalfa, and which may cause considerable damage to crops. One of the most common native dodders is *Cuscuta gronovii*, a parasite of many herbaceous and woody plants, and found from N.S. to Man., south to Fla. and Ariz. It forms coarse, deep yellow stems with clusters of small, bell-shaped, white flowers.

Dodder
Cuscuta gronovii

Waterleaf family

Wild Heliotrope
Phacelia distans

Hydrophyllaceae A small family with about 20 genera and 250 species of herbs, many of them from western North America. Some are grown in summer bedding schemes.

Family Features Flowers regular, hermaphrodite, borne in cymes. Sepals 5, joined at least at the base; corolla tubular or flat, with 5 petal-lobes; stamens 5, inserted on corolla and alternating with petal-lobes; ovary superior, with 1 or 2 cells. Fruits are capsules. Leaves entire or pinnate, in a rosette or arranged alternately on stems. Plants are often hairy.

Over 200 species of *Phacelia* are found in North America, many in the west. They are hairy, often glandular plants. Their flowers are tubular, funnel-shaped or bell-shaped, often with protruding stamens, and mostly blue, purple or white. The flowers grow in curled clusters, which uncurl as they open.

Variable Phacelia
Phacelia heterophylla

Wild Heliotrope or Common Phacelia, *Phacelia distans*, is an annual plant, 2–3ft tall, with erect or sprawling stems and almost fern-like leaves. Its bell-shaped, blue flowers are borne in early summer, in a few terminal coiled clusters. Wild Heliotrope grows in fields, on slopes and among brush, in deserts in much of Calif., and into Nev. and Ariz.

Variable Phacelia, *Phacelia heterophylla*, is found in dry rocky places in the Rocky Mountains from B.C. to Calif. It is usually biennial, and often has a single, rather coarse and leafy stem up to 6ft tall. Each gray-green, three-lobed leaf has a large ovate leaflet and two smaller ones at the base. The flowers grow in coiled clusters in leaf axils; they are white to greenish-yellow, bell-shaped with projecting stamens.

Baby Blue-eyes, *Nemophila menziesii*, flowers in spring. It is an annual plant, only 6in tall, with slender, somewhat succulent, branched stems and pinnate leaves. Its bowl-shaped, bright blue flowers are borne singly on thin stalks near the ends of the stems. Plants grow in flats and on grassy hillsides, in chaparral and sage scrub, on the coast and in the foothills in Calif. and Ore.

Baby Blue-eyes
Nemophila menziesii

Purple Mat, *Nama demissum*, forms a mat of prostrate stems, branching toward their ends to form clusters of spoon-shaped leaves. Red-purple, bell-shaped flowers grow in the axils of the leaves and branches. This annual plant grows in desert flats and washes, and in Creosote Bush scrub from Calif. to Ut. and Ariz., south into Mexico.

Purple Mat
Nama demissum

The **Waterleafs**, *Hydrophyllum* species, are perennials found in moist and shady places throughout the US and in southern Canada. They have clumps of broad, pinnately lobed or divided leaves, often with lighter patches of green, as if stained by water. The leafy stems bear terminal clusters of bell-shaped flowers with long stamens; the flowers vary from greenish-white to blue-violet. The young basal leaves make a good vegetable.

Virginia Waterleaf, *H. virginianum*, is an eastern species found in moist woods or open wet places, from Que. to N.D., and south to N.C. and Ark. Fendler's Waterleaf, *H. fendleri*, grows in shady places in the Rocky Mountains. It has white or violet flowers.

Virginia Waterleaf
Hydrophyllum virginianum

Forget-me-not or Borage family

Salt Heliotrope
Heliotropum curassavicum

Hoary Puccoon
Lithospermum canescens

Houndstongue
Cynoglossum officinale

Boraginaceae About 100 genera and 2000 species of herbaceous plants found in tropical and temperate regions. Forget-me-nots and heliotropes are grown in gardens.

Family Features Flowers regular, hermaphrodite; borne in one-sided clusters, tightly curled at first, uncoiling as the flowers open one by one from the bottom. Calyx of 5 fused sepals; corolla of 5 fused petals; stamens 5, inserted on corolla and alternating with petal-lobes; ovary superior with 2 or 4 cells, entire or four-lobed, with the style protruding from the center. Fruit consists of four nutlets. Leaves simple, usually alternate. Stipules 0. The plants are often coarsely hairy or bristly.

Puccoon is a name given to several *Lithospermum* species by the Indians, who extracted red dye from the roots to use as face paint. The plants grow in woods and prairies in the east and midwest. Most are perennials, with leafy stems and clusters of funnel-shaped, yellow or orange flowers. **Hoary Puccoon**, *Lithospermum canescens*, is found from Ont. to Sask., south to Tex. and Tenn., east along the Allegheny Mountains. Its 18-in tall stems have narrow leaves, and the plant is covered with grayish hairs, giving it a hoary appearance. In late spring it bears sprays of yellow flowers.

Salt Heliotrope, *Heliotropium curassavicum*, is a perennial plant with prostrate fleshy stems and succulent leaves. Its flowers grow in double coiled clusters in the leaf axils. The flowers are funnel-shaped, white or tinged with blue, often with yellow spots in the throat, and a yellow or purple center. This plant grows in alkaline and salty soils from B.C. to Man., south to Calif. and N.M., into South America. It is also called Quail Plant since the birds eat it.

Blue-weed
Echium vulgare

Houndstongue, *Cynoglossum officinale*, is a European plant naturalized in much of North America, in waste places and on roadsides, in open woods, fields, and meadows, probably introduced for use in herb medicine. This is an upright, leafy plant up to 3ft tall, with large, lance-shaped leaves all covered with soft gray hairs. Its stems branch near the top to end in curled clusters of dull red, funnel-shaped flowers.

Blue-weed, *Echium vulgare*, is another European medicinal plant naturalized in North America, growing in waste places and on roadsides. It is a roughly hairy biennial plant with a rosette of large, lance-shaped leaves, and an erect leafy flowering stem up to 3ft tall, in the second year. The funnel-shaped flowers are borne in many coiled clusters in the leaf axils; they are pink in bud, opening bright blue.

Virginia Bluebell
Mertensia virginica

Virginia Bluebell, *Mertensia virginica*, is a spring flower, most abundant in the midwest. It grows in moist places and woodland, from N.Y. to Wis., south to Ala. and Kan. It is a hairless perennial plant with a clump of large, lance-shaped leaves, and erect leafy stems 2–3ft tall. At the tops of the stems hang clusters of bell-like flowers, pink in bud and opening blue. Similar, generally less showy *Mertensia* species occur throughout the U.S. and in Canada.

Forget-me-not or Borage family

Water Forget-me-not
Myosotis scorpioides

There are about 50 **Forget-me-nots**, *Myosotis* species, in the temperate regions of the world, with about 12 in North America, some native, others introduced from Europe. *Myosotis sylvatica* is the species grown in gardens. The **Water Forget-me-not**, *M. scorpioides*, is a European species which grows in wet places and in water; it is naturalized in eastern and northwestern areas of the U.S. and in Canada. This is a perennial plant, with sprawling leafy stems which turn upward to unfurl coiled clusters of blue, yellow-eyed flowers. It is a small plant, only 2ft tall at most and often smaller.

Many-flowered Stickseed
Hackelia floribunda

Stickseeds, *Hackelia* species, are a group of mostly western plants which resemble forget-me-nots and are sometimes called false forget-me-nots. **Many-flowered Stickseed**, *Hackelia floribunda*, is a perennial plant, with an erect stem up to 3ft tall, lance-shaped leaves, and terminal coiled clusters of bright blue, funnel-shaped flowers. The nutlets, which follow the flowers, have prickly edges, a characteristic of Stickseeds and the feature that gives them their common name. The nutlets catch in the fur of passing animals and so are dispersed. Many-flowered Stickseed grows in coniferous woodland in the Rocky Mountains, from Wash. to Mont., and south to Calif. and N.M.

There are over 80 species in the genus *Cryptantha*, many of them found in western North America. They are hairy plants, sometimes known as **White Forget-me-nots**, with white flowers usually borne in the typical coiled clusters. **Common White Forget-me-not**, *Cryptantha intermedia*, is a stiff, very hairy annual plant, which grows up to 2ft tall; it has linear or lance-shaped leaves, and leafless flower stalks in spring and early summer. It is found in the chaparral, coastal sage and pinyon scrub, etc. on the western side of the Rocky Mountains from Calif. to B.C.

Common White Forget-me-not *Cryptantha intermedia*

Fiddleneck is a name given to several *Amsinckia* species. They are western plants, bristly-hairy, often acrid annuals with branched stems leafy at the base, and terminal coiled clusters of yellow, funnel-shaped flowers, like fiddlenecks. The yellow color of their flowers is unusual in this family. Fiddlenecks grow throughout the west, mostly in grassy places, on the lower slopes in the mountain areas, and in the plains, but they are also found in deserts, in scrub, and one species grows in salt-marshes on the Pacific coast. They are all quite similar in appearance.

Rough Fiddleneck *Amsinckia intermedia*

There are about 100 species of *Plagiobothrys* in western North America and South America. They resemble the *Amsinckia* species but have white flowers and are usually softly hairy, never with acrid hairs. **Popcorn Flower**, *Plagiobothrys nothofulvus*, is an annual plant, with a rosette of lance-shaped leaves and a sparsely leafy erect stem, branched near the top to end in coiled clusters of flowers. The flowers have dense red-brown hairs on their calyces, and white, funnel-shaped corollas with broad, more or less flat petal-lobes. This plant is common in grassy places, in fields and on hillsides throughout much of Calif. and north into Wash.

Popcorn Flower *Plagiobothrys nothofulvus*

Wood Sage
Teucrium canadense

Vinegar Weed
Trichostema lanceolatum

Giant Hyssop
Agastache urticifolia

Mint family

Labiatae or Lamiaceae A large family, with about 180 genera and 3500 species, mostly herbs and some shrubs, found in tropical and temperate regions, especially in the Mediterranean area. Many are used as kitchen herbs, including mint, basil, sage, rosemary, and thyme. Lavender, clary, and patchouli are all important in the perfume industry. Garden plants include salvias, lavender, catnip, and monardas.

Family Features Flowers often in spikes, made up of whorls of flowers in the axils of bracts; bilaterally symmetrical, hermaphrodite. Calyx tubular, toothed, often 2-lipped, formed of 5 fused sepals; corolla tubular, 5-lobed, often 2-lipped; stamens 4 or 2, inserted on corolla-tube; ovary superior, with 2 deeply lobed cells and a divided style arising from the cleft in the center. Fruit consists of 4 nutlets, free or in pairs. Leaves usually opposite. Stems square. Stipules 0. The plants in this family are often aromatic.

Wood Sage, *Teucrium canadense*, grows in moist places in most of the U.S. and southern Canada. It is a perennial plant, with creeping rhizomes and erect, downy, leafy stems. The leaves are lance-shaped, toothed and densely hairy beneath. The flowers are borne in a terminal spike, and are pink with four small lobes and one large flattened lip hanging downward.

Vinegar Weed, *Trichostema lanceolatum*, is one of several species known as bluecurls. The name comes from the long, blue curling stamens in their blue flowers. Vinegar Weed grows in dry, open places and fields, from Ore. to Baja Calif. It is a bushy annual plant,

2ft or more tall, glandular-hairy, and with an unpleasant scent. It has lance-shaped leaves and long spikes of blue flowers with hairy calyces. Each tubular flower has a long lower lip.

Giant Hyssop, *Agastache urticifolia*, is a perennial plant, with several branched stems up to 5ft tall, and nettle-like leaves – another name for it is Nettleleaf Horsemint. It grows in moist soil in the Rocky Mountains from B.C. to Mont., and south to Calif. It has dense flower spikes terminating its stems, each spike made up of whorls of pale lavender flowers with protruding stamens. This is one of several *Agastache* species in North America, distinguished by their dense terminal flower spikes.

White Horehound
Marrubium vulgare

White Horehound, *Marrubium vulgare*, is found in disturbed places in much of the U.S. and southern Canada, introduced from Eurasia, probably as a medicinal herb. It is used in cough medicines and teas to treat coughs and bronchitis. It is an aromatic perennial plant with erect stems, 2–3ft tall, and wrinkled, ovate leaves, thickly covered with woolly white hairs. It bears dense whorls of white, two-lipped flowers in the axils of the upper leaves in summer.

Catnip
Nepeta cataria

Catnip, *Nepeta cataria*, is another medicinal plant, also grown in gardens, and native to Europe. It gets its name from the attraction it has for cats who seem to love its scent. It is a perennial plant, whitened in color by soft dense hairs which cover the toothed ovate leaves. It has more or less erect stems, with clusters of white, red-spotted, two-lipped flowers in the axils of the upper leaves and terminating the stems.

Mint family

Gill-over-the-ground
Glechoma hederacea

Selfheal
Prunella vulgaris

Hemp-nettle
Galeopsis tetrahit

Called **Gill-over-the-ground** in the east or Creeping Charlie in the west, *Glechoma hederacea* is a low-growing perennial plant, with stems up to 2ft long, and rounded heart-shaped leaves with wavy margins. Its stems turn upward at the ends to bear blue-purple, two-lipped flowers in twos or fours in the axils of the leaves. In North America it grows in moist, shady places, usually in disturbed habitats. This is yet another medicinal plant in this family of culinary and medicinal herbs. In its native Britain it was used to give the bitter flavor to beer, before the introduction of hops.

Selfheal, *Prunella vulgaris*, sounds from its name as if it ought to be a medicinal plant; at one time it was, and highly recommended for the treatment of wounds, but is little used today. It is native to both Europe and North America, growing throughout much of this continent in fields, on roadsides, and as a weed in gardens. It is a small perennial plant, with erect stems up to 20in tall, and ovate or lance-shaped, irregularly toothed leaves. Its blue-violet, two-lipped flowers are borne in dense clusters amid hairy bracts, at the tops of the stems.

Hemp-nettle, *Galeopsis tetrahit*, is another introduced European labiate in North America, so well naturalized that it appears to be native in some areas. It grows in moist places across the continent, much more commonly in the north, and absent from the southwest. This is a hairy annual plant, with a branched stem and coarse, toothed leaves like those of nettles, but without the stinging hairs. The flowers grow in whorls in the axils of the upper leaves;

they are two-lipped, pink or purple in color, with yellow spots in the center of the lower lip.

Henbit, *Lamium amplexicaule*, is an annual plant, with branched, rather sprawling stems, and scalloped, rounded leaves, the lower ones with long stalks, the upper ones clasping the stems. Whorls of two-lipped, purple flowers grow in the axils of the upper leaves; the flowers are hairy on the outside. This plant grows as a weed in waste places, fields, and on roadsides across much of North America, but is not a native plant, being naturalized from Europe. It is related to White Deadnettle, *Lamium album*, with white flowers, and Purple Deadnettle, *Lamium purpureum*, with purple flowers, both European plants found occasionally as weeds.

Henbit
Lamium amplexicaule

Obedient Plant, *Physostegia virginiana*, has earned its common name from the story that its flowers will stay in the new position for a short time if they are moved. The plant is also called False Dragonhead, its flowers similar to those of snapdragons, and resembling the head of a dragon with a large mouth. It is an eastern and midwestern plant, growing in relatively moist places, in woods and thickets, and in prairies, from Me. to Alta., and south to S.C. and Tex. It is a perennial plant, with a clump of erect leafy stems, with opposite, narrowly elliptical, serrated leaves, and terminal spikes of flowers in the latter half of summer. The flowers are tubular, two-lipped, and vary in color from pale mauve, almost white, to pink or rose purple. This is an attractive plant which is grown in gardens, in several different color varieties.

Obedient Plant
Physostegia virginiana

Mint family

Purple Sage
Salvia dorrii

There are about 700 kinds of **Sage**, *Salvia* species, in the warmer temperate and tropical regions of the world. Over 50 are found in North America, the majority in the south. Some are grown in gardens, a few are used in herb medicine and as kitchen herbs. Many are small leafy shrubs, others are small herbs; but all have flowers which grow in whorls in the axils of the upper leaves, forming a terminal spike. Many are aromatic.

Purple or **Desert Sage**, *Salvia dorrii*, is a western species, a broad, low-growing, shrubby plant. It has spiny branches, silvery leaves, and bright blue, two-lipped flowers growing in the axils of conspicuous purplish bracts. This plant often grows with sagebrush and in western deserts. Chia, *S. columbariae*, is an annual sage, with a rosette of coarsely toothed leaves. Its blue flowers grow in dense, widely spaced whorls. It grows in dry, disturbed places, in chaparral and scrub in the southwest.

Woundwort
Stachys palustris

Woundwort, *Stachys palustris*, grows in moist places and marshes across Canada, and south into the U.S. as far as N.Y., Mo., and Ariz. This is a hairy perennial plant with erect stems up to 3ft tall, and opposite, lance-shaped leaves with serrated edges. Its purple flowers grow in whorls in the upper leaf axils; they are two-lipped, with a hooded upper lip, and white markings on the spreading lower lip. Woundwort has antiseptic properties and its leaves have traditionally been used to bind wounds.

Bee-balm or Oswego Tea, *Monarda didyma*, is a North American native plant, a garden flower, and the source of oil of bergamot, used to flavor tea. It grows wild in moist woods in the east from Me. to Mich., south to N.J. and O., and in the mountains to Ga. This perennial plant forms a clump of erect stems up to 5ft tall, with opposite, coarsely toothed, lance-shaped leaves. At the top of each stem is the bright red, head-like cluster of flowers above a circle of reddish bracts. Hummingbirds and bees are attracted to the blossoms. Bergamot, *M. fistulosa*, is similar but has pale lavender flowers; it grows in woods and prairies across much of southern Canada and the U.S.

Bee-balm
Monarda didyma

Cut-leaved Water Horehound, *Lycopus americanus*, is one of about six widespread *Lycopus* species in North America, found in wet places. They are like scentless mints, spreading perennials with erect, leafy stems. Cut-leaved Water Horehound gets its name from its coarsely toothed, almost lobed leaves. It is found across the U.S. and southern Canada, but not in the southwestern deserts. Its white flowers grow in dense whorls in the upper leaf axils; each flower is tubular with four lobes.

Cut-leaved Water Horehound
Lycopus americanus

Wild Mint, *Mentha arvensis*, is one of about 10 mints found in North America. It grows in moist places all around the North Pole, south to Va. and Calif. It is a perennial plant, with long creeping stems and also erect stems up to 2ft tall, and toothed, ovate or elliptical leaves. Its flowers grow in dense, widely spaced whorls in the axils of the upper leaves; they are tubular, very small, and white to pale lavender or pink. This mint has a strong, rather sickly scent. It grows in similar places to peppermint, and has to be removed from fields of cultivated peppermint, since it spoils the flavor.

Wild Mint
Mentha arvensis

Nightshade family

Black Nightshade
Solanum nigrum

Jimsonweed
Datura stramonium

Henbane
Hyoscyamus niger

Solanaceae A large and important family, with about 90 genera and 2000 species, mostly herbs and twining plants, the majority found in the tropics and warm temperate regions, especially in Central and South America. Food plants in this family include potato, tomato, chilies, and peppers. Some species are poisonous, like Belladonna, Henbane, and the tobaccos.

Family Features Flowers solitary or in cymes, usually regular, hermaphrodite. Calyx with 3–6 lobes; corolla usually 5-lobed; stamens inserted on corolla and alternating with corolla lobes; ovary superior with 2 cells. Fruit a berry or capsule. Leaves alternate, simple. Stipules 0.

By far the largest genus is *Solanum*, the **Nightshades**, with about 1500 mainly tropical species. Over 40 grow in North America, most commonly in the south. **Black Nightshade**, *Solanum nigrum*, is a cosmopolitan weed, a leafy annual plant, with drooping clusters of white flowers and dull black berries. The stamens in nightshades are characteristic, with short filaments and large yellow anthers protruding from the flower. Many nightshades have poisonous berries which are dangerous to children.

Jimsonweed, *Datura stramonium*, is much more poisonous; a few of the rough black seeds can be lethal to children and adolescents. It is a coarse annual, with an unpleasant scent, a branched purplish stem up to 5ft tall, and large, coarsely toothed leaves. Each flower has an elongated winged calyx and a long, funnel-shaped white corolla. The plant grows in dry waste ground and pastures in the U.S. and southern Canada.

Henbane, *Hyoscyamus niger*, is another very poisonous species. This plant is native to Europe, but grows on roadsides and in waste places in northern U.S. and southern Canada. It is a coarse annual, with an unpleasant scent, and is stickily hairy. Its erect, branched stems grow up to about 3ft tall and are very leafy, with very coarsely toothed leaves. In late summer it bears conspicuous flowers — funnel-shaped, with purple veins on a greenish-yellow background.

Desert Tobacco
Nicotiana trigonophylla

About 60 species of **Tobacco** belong to the genus *Nicotiana*, most of them native to North and South America, and all poisonous plants, with distinctive heavy scents. **Desert Tobacco**, *Nicotiana trigonophylla*, is a western species, found from the Mojave and Colorado deserts to Tex. and Nev. It is usually perennial, with a sparsely branched stem 2–3ft tall, and lance-shaped leaves with bases clasping the stem; the whole plant is covered with sticky hairs. In spring and early summer loose clusters of white, trumpet-shaped flowers appear at the tops of the stems.

Clammy Ground Cherry
Physalis heterophylla

Ground Cherries, *Physalis* species, have brightly colored berries enclosed in papery sacs formed from the inflated calyces. Some are poisonous, others edible. **Clammy Ground Cherry**, *Physalis heterophylla*, has yellow, tomato-like berries which are good to eat. It is a perennial, with spreading stems up to 3ft tall, and heart-shaped, sticky-hairy leaves. Its solitary bell-shaped flowers grow in the leaf axils; they are greenish-yellow with purple centers. This plant grows in dry sandy soil, in upland woods and prairies, from N.S. to Minn. and Ut., south to Fla. and Tex.

Common Monkey-flower
Mimulus guttatus

Square-stemmed
Monkey-flower
Mimulus ringens

Turtlehead
Chelone glabra

Snapdragon or Figwort family

Scrophulariaceae A large family with about 220 genera and 3000 species of herbs and shrubs, found almost throughout the world. Many have showy flowers. Some, like speedwells, snapdragons, and penstemons, are grown in gardens.

Family Features Flowers usually bilaterally symmetrical, hermaphrodite. Calyx 4–5 lobed; corolla 5–8 lobed, regular to 2-lipped; stamens normally 2–4, inserted in pairs on the corolla — if a fifth stamen is present, it is usually sterile and different from the others; ovary superior with 2 cells. Fruits are capsules or berries. Leaves simple or pinnate, alternate, opposite or in whorls. Stipules 0.

Monkey-flowers, *Mimulus* species, have showy flowers, and some are grown in gardens. There are over 80 species in North America, most from Pacific and southwestern states, many growing in wet places, others in dry, sandy and rocky places, disturbed ground, and chaparral. Their flowers have a broad, two-lipped corolla, its throat more or less closed by a palate formed of two ridges. These ridges may be covered in hairs (bearded) or hairless.

Common Monkey-flower, *Mimulus guttatus*, is typical of many in having yellow flowers and growing in wet places. It is found throughout the Rocky Mountains from Alas. to Calif. This is a perennial, hairless plant, with creeping leafy stems which root at the nodes. In summer the shoots turn upward and bear yellow, orange-spotted flowers.

Square-stemmed Monkey-flower, *M. ringens*, grows in wet places, along streams and in marshes, from N.S. to Sask., south to Ga. and Tex. It has four-angled stems, opposite, lance-shaped leaves, and two-lipped blue flowers with yellow palates.

Turtlehead, *Chelone glabra*, is a stiff-looking plant, with a dense terminal spike of two-lipped, white flowers resembling turtles' heads. It is a perennial, with erect stems up to 5ft tall, and narrow, toothed leaves in opposite pairs. It grows in wet places and woods from Nf. to Minn., south to Ga. and Ala. The less common *C. obliqua* is sometimes grown in gardens; it has purple flowers and grows on the coastal plain in the east.

Mulleins, *Verbascum* species, are biennial plants, with a rosette of leaves in the first year, and a tall flowering stem in the second. Several are grown in gardens. **Common Mullein**, *Verbascum thapsus*, is native to Europe but is widely naturalized in North America, in disturbed places, roadsides, and fields. Its woolly leaves are arranged so that they direct water down the stem and into the roots, and they cut down water loss — useful for a plant that grows in dry places. The 6-ft tall flowering spikes bear many yellow flowers.

Figwort, *Scrophularia lanceolata*, is a hairless plant with an erect leafy stem up to 6ft tall, opposite, long-stalked leaves, and many small flowers. The flowers are two-lipped, shiny brown outside and green inside, with five stamens. It grows in open woods and on roadsides from Que. and Minn., south to Ga. and La.

Common Mullein
Verbascum thapsus

Figwort
Scrophularia lanceolata

Snapdragon or Figwort family

Southwestern Penstemon
Penstemon barbatus

Bush Penstemon
Penstemon fruticosus

The **Beardtongues**, *Penstemon* species, are a large western North American group, with over 150 species. They are perennial plants or shrubs, with opposite leaves and showy flowers, several so showy that they are grown in gardens. The flowers are tubular in shape, often with an inflated throat and with a two-lipped opening. The upper lip is often much weaker, with only two lobes; the lower lip is large and has three lobes. The sterile stamen is well developed in these plants and is often bearded (forming the beardtongue).

Some of the most colorful penstemons are those with bright red flowers. There are several such species in the west and southwest, including **Southwestern Penstemon**, *Penstemon barbatus*, a plant which is attractive enough to be grown in gardens. It forms a clump of erect stems up to 3ft tall, with grass-like, linear leaves, and many drooping flowers in a long terminal inflorescence. It grows in open rocky areas in the forests of the southwestern mountains, from Colo. to Tex., and into Mexico.

Many of the penstemons are low, bushy or mat-forming plants, with a woody base and many branching, leafy stems. Some are grown in rock gardens. **Bush Penstemon**, *Penstemon fruticosus*, is a low-growing, shrubby plant, only 15in tall at most, and forming dense patches of woody stems, with opposite, lance-shaped leaves and showy lavender flowers. It is found on damp, rocky slopes from B.C. to Mont., and south to Ore. and Wyo.

Blue-eyed Mary, *Collinsia verna*, is a winter annual plant which flowers in spring. It has weak stems and triangular-ovate leaves, with whorls of flowers in the axils of the uppermost. Each flower is two-lipped, with two white upper petal-lobes and three blue lower ones; the middle lobe of the three lower ones forms a pouch enclosing the stamens. The plant grows in rich woods from N.Y. to Wis., and south to W.Va. and Ark.

Blue-eyed Mary
Collinsia verna

Several **Toadflax**, *Linaria* species, grow in North America. **Butter-and-eggs**, *Linaria vulgaris*, is a European species, naturalized along roadsides and railroads, and in waste places in temperate areas of the continent. It is a perennial plant which forms colonies of erect stems 1–3ft tall, with linear leaves and spikes of bright yellow and orange flowers. Each is two-lipped, with a straight spur and an orange palate. Butter-and-eggs has a long history of use in herbal medicine. Steeped in milk it makes a good fly poison.

Butter-and-eggs
Linaria vulgaris

Blue toadflax, *Linaria canadensis,* is a slender annual with leafy flowering stems, 5–20in tall. The flowers grow along the erect stems in summer, and are light blue, two-lipped and spurred, with two white spots on the palate. Blue Toadflax grows in sandy soil throughout much of the U.S., and in parts of southern Canada, most often in the east.

Several **Snapdragons**, *Antirrhinum* species, grow in the chaparral and mountains in the west. They are mostly annual plants with two-lipped, sac-like flowers. **Common Snapdragon**, *Antirrhinum majus*, is the garden annual which sometimes escapes into the wild.

Common Snapdragon
Antirrhinum majus

Snapdragon or Figwort family

Thyme-leaved Speedwell
Veronica serpyllifolia

American Brooklime
Veronica americana

Foxglove
Digitalis purpurea

Many of the **Speedwells**, *Veronica* species, found in North America are weeds. They are small spreading plants, with opposite leaves, and blue or white flowers. Speedwell flowers are distinctive, with a short tube and four lobes, looking like four petals in the form of a broad, upright cross. The upper lobe is larger than the others.

Thyme-leaved Speedwell, *Veronica serpyllifolia*, is typical of many of these little weedy plants. It is a perennial, with creeping, rather hairy, somewhat sticky stems, and small flowers in the axils of the upper leaves. The flowers are white, with dark blue lines. Other weedy species include Common Speedwell, *V. officinalis*, with pale blue flowers, and Germander Speedwell, *V. chamaedrys*, with conspicuous bright blue flowers.

American Brooklime, *Veronica americana*, is a native species that grows in marshes and along streams in much of North America, except the extreme south. It is a fleshy, hairless plant with sprawling stems which root in the mud, and opposite, lance-shaped leaves. Racemes of blue flowers grow on long stalks in the upper leaf axils. Young shoots of this plant can be used in salads.

Foxglove, *Digitalis purpurea*, is a European plant naturalized in open places and on roadsides from B.C. to Calif., and also, less commonly, in the northeastern states and eastern Canada. It is a biennial plant, with a rosette of softly hairy, large lance-shaped leaves in the first year, and an erect, leafy flowering stem 3–6ft tall in the second. The large tubular flowers are mauve-pink, lighter on the inside, with pink spots. Foxgloves contain digitoxin, a poison and a vital medicine in the treatment of heart disease.

Many members of this family are semi-parasites. They have green stems and leaves but attach themselves by their roots to roots of other plants, especially grasses, and obtain water and nutrients from their hosts. **Louseworts**, *Pedicularis* species, have such a lifestyle. There are more than 30 species of these plants in North America, many in the west and north. They are perennials, with opposite, divided leaves, and spikes of two-lipped flowers.

Wood Betony
Pedicularis canadensis

Wood Betony, *Pedicularis canadensis*, grows in woods and prairies, from Que. to Man., and south to Fla. and Tex. It has dense clusters of red or yellow flowers topping stems with opposite, finely cut leaves. Elephant Heads, *P. groenlandica*, is a western species, found in wet meadows in the Rocky Mountains. It has narrow, pinnate leaves, and dense spikes of pink flowers, which resemble elephants' heads. The upper lip forms the trunk, the side lobes of the lower lip form the ears.

Purple Gerardia
Agalinis purpurea

Purple Gerardia, *Agalinis* (or *Gerardia*) *purpurea*, is one of several semi-parasitic species found in the east. They are mostly wiry plants with small, opposite, linear leaves, and pink or purple bell-shaped flowers in late summer. Purple Gerardia is one of the most common, a much branched plant, 1–4ft tall, which grows on shores and in bogs from N.S. to Mexico.

Snapdragon or Figwort family

Yellow Rattle
Rhinanthus crista-galli

Yellow Rattle, *Rhinanthus crista-galli*, is another semi-parasite, growing in moist places around the North Pole, south in North America to Colo. and N.Y. It has unbranched stems with opposite, triangular leaves, and yellow flowers in the upper leaf axils. The flowers have characteristic inflated calyces, which become even more inflated in fruit, enclosing the capsules with their winged seeds. As the capsules mature, they dry out, and the seeds rattle inside.

Eyebright
Euphrasia americana

Eyebright, *Euphrasia americana*, is used in herb medicine to treat sore and tired eyes. This European native is widely naturalized in North America, on roadsides and in grassy places, from Nf. to Que., and south to N.Y. It has branched stems, only about 1ft tall, and opposite, ovate leaves, with three teeth on the margin. The flowers grow in the axils of the upper leaves; each flower is two-lipped, the white lower lip with three notched lobes and purple veins, the bluish upper lip hooded.

Desert Paintbrush
Castilleja chromosa

Indian Paintbrushes get their name from an Indian legend about a brave who was trying to paint a prairie sunset and threw down his brushes. Where they landed there the flowers grew. There are over 200 species of paintbrushes in the New World, belonging to the genus *Castilleja*, many in the prairies and mountains of the west. Wyoming Paintbrush, *C. linariaefolia*, is the state flower of Wyoming.

Indian Paintbrushes are annual or perennial plants, some of them almost shrubby, with alternate, lance-shaped or narrowly segmented leaves. Their distinctive flower clusters, with colored, often three-lobed bracts, grow at the tips of the stems. The actual flowers are small, and the bracts and calyces form the "paintbrush."

Desert Paintbrush, *Castilleja chromosa*, is a common plant of sagebrush and other dry places in the Rocky Mountain area, from Ida. across to Ore., and south to Calif. and N.M. It has erect, unbranched stems up to 15in tall, with leaves divided into three or five lobes, and bright orange or scarlet three-lobed bracts and calyces in the flower clusters. Giant Red Paintbrush, *C. miniata*, is found in wet places from B.C. to Calif. It grows up to 3ft tall, with unbranched stems, and bright scarlet, deeply cleft bracts and calyces.

Indian Paintbrush
Castilleja coccinea

The only paintbrush in the east, and known there just as **Indian Paintbrush** or Painted Cup, is *Castilleja coccinea*. It grows in woods, meadows and prairies from Ont. to Man., south to S.C. and Okla. This paintbrush is an annual plant, with an unbranched stem and three-lobed, scarlet-tipped bracts.

Owl's-clovers, *Orthocarpus* species, are western plants which resemble Indian Paintbrushes, but their flowers are more conspicuous, and the bracts less significant. Each flower has an arched upper lip, and a three-lobed, pouched lower lip. **Yellow Owl's-clover**, *O. luteus*, is an annual plant with unbranched stems up to 15in tall, alternate, narrow leaves, and long spikes of yellow flowers. It grows in sandy soil, in plains and prairies, from B.C. to Man., south to Ariz. and N.M.

Yellow Owl's-clover
Orthocarpus luteus

Broomrape family

Orobanchaceae A small family of parasitic herbs with about 10 genera and 170 species, mainly from warm temperate regions of the Old World. They lack chlorophyll and are parasitic on the roots of flowering plants and trees. Some cause damage to crop plants.

Family Features Flowers bilaterally symmetrical, hermaphrodite, in dense terminal spikes. Calyx toothed or lobed; corolla 5-lobed, often curved or 2-lipped; stamens 4, alternating with corolla lobes — if a fifth stamen is present it is sterile; ovary superior with 1 cell. Fruit is a capsule with many tiny seeds. Their erect stems have colorless, alternate scale leaves at the base.

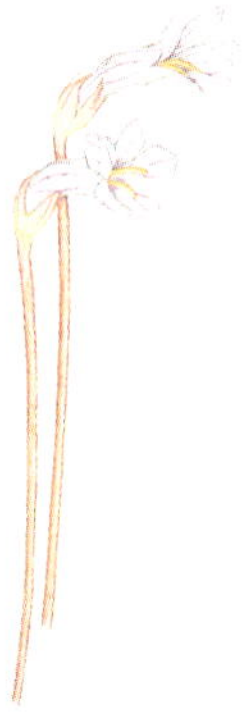

Cancer-root
Orobanche uniflora

There are few representatives of this family in North America, the majority being about 12 species of **Broomrapes** in the genus *Orobanche*. **Cancer-root**, *Orobanche uniflora*, produces erect, slender stems in early summer, each one about 8in tall with a single white or violet, fragrant flower. This delicate plant grows in moist woods in much of North America.

Spike Broomrape
Orobanche multiflora

Spike Broomrape, *Orobanche multiflora*, is more substantial. It has thick, brownish stems up to 20in tall, with many scale-like bracts. Purplish, two-lipped flowers grow in the axils of the bracts. The plant is parasitic on members of the daisy family, including artemisias. It is found in prairies and deserts, from Wash. south to Mexico, and east to Tex.

Squawroot, *Conopholis americana*, is parasitic on trees, mostly oaks and beech, and is found in woods, from N.S. to Mich., south to Fla. and Ala. In early summer it produces fleshy stems covered with brownish scales and resembling 6-in long pine cones. These bear hooded, yellowish flowers.

Plantain family

Plantaginaceae A small family found throughout the world, mainly in the northern temperate regions, with 3 genera and about 270 species of herbs.

Squawroot
Conopholis americana

Plantains, inconspicuous plants belonging to the genus *Plantago*, account for 260 of these. They are annual or perennial plants, mostly with a rosette of basal leaves and leafless, unbranched flower stalks. The flowers are inconspicuous, each with four green sepals and four membranous petals. The stamens are colored and noticeable, often protruding from the flowers. Young leaves of many plantains can be cooked as a vegetable and their seeds can be ground into flour.

Common Plantain
Plantago major

Several plantains are cosmopolitan weeds. **Common Plantain**, *Plantago major*, is one of these, a plant most often found in open waste places and bare ground. It is a perennial with rosettes of long-stalked, broadly ovate, almost hairless leaves. In summer the plant bears long narrow spikes of green flowers with purple anthers.

English Plantain
Plantago lanceolata

English Plantain, *Plantago lanceolata*, is another weed found in many parts of the world. Its leaves are lance-shaped with short stalks, held more or less upright. The summer flowering stalks have short terminal spikes of green flowers, with whitish stamens. The stems and leaves have long silky hairs.

Vervain family

Verbenaceae A mainly tropical and subtropical family, with about 75 genera and 3000 species of herbs, shrubs and trees. Teak comes from an Asian member of the family.

Family Features Flowers bilaterally symmetrical, hermaphrodite. Calyx lobed or toothed, with 4–5 fused sepals; corolla lobed, often 2-lipped, with 4–5 fused petals; stamens usually 4, inserted on the corolla tube; ovary superior, often 4-lobed. Fruit usually formed of 4 nutlets. Leaves opposite or in whorls, simple or compound. Stipules 0. The terminal branches of the stem are often four-angled.

Blue Vervain
Verbena hastata

Blue Vervain, *Verbena hastata*, is one of over 40 vervain species in North America. It grows in wet meadows and prairies, from N.S. to B.C., and south to Fla. and Ariz. It is a perennial plant up to 5ft tall, with stiff, four-angled stems resembling a candelabrum, and opposite, lance-shaped, rough leaves. Its small, tubular flowers grow in long terminal spikes. European Vervain, *V. officinalis*, is widely naturalized in the east.

Acanthus family

Acanthaceae A mainly tropical family with about 250 genera and 2500 species of herbs and shrubs. Some, like gloxinias, are grown as house plants or in greenhouses.

Family Features Flowers bilaterally symmetrical, hermaphrodite, often with conspicuous colored bracts. Calyx with 4–5 lobes; corolla tubular, usually 2-lipped; stamens 4 or 2, alternating with corolla-lobes; ovary superior with 2 cells. Fruits are capsules. Leaves opposite. Stamens 0.

Ruellia
Ruellia caroliniensis

Ruellia, *Ruellia caroliniensis*, is a perennial plant, with erect stems up to 3ft tall, opposite, ovate leaves, and clusters of light mauve flowers in the upper leaf axils. This plant grows in open woods from N.J. to Ind., south to La. and Tex. Similar species grow in the east and midwest.

Lopseed family

Phrymaceae The single species in this family is **Lopseed**, *Phryma leptostachya*. It is a perennial, found in moist woods from Que. to Man., south to Fla. and Okla. It has a branched stem up to 3ft tall, with opposite, serrated leaves, and narrow spikes of paired, white or lavender flowers. Each flower has a two-lipped calyx, and a two-lipped corolla, with a short upper lip and a longer, spreading, three-lobed lower lip. When the flowers are over, the calyx remains, drooping against the stem and enclosing the seed-like fruits.

Lopseed
Phryma leptostachya

Moschatel family

Adoxaceae The only species in this family is **Moschatel**, *Adoxa moschatellina*, a small perennial plant, with three-lobed leaves and extraordinary flowers growing in terminal clusters on stems that have a single leaf about half way up. It is the form of the flower cluster that makes this plant so unique, for each cluster has five yellow-green flowers, four forming the sides of a square, and the fifth on top. The side flowers have three sepals and five petals, the top flower two sepals and four petals. Moschatel grows in woods and forests around the North Pole, in North America south to Colo., Io., and Del.

Moschatel
Adoxa moschatellina

Trumpet Honeysuckle
Lonicera sempervirens

Twinflower
Linnaea borealis

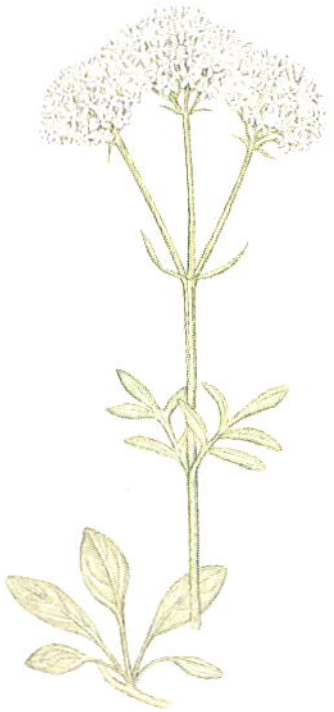

Downy-fruited Valerian
Valeriana acutil oba

Honeysuckle family

Caprifoliaceae A small family of shrubs and herbs, with 13 genera and about 490 species, many in north temperate regions. Viburnums and honeysuckles are garden plants.

Family Features Flowers regular or bilaterally symmetrical, hermaphrodite, usually in cymes. Calyx 5-toothed, usually joined to ovary; corolla tubular, formed of 4 or 5 fused petals; stamens 4 or 5, alternating with corolla-lobes; ovary inferior with 2–5 cells. Fruit is a berry. Leaves opposite, simple or divided. Stipules 0.

There are about 200 **Honeysuckles**, *Lonicera* species. **Trumpet Honeysuckle**, *L. sempervirens*, is a woody climber, with broadly ovate leaves fused into pairs below the trumpet-shaped flowers. The flowers are red outside, yellow inside. This plant grows in woods in the eastern U.S., and is grown in gardens.

Twinflower, *Linnaea borealis*, is a delicate creeping plant of northern woods and bogs, with trailing leafy stems, and pairs of nodding, pink or white flowers on erect stalks.

Valerian family

Valerianaceae A small family with about 13 genera and 400 species of herbs, found in much of the world. Valerian is used in herb medicine.

Family Features Flowers usually bilaterally symmetrical and hermaphrodite, borne in cymes or heads. Calyx formed of 1–3 minute or inrolled sepals; corolla mostly 5-lobed, often 2-lipped; stamens 1–4, alternating with corolla-lobes; ovary inferior with 1–3 cells. Fruit is dry and indehiscent. Leaves alternate, opposite or forming a rosette. Stipules 0.

Valerians, *Valeriana* species, are perennial plants, often with a distinctive scent. Their leaves may be entire or pinnately divided, and their pink or white flowers are borne in compound inflorescences, often resembling heads or umbels. *Valeriana acutiloba* is a northwestern species from high in the Rocky Mountains. It has mostly basal leaves, and white flowers growing on 2-ft tall stalks in summer.

Teasel family

Dipsacaceae A small family with 9 genera and about 155 species, mostly herbs from Europe and Asia.

Family Features Flowers bilaterally symmetrical, hermaphrodite, often in dense heads. Calyx small, cup-like, deeply divided; corolla 4–5 lobed, often 2-lipped; stamens 2 or 4, alternating with corolla lobes, filaments free or joined in pairs; ovary inferior, with 1 cell. Fruits are indehiscent. Leaves opposite or in whorls. Stipules 0.

Teasel
Dipsacus fullonum

Teasel, *Dipsacus fullonum*, grows in wet places in many parts of North America. It is a biennial, with an erect, prickly flowering stem in the second year, up to 6ft tall, with prickly leaves, the lower ones joined across the stem, making a cup. In the flower heads flowers open from the center outward.

Bluebuttons
Knautia arvensis

Bluebuttons, *Knautia arvensis*, grows in grassy places in northeastern U.S. and eastern Canada. It is a small perennial, with erect stems, divided leaves, and heads of lilac flowers in late summer.

Bellflower or Bluebell family

Campanulaceae Also called the Harebell family. About 60 genera and 2000 species, mostly herbs, found throughout much of the world. The family contains many garden plants, including campanulas and lobelias.

Family Features Flowers often showy, regular or bilaterally symmetrical, hermaphrodite. Calyx usually 5-lobed and joined to ovary; corolla tubular, bell-shaped or 1- or 2-lipped; stamens as many as corolla-lobes and alternating with them; ovary inferior, with 2 or more cells. Fruit a capsule with many tiny seeds. Leaves alternate, simple. Stipules 0. Plants usually have milky juice.

Many **Bellflowers**, *Campanula* species, are perennial plants, with tall leafy stems and bell-like flowers in the axils of the upper leaves. **Tall Bellflower**, *Campanula americana*, is one such plant, but is an annual, with stems growing up to 3ft tall, and clusters of light blue, starry flowers in the latter half of summer. This plant grows in moist woods from Ont. to Minn., south to Fla. and Okla.

Harebell, *Campanula rotundifolia*, is a small perennial forming a clump of long-stalked leaves with rounded blades. From this clump grow slender stems, no more than 15in tall, with narrow leaves and nodding blue, bell-like flowers in the latter half of summer. Harebell grows in dry grassland, on cliffs and dunes, often on poor shallow soils, all around the North Pole, across Canada, and south in the U.S. to N.J., Ind., and Ore.

Tall Bellflower
Campanula americana

Harebell
Campanula rotundifolia

Venus' Looking-glass
Triodanis perfoliata

Venus' Looking-glass, *Triodanis perfoliata*, is an annual plant, with a leafy stem up to 18in tall. Its leaves are toothed and cupped around the stem. Its flowers grow in clusters in the leaf axils, the lower ones unopening, the upper ones pale lavender to deep purple, with five spreading petal-lobes. This plant often grows in disturbed habitats across the U.S. and into southern Canada.

Members of the Bellflower family which have bilaterally symmetrical flowers, like *Lobelia* species, are sometimes placed in the Lobeliaceae.

Cardinal Flower
Lobelia cardinalis

Cardinal Flower, *Lobelia cardinalis*, is exceptional among North American lobelias, in having brilliant red flowers. Most of the others have blue or white flowers. Cardinal Flowers grow in wet places from N.B. to Minn., south to Fla. and Tex. This is a perennial plant, with erect stems up to 5ft tall, narrow, toothed leaves, and a spike of flowers terminating the stem. Each flower is two-lipped, with an erect upper lip and a spreading, drooping, three-lobed lower lip.

Toothed Downingia
Downingia cuspidata

About 12 species of *Downingia* are found in the Pacific west, usually associated with muddy flats and vernal pools. They are rather succulent annual plants, no more than 10–15in tall, with soft stems, entire leaves, and two-lipped flowers. The flowers are generally blue, with a small upper lip, and often with a yellow and white lower lip. The flowers "perch" on the tips of elongated ovaries that look like long stalks. **Toothed Downingia**, *Downingia cuspidata*, has light blue flowers blotched with yellow and white on the lower lip. It is found on wet and drying muddy soils in Calif.

Common Sunflower
Helianthus annuus

Ox-eye
Heliopsis helianthoides

Sunflower or Daisy family

Compositae or Asteraceae. By far the largest family of flowering plants, with over 900 genera and 14,000 species found throughout the world. Most are herbs. The many decorative plants in the family include chrysanthemums, heleniums, marigolds, and many others. Important food plants include lettuce, chicory, and sunflowers, among others. Some, like dandelions and thistles, are weeds, and ragweeds cause hayfever.

Family Features The flower structure of this family is unique. Individual flowers (called florets) are small but gathered into flower heads surrounded by bracts; the heads look like single flowers. Florets have a corolla, which may be tubular in form (disk florets), or strap-shaped (ray florets). A flower head may be made up of all disk florets or all ray florets, but often the disk florets form the center of the head, with ray florets around the margin. Each floret has a calyx, which may be formed of hairs, bristles, teeth, or a membranous ring. Florets may be male, with 5 stamens, or female with an inferior ovary, or have both male and female parts. The fruits are achenes, crowned by a pappus, the remains of the calyx.

Sunflowers are familiar composite flowers, with over 40 species in the genus *Helianthus* in North America. Most are perennials and have all yellow flower heads. **Common Sunflower**, *Helianthus annuus*, however, is an annual plant. It has an erect branching stem which can reach 10ft tall, many alternate, toothed, roughly hairy leaves up to 1ft long, and several flower heads, each with brownish-purple disk florets and bright yellow ray florets. The heads may measure 6in across. The seeds are edible. It is found in dry places and prairies from Minn. to Wash., and south to Mo. and Calif. Jerusalem Artichoke, *H. tuberosus*, is a midwestern species, with roots that swell to form edible tubers.

Black-eyed Susan
Rudbeckia hirta

Ox-eye, *Heliopsis helianthoides*, may be mistaken for a sunflower, except that its flower heads have conical disks. This short-lived perennial plant grows in dry woods, prairies, and waste places across southern Canada, more commonly in the east than in the west, south in the U.S. to Ga. and N.M. It has erect stems up to 5ft tall, with opposite ovate, serrated leaves, and terminal, usually solitary, yellow flower heads in summer.

Black-eyed Susan, *Rudbeckia hirta*, grows on hillsides and prairies, in open woods, on roadsides, and in fields, from Nf. to B.C., south to Fla. and Mexico. It is a biennial plant, with a rosette of leaves in the first year and flowering stems in the second, with variably toothed lance-shaped or elliptical, roughly hairy leaves. Its flower heads are 2–3in across, with up to 20 golden yellow ray florets, and a purple or brown, domed disk in the center of each head.

Plains Zinnia
Zinnia grandiflora

Plains Zinnia, *Zinnia grandiflora*, also has bright golden-yellow flowers, but with reddish disk florets, and only 3–6 almost round ray florets to each head. Its low-growing clumps are transformed by the numerous flower heads in late summer. This is a perennial plant with branched stems and opposite, linear leaves. It grows in dry plains and deserts from Kan. to Colo., south into Mexico.

Sunflower or Daisy family

Stemless Goldflower
Hymenoxis acaulis

Showy Gaillardia
Gaillardia pulchella

Plains Tickseed
Coreopsis tinctoria

Stemless Goldflower, *Hymenoxis acaulis*, grows in dry open places, on hillsides and plains, mainly in the midwest and west, from Ida. to Calif., and eastwards to Ont. and O. It is most common in Colo. and Wyo. This is a perennial plant, with a tuft of lance-shaped, basal leaves, and solitary yellow flower heads borne in early summer. There are 5–35 broad, three-toothed ray florets on each flower head.

Blanket Flowers, *Gaillardia* species, are colorful plants for late summer gardens. They have bright flowers in shades of red, yellow, and purple, with broad ray florets and three deep teeth in each ray. Several are native to North America. **Showy Gaillardia** or Indian Blanket, *G. pulchella*, is one of the most widespread, growing in dry sandy places, in fields and on roadsides across the plains states from Mo. to Colo., north to Minn., and south into northern Mexico; it also extends east along the coast from Tex. to Va. This is an annual plant, with branched stems 12–18in tall, bristly leaves, and many solitary flower heads.

Tickseeds, *Coreopsis* species, are also grown in gardens. Most are short-lived perennials with showy yellow flowers. **Plains Tickseed** or Garden Coreopsis, *Coreopsis tinctoria*, is an annual grown in summer bedding schemes and for cut flowers. It is a native North American plant, along with about 30 other species in the genus. Plains Tickseed is found in low-lying ground and waste places from Man. to Alta., and south to Tex. and Ariz. It may grow elsewhere as a garden escape. It is a branched plant, 2–4ft tall, with leaves divided into long linear segments, and many flower heads in summer. The flower heads have a purple disk, and about eight broad yellow ray florets, each one purple-blotched at the base and with three teeth at the tip.

Nodding Bur-marigold
Bidens cernua

Nodding Bur-marigold, *Bidens cernua*, grows in marshes, ditches, and other wet places throughout much of North America, Europe, and Asia, although it is never common. It is an annual plant, with branched stems up to 2ft tall, many lance-shaped, toothed leaves borne in opposite pairs, and many flower heads on long stalks, nodding as they get older. Each flower head has a large yellow disk and broad yellow ray florets; behind the head the green leafy bracts project beyond the rays. Like all members of the genus, the plant produces fruits with barbed spines which catch on clothes. Nodding Bur-marigold fruits have four spines. Tickseed-sunflower, *Bidens aristosa*, is a common eastern plant of wet meadows, ditches and marshes. Its fruits have two spines.

Golden Crownbeard
Verbesina encelioides

Golden Crownbeard, *Verbesina encelioides*, is found from Fla. to Calif., north to Kan. and Mont., and south into Mexico. It grows in rangeland and pastures, and as a weed along roadsides and field edges. This annual plant has much-branched stems and gray-green, triangular leaves. The many flower heads grow on long stalks; they have broad, bright yellow, toothed ray florets and a central yellow disk. Related plants from the eastern states are the wingstems, like *V. occidentalis*, a perennial plant with winged stems and flower heads with only 2–5 uneven ray florets.

Sunflower or Daisy family

Sneezeweed
Helenium autumnale

Sneezeweed, *Helenium autumnale*, is the most common and widespread of about 20 North American *Helenium* species. It grows in wet meadows, marshes, and ditches from Que. to B.C., south to Fla. and Ariz. This perennial plant has a clump of erect leafy stems about 5ft tall, and lance-shaped leaves which appear to run down the stems as wings. In late summer and fall it bears many terminal flower heads, each with 10–20 reflexed yellow ray florets and an almost globular, greenish-yellow disk. The effect is of a round button with streamers attached. This is one of three *Helenium* species seen in gardens in late summer and fall.

Woolly Sunflower
Eriophyllum lanatum

Woolly Sunflower, *Eriophyllum lanatum*, grows in dry places from southern Calif. to B.C., and through the Rocky Mountains. It is a study in gray and yellow, with leaves made gray-white by woolly hairs, and many solitary yellow flower heads. It is an excellent mound-forming plant for a dry sunny garden. It is a perennial, with a woody base, several branched stems, narrowly divided lower leaves, and linear upper leaves. Each flower head has 8–13 broad yellow ray florets and a yellow disk. There are about 12 *Eriophyllum* species in the west, all more or less woolly perennial plants or shrubs, with yellow or white flowers.

Dusty Maiden, *Chaenactis douglasii*, is one of about 25 *Chaenactis* species, all from the west, and known as pincushion flowers. This little plant is a usually a biennial, forming rosettes of cottony-glandular, lacy leaves and flowering around midsummer. The 15-in tall flowering stalks branch near the top to bear pink or white, top-shaped flower heads. They are formed solely of disk florets. Dusty Maiden grows on gravelly slopes and sandy plains, in chaparral and pine woods, from Calif. to B.C., and in the inner ranges to Ariz. and Mont.

Dusty Maiden
Chaenactis douglasii

Common Ragweed, *Ambrosia artemisiifolia*, and Great Ragweed, *A. trifida*, are both annual weeds that grow in waste places, fields, and roadsides – Common Ragweed throughout the U.S. and southern Canada, Great Ragweed mainly in the U.S. east of the Rockies. Because they are wind pollinated, they produce huge amounts of pollen and are a major cause of hayfever. They are coarse plants, with male and female flowers in separate heads, the numerous yellow-green male heads in elongated inflorescences at the top of the plant, and the green female heads in the leaf axils lower down. Common Ragweed grows 3–5ft tall and has dissected, light green leaves. Great Ragweed is 6–8ft tall, with palmate, three-lobed leaves.

Common Ragweed
Ambrosia artemisiifolia

Galinsoga parviflora is a cosmopolitan weed that grows in cities in the east and in Europe, in waste places and disturbed ground. In England it is known as **Gallant Soldier**, a corruption of the Latin *Galinsoga*. It is an inconspicuous, little annual plant, no more than 2ft tall, with many branching stems, ovate, toothed leaves, and flowers only a quarter inch across, usually with five white ray florets and a yellow disk. Its tiny fruits are flattened and bristly; they may cling to clothing and are also blown far and wide by the wind. It originates from Mexico and South America.

Gallant Soldier
Galinsoga parviflora

Sunflower or Daisy family

Cocklebur
Xanthium strumarium

Cocklebur, *Xanthium strumarium*, is a strange plant that grows in waste places and fields, on coastal beaches and beside lakes, in the U.S. and southern Canada. It is probably native to South America, but now grows as a weed in most warm temperate and subtropical regions. This is an annual plant, with rough branched stems and broad, rounded-triangular leaves. Its male and female flowers are borne separately in rounded heads in the leaf axils, the male heads on the upper part of the plant, the females below. The prickly female heads enlarge in fruit to form inch-long, ovoid burs which catch on the fur of animals or on clothes.

Common Madia
Madia elegans

The name **Tarweeds** is given to the *Madia* species because of their glandular nature and heavy scent. **Common Madia**, *M. elegans*, is found in foothills and valleys, dry open slopes and grassland in the Western Cascades and Sierra Nevada of Ore. and Calif. It is a branched plant up to 4ft tall, with hairy linear leaves. Its colorful flower heads are borne in loose compound clusters. They grow up to 2in across and have 8–16 yellow ray florets, often blotched with maroon at the base, yellow or maroon disk florets, and black anthers. The plant has several varieties: one flowers in spring and early summer, another through the summer, and a third in fall.

The *Hemizonia* species are a group of about 30, all found in Calif. Many are called tarweeds, like the *Madia* species, while some are known as spikeweeds. They are glandular, aromatic plants, with lobed or entire basal leaves, and most produce their yellow or white flowers in the fall. **Common Spike-weed,** *H. pungens*, is the most widely distributed, growing in dry places in the interior valleys and foothills in Calif, Ore., and sometimes in Wash. This pungent plant has stiffly rigid, much-branched stems up to 4ft tall, with yellow-green, spine-tipped leaves. The lower leaves are lobed, the upper leaves entire, and clusters of yellow flower heads grow in their axils.

Common Spikeweed
Hemizonia pungens

About 40 *Dyssodia* species are found in the southwest. They are herbaceous or subshrubby plants, strongly scented and with numerous oil glands on their leaves. Their terminal flower heads have a ring of ray florets around a disk. **Common Dogweed**, *Dyssodia pentachaeta*, is a small mound-like plant, no more than 8in tall. Its wiry stems have opposite leaves at the base and a single yellow flower head at the top, well above the foliage. The leaves are pinnately divided with prickly lobes. The plant grows in arid, rocky areas and deserts from Ut. to Ariz., across to Tex. into Mexico.

Common Dogweed
Dyssodia pentachaeta

Rosinweeds, *Silphium* species, are found in woods and prairies of the east and midwest. They are leafy perennial plants with erect stems, often 5–7ft tall. They contain resinous sap which hardens into gum when exposed to air, used by the Indians as chewing gum. **Cup Plant**, *S. perfoliatum*, may grow 8ft tall; it has square stems and its rough leaves are opposite, the upper ones joined across the stem to form a cup. The flower heads grow in loose terminal clusters on long stalks, apparently from the cupped upper leaves. Each head has 20–30 narrow ray florets and a yellow disk.

Cup Plant
Silphium perfoliatum

Sunflower or Daisy family

Canadian Goldenrod
Solidago canadensis

Goldenrods have glowing yellow flowers in late summer and fall. They are members of the genus *Solidago*, a large group mostly found in the east. These are perennial plants, with erect leafy stems growing up to 4ft tall, and simple, often toothed, alternate leaves. Their flower heads are small, with yellow ray florets and a yellow disk, but they are grouped into striking inflorescences. Many goldenrods have inflorescences like plumes, with branches arched and nodding, or straight; the flower heads are usually all on the upper side of the stem. Others have club-like or spike-like, erect inflorescences; the flowers are often arranged all around each branch. A third kind of inflorescence is the flat-topped cluster. A few species have clusters of flower heads in their leaf axils, giving the plants a zigzag appearance.

Canadian Goldenrod, *Solidago canadensis*, is a tall species, with erect stems up to 5ft tall and lance-shaped leaves. It has large, plume-like inflorescences with arching branches, and each flower head has 10–17 ray florets. This is one of the most widespread species, growing in woodland clearings and open places across most of the U.S. and Canada, only missing from the southern states like Tex.

Stiff Goldenrod
Solidago rigida

Stiff Goldenrod, *S. rigida*, has hard, rigid oval leaves clasping the upper part of the stem. It grows about 5ft tall, making clumps of hairy, erect stems with flat-topped inflorescences. The flower heads have 7–10 ray florets each and are arranged all along the upper side of each stem. Stiff Goldenrod is found in dry open places, woods, and prairies from Conn. to Alta., south to Ga. and N.M., more commonly in the west.

Showy Goldenrod, *S. speciosa*, has a pyramidal inflorescence made up of ascending branches crowded with flower heads on all sides. Each head has 6–8 ray florets. This is one of the last goldenrods to flower, coming into bloom between August and October. It is a tall plant, with a thick, erect, rather reddish stem, and smooth elliptical leaves. Showy Goldenrod grows in prairies, fields, woods, and thickets, from N.H. to Wyo., south to Ga. and Tex.

Rabbit Brush, *Chrysothamnus nauseosus*, covers large areas of dry hills and plains in the west, from B.C. to Sask., south to Tex. and Calif., and into Mexico. It forms a much-branched, gray-white shrub, 2–3ft tall, with stems thickly covered in gray or white hairs, and has many linear leaves. The plant has a rather unpleasant scent. Its late summer flowers are borne in terminal clusters; the heads are formed only of disk florets. Rabbit Brush is one of about 12 *Chrysothamnus* species, a genus found only in western North America.

Tansy Aster, *Machaeranthera tanacetifolia*, grows in dry open places in the plains and deserts, from Alta. to S.D., south to Mexico. This annual plant has finely divided leaves and numerous flower heads, each one with narrow, bright blue-purple ray florets around a yellow disk. This is one of about 20 species of *Machaeranthera*, many of them known as spine asters, with spiny-edged leaves and blue or purple flowers.

Showy Goldenrod
Solidago speciosa

Rabbit Brush
Chrysothamnus nauseosus

Tansy Aster
Machaeranthera tanacetifolia

Sunflower or Daisy family

Curlycup Gumweed
Grindelia squarrosa

Gumplants, *Grindelia* species, are western plants with sticky flower heads and leaves. **Curlycup Gumweed,** *G. squarrosa,* grows in dry open and waste places, invading overgrazed rangeland. Native to the Great Plains, it is now found from B.C. to Que., and south to Calif. and Tex. It is a biennial or perennial plant, with branched stems up to 3ft tall, and stalkless, toothed, often sticky leaves. In the latter half of summer it bears many yellow flower heads. Each head has 24–40 ray florets and is cupped in sticky bracts which curl backward at their tips. This plant has a use in Indian herb medicine, as a remedy for asthma and bronchitis. However, plants that grow in selenium-rich soils can absorb selenium, and are poisonous.

Broom Snakeweed
Gutierrezia sarothrae

Broom Snakeweed, *Gutierrezia sarothrae,* is another plant of overgrazed rangeland and is also used in Indian herb medicine. It grows in dry plains and foothills, from Sask. to Ore., south to Calif. and Mexico, most commonly in the southwest. It is a sticky perennial, with a woody base and slender, brittle stems clothed with narrow leaves. In late summer it bears many yellow heads in flat-topped inflorescences, like those of some goldenrods. Individual heads are very tiny, with 3–8 ray florets and the same number of disk florets.

Golden Aster, *Chrysopsis villosa,* is a low-growing plant, with rounded mounds of branched, leafy stems, at most 20in high, growing from a woody base. The mounds look gray from the dense covering of hairs on the small, lance-shaped leaves, but in summer they turn yellow with flowers. The flower heads grow in small clusters on the ends of all the branches; each has 10–16 ray florets which roll under as the flowers age. This common plant grows in dry, open places, on plains, slopes, and hills from Minn. to B.C., and south through the Great Plains and the Rocky Mountains to Mexico.

Golden Aster
Chrysopsis villosa

There are about 150 *Haplopappus* species in western North and South America. They are a variable group of herbs and shrubs, many with erect or sprawling stems. However, **Stemless Goldenweed**, *H. acaulis*, forms a tufted, leafy mat up to 3ft across, studded in early summer with solitary, terminal yellow flower heads on 8-in tall, bare stems. The leaves are narrow, linear or spoon-shaped, rigid and held erect, roughly hairy to the touch. Each flower head has 6–10 ray florets. This plant grows on dry rocky ridges and slopes, from foothills to high mountains, in sagebrush scrub and pine forests, from Calif. to Ore., east to Colo. and Mont., then in dry eroded hills into Sask.

Stemless Goldenweed
Haplopappus acaulis

Horseweed, *Conyza canadensis*, grows in disturbed ground, waste places, roadsides, and open fields across the U.S. and southern Canada, and because of its use in herb medicine, is now also found in Europe and other parts of the world. It was known to the Indians long before its uses became more widely accepted. This is a coarse, bristly, annual plant, with a rosette of basal leaves at first, and a stem up to 5ft tall, very leafy with many lance-shaped, more or less toothed leaves. From the axils of the upper leaves grow clusters of tiny flowers, each one with white ray florets and a yellow disk.

Horseweed
Conyza canadensis

Sunflower or Daisy family

New England Aster
Aster novae-angliae

There are over 100 species of **Michaelmas Daisies** or Wild Asters, *Aster* species, in North America, mostly perennial plants, with erect stems, simple, alternate leaves, and many small flower heads. Their flowers are blue, white or purple, with narrow ray florets and red, purple or yellow disk florets. Many hybrids are grown in flower gardens, flowering in late summer or fall.

New England Aster, *Aster novae-angliae*, grows in wet meadows and swamps from Que. to Sask., and south to Ala. and N.M. It forms a clump of hairy stems up to 7ft tall, with many lance-shaped leaves, their bases clasping the stem. The flower heads are borne on long, sticky stalks growing in the axils of the upper leaves; they have many red-purple ray florets, 45–100 on each flower head, and a central yellowish disk.

Smooth Aster
Aster laevis

Smooth Aster, *Aster laevis*, is a smaller plant, only 3ft tall at most, with smooth stems and leaves, often with a grayish bloom on the stem. Its leaves are small, with clasping bases, and it has a terminal open cluster of blue or purple flowers. Each flower head has 15–25 ray florets and yellow disk florets. This plant grows in dry, open places across southern Canada, and south to Ga. and N.M.

Many *Aster* species have small white flowers, like **Small White Aster**, *Aster vimineus*. This plant forms clumps of erect stems 2–5ft tall, with many linear leaves which become smaller higher up the stem, and with smaller leaves in the axils of the main ones. The flower heads are borne on many branches on the upper part of the stem. Each has 15–30 white rays and a yellow disk. This plant grows in moist, open places from Ont. to Me., along the coastal plain, and up the Mississippi River Valley to Mo. and O.

Small White Aster
Aster vimineus

Fleabanes, *Erigeron* species, are another large group, with over 100 North American species. Many modern hybrids are grown in gardens. One of their most attractive features is the large number of narrow ray florets in each flower head, 100–200 being not uncommon; the rays are usually arranged in two rows. Fleabanes are not unlike asters but they flower in spring and early summer. They may be annual or perennial plants, have narrow leaves, and their flower heads may be solitary or borne in clusters.

Daisy Fleabane
Erigeron annuus

Daisy Fleabane, *Erigeron annuus*, is an annual, with a leafy stem and a terminal cluster of white, or sometimes pink, flower heads. Its stems and lance-shaped, toothed leaves are covered with spreading hairs. Each flower head has 80–120 ray florets forming a relatively narrow ring around a wide yellow disk. This plant is a weed in the northern and eastern U.S., and southern Canada, growing in fields and waste places.

Seaside Daisy
Erigeron glaucus

Seaside Daisy, *Erigeron glaucus*, is a perennial, with prostrate branches and many rosettes of spoon-shaped leaves. From these arise the leafy flowering stems, growing 15in tall, each one with a solitary, terminal flower head. Each head has about 100 lavender ray florets and a yellow disk. Seaside Daisy grows on bluffs and in coastal scrub, sandhills, and beaches from Ore. to southern Calif.

Sunflower or Daisy family

Big Sagebrush
Artemisia tridentata

There are many species of *Artemisia* in North America, some naturalized European species, others native to this continent, especially in the west. They are herbs or shrubs, aromatic plants, each with its own distinctive scent. They have alternate, entire, toothed or dissected leaves, and small flower heads made up entirely of disk florets. The heads are gathered into large inflorescences. Wormwood, *Artemisia absinthium*, a European member of the genus, is a medicinal herb, very bitter, and used to remedy digestive problems. Tarragon, *A. dracunculus*, is a kitchen herb, used mostly in chicken dishes.

Big Sagebrush, the gray-green plant which covers so many valley floors in the Rocky Mountains, is *Artemisia tridentata*. Like many of the western species, it is an evergreen shrub, but can be recognized by its size (it grows up to 10ft tall) and its leaves. These are wedge-shaped, with three teeth on the end, silver-gray hairs, and quite a pleasant scent. Typically, this shrub has a short single trunk, then several sprawling branches which end in a mass of leafy stems. The branches are covered with shredding, gray-green bark. In late summer and fall tiny yellow-white flower heads open in dense, elongated clusters near the ends of the stems; their pollen causes hayfever. This plant has a long history in Indian herb medicine and makes a good insect repellent.

Mugwort
Artemisia vulgaris

Mugwort, *Artemisia vulgaris*, is a creeping perennial plant, a weed of roadsides, waste places, and fields found throughout most of the eastern U.S. and Canada. It has strong, erect stems, with many clasping, deeply cleft leaves. These leaves are smooth and very dark green above, white with cottony hairs below. The plant produces many flower heads, growing on long branched, leafy stems from every leaf axil, each one small, reddish-brown and inconspicuous. This European plant is very dull, but very obvious with its dark and light leaves.

Yarrow
Achillea millefolium

Yarrow, *Achillea millefolium*, is a plant that grows all around the northern hemisphere. It is aromatic, like the wormwoods, and has traditionally been used as a wound herb. It is a very variable plant, growing tall in shady positions but flat to the ground in exposed sites, found most often in disturbed places like roadsides and fields. Its creeping underground stems form large colonies if left alone, with soft, ferny, much dissected, dark green leaves. The erect stems bear terminal, more or less flattened clusters of white flower heads. Each head is small, with five broad ray florets and a central disk.

Tansy
Tanacetum vulgare

Tansy, *Tanacetum vulgare*, is another medicinal plant brought from Europe and now naturalized in waste places, in fields and on roadsides in much of the U.S. and southern Canada. It is used as a wash for sprains and bruises, and as an insect repellent. This is a perennial plant, with creeping underground stems from which grow many erect, robust stems with soft, ferny, pinnately divided leaves. When they are about 3–4ft tall, the stems bear terminal, branched clusters of yellowish flower heads; the heads contain only disk florets, many of them packed densely together.

Sunflower or Daisy family

Mayweed
Anthemis cotula

The **Mayweeds** and Chamomiles are a confusing group, not least because they keep changing their botanical names. For instance, the old name for Chamomile (of Chamomile tea fame) is *Anthemis nobilis*, and it has still kept this name in many herbal books. But in botanical books it has been called *Chamaemelum nobile* for many years.

Mayweed or Stinking Chamomile, *Anthemis cotula*, is a common weed of fields, waste places, and roadsides in many parts of the world, including North America, although it originated in Europe. The plant has an unpleasant odor that comes from glands on its leaves; their acrid secretion can cause blisters. It is an annual, with a branched erect stem up to 2ft tall, and soft, finely dissected, quite smooth leaves. It bears daisy-like flowers in summer, each with 10–20 white ray florets and a dome-shaped, yellow disk. Corn Chamomile, *A. arvensis*, is a similar weed, but has hairy leaves and no scent.

Scentless Chamomile
Tripleurospermum inodora

Scentless Chamomile, *Tripleurospermum inodora*, has had several complex changes to its Latin name in the past. The changes may seem unimportant, and in a sense they are for the plant remains the same, even if the name changes. But the problem that arises when a plant has such a history is tracking it down, for it may be found under any of its previous names in different books, and then it may appear that the books are describing different plants, when in fact they are the same one with different names. Scentless

Chamomile is an annual, almost scentless, hairless plant, with a branched, sprawling stem up to 2ft tall, and leaves divided into linear segments. It bears many daisy-like flowers in the latter part of summer. Each head has 12–25 white ray florets which droop as they age, and a dome-shaped yellow disk. It is native to Europe, but has been introduced and become naturalized in roadsides and waste places throughout much of the northern U.S. and Canada.

Pineapple Weed
Matricaria matricarioides

Pineapple Weed, *Matricaria matricarioides*, can sometimes be found under the name *Chamomilla suaveolens*. It is native to the west but now grows as a weed in waste places and on roadsides almost throughout North America. It is a scented, hairless, annual plant, its crushed foliage smelling of pineapples. It has a branched, often sprawling stem, only about 2ft tall, and pinnate leaves divided into linear segments. It bears many distinctive flower heads, each with a highly domed, greenish-yellow disk and no ray florets. The disk is cupped by green bracts with papery edges.

Ox-eye Daisy
Chrysanthemum leucanthemum

Ox-eye Daisy, *Chrysanthemum leucanthemum*, is a perennial grown in flower borders. It comes originally from Europe and Asia, but is now naturalized in fields, waste places, and roadsides in much of the northern hemisphere. It forms spreading patches of leaf rosettes, and erect stems up to 3ft tall, with dark green, pinnately divided leaves. The single large flower head has 15–30 white ray florets and a flat yellow disk. The plant has many garden names, including Moon Daisy, Shasta Daisy, and Marguerite. It has another Latin name too — *Leucanthemum vulgare*.

Common Groundsel
Senecio vulgaris

Golden Ragwort
Senecio aureus

Sunflower or Daisy family

The genus *Senecio* is a large one, with about 1000 species worldwide. Many of the plants have bright yellow ray florets on their flower heads (when they are usually called ragworts or butterweeds), but others lack ray florets altogether (when they are called groundsels). There are nearly 100 species in North America, the majority with bright yellow ray-floretted flowers, like butterweeds. They often grow in wet places, swamps, streambanks, and wet woods, in prairies and mountains, but some of the western ones are desert and scrub species.

Some groundsels are cosmopolitan weeds found throughout the world. **Common Groundsel**, *Senecio vulgaris*, is one such, growing in disturbed places everywhere. It is a small annual plant, no more than 1ft tall, with a branched stem and crisp, irregularly toothed leaves. It bears many small flower heads, each one with a cup of green bracts and many yellow disk florets, so that the head resembles a shaving brush. After flowering, each head produces a dome of white-haired fruits.

Golden Ragwort, *Senecio aureus*, is a perennial, with creeping stems and clumps of heart-shaped leaves. From these clumps grow erect stems up to 3ft tall, with irregularly toothed leaves and terminal branched clusters of bright yellow flowers. Each flower head has 8–12 ray florets and a central yellow disk cupped in green, purple-tipped bracts. The plant grows in swamps, wet meadows, and woods from Lab. to Minn., south to Ga. and Ark.

Threadleaf Groundsel, *Senecio douglasii*, grows on dry rocky plains and in deserts from Ariz. and Colo. to Tex., south into Mexico. It also multiplies on rangeland but cattle avoid it since it is toxic. It forms bushy clumps of branched stems 1–3ft tall and clothed with narrowly divided leaves, all bluish-green in color, with woolly hairs when young. In summer it bears numerous yellow flower heads, each with a narrow disk and 10–13 ray florets.

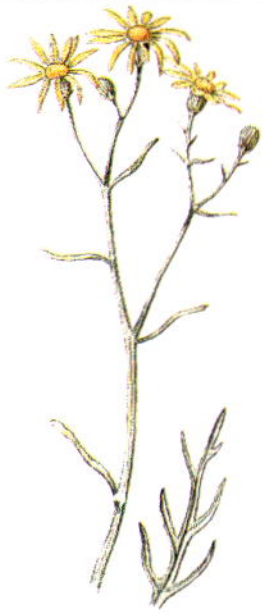

Threadleaf Groundsel
Senecio douglasii

Around 30 species of *Arnica* grow around the North Pole, many of them in Canada and in the Rocky Mountains. Like the European Arnica, *A. montana*, some of the North American species can be used to treat bruises and strains. This is also true of **Heartleaf Arnica**, *A. cordifolia*, a widespread western species. It grows in open woods in the foothills and mountains from Alas. to Calif., east to Mich. and N.M. It forms spreading colonies, with stems growing up to 2ft tall, opposite, heart-shaped leaves, and 1–3 terminal, yellow flower heads in early summer.

Heartleaf Arnica
Arnica cordifolia

Sweet Coltsfoot, *Petasites palmatus*, grows in shady wet meadows and damp woods below 1000ft, across Canada, south to Minn., Mich. and Mass., and in the Coast Ranges of the Rockies to Calif. In spring its creeping rhizomes send up thick, 2-ft tall flowering shoots, with many linear, parallel-veined bracts, and terminal clusters of white or pinkish flowers formed of disk florets and small ray florets. Large basal leaves follow in summer. They grow on long stalks and have broad, palmately lobed blades with dense white hairs on the underside; they may grow up to 15in across.

Sweet Coltsfoot
Petasites palmatus

Sunflower or Daisy family

Elecampane
Inula helenium

Elecampane, *Inula helenium*, is an old herbal plant used to treat chest complaints. It is native to Europe but now grows wild in scattered places from Que. to Minn., south to N.C. and Mo. It favors rough, damp places on roadsides, in fields, and waste places. It is a stout perennial up to 6ft tall, with a basal rosette of large, pointed-ovate leaves, and thick stems bearing similar but smaller leaves, their bases clasping the stem. The stems and the undersides of the leaves are softly hairy. Near the top of the stem are clusters of bright yellow flower heads, like small sunflowers.

Pearly Everlasting
Anaphalis margaritacea

Some members of the daisy family have flowers with a curious papery texture. They are often known as everlasting flowers, for their naturally dry blooms last far longer than most flowers. Some, like **Pearly Everlasting**, *Anaphalis margaritacea*, are used in dried arrangements. This is grown in gardens, as well as being a native plant. It grows in dry, open places across Canada and the northern U.S., south to N.C., Kan., and Calif. It is a pale green, perennial plant, forming patches of erect stems 2–3ft tall, its stems and linear leaves covered with white woolly hairs. The flower heads grow in branched clusters at the tops of the stems, male and female flowers on separate plants. Each head is globe-shaped, with yellow disk florets surrounded by white, papery bracts.

Low Cudweed
Gnaphalium uliginosum

Cudweeds are a group of about 100 species in the genus *Gnaphalium*, with 25 in North America. They are woolly-haired, with alternate, entire leaves, and clusters of "everlasting," whitish or yellowish flower heads, all formed of disk florets. The bracts which surround the flower heads may be completely papery, or may have only papery tips. **Low Cudweed**, *G. uliginosum*, grows in damp waste places and roadsides, beside streams, and in ditches, especially on acid soils, across Canada and into the U.S., south to Ind. and Va. It is an annual plant, only 8in tall, with branched, gray woolly stems, and linear leaves. In late summer curious little brownish-white flower heads are borne in small clusters, in the leaf axils, and terminating the stems.

Plantain-leaved Pussytoes
Antennaria plantaginifolia

Pussytoes, *Antennaria* species, also have "everlasting" flowers. They are a group of about 30 species, many found in North America. These small perennial, woolly-stemmed plants mostly form rosettes of simple leaves and erect flowering stems. The few stem leaves may be reduced to little more than scales, and the flower heads are borne in dense terminal clusters. **Plantain-leaved Pussytoes**, *A. plantaginifolia*, is found in open woods and dry places from Que. to Minn., south to Fla. and Tex.

New York Ironweed
Vernonia noveboracensis

Ironweeds are a group of about 15 species belonging to the genus *Vernonia*, found in woods and prairies of the east and midwest. They are perennial plants, with erect stems growing 3–6ft tall, alternate, simple leaves, and complex, open clusters of medium-sized, purple flower heads terminating the stems in late summer and fall. The heads contain only disk florets. **New York Ironweed,** *V. noveboracensis*, grows along streams, in marshes, and wet woods from Mass. along the coastal plain to Fla. and Miss.

Sunflower or Daisy family

Boneset
Eupatorium perfoliatum

There are several kinds of **Thoroughwort**, white-flowered species of the genus *Eupatorium*, in eastern North America. They are perennial plants flowering in late summer and fall, their fuzzy flowering heads borne in complex, branched clusters at the top of erect, leafy stems. The leaves are entire and grow in opposite pairs. Their flower heads contain only disk florets.

Boneset, *Eupatorium perfoliatum*, is a thoroughwort well known to Indians and to settlers for its use in the treatment of fevers. Boneset forms clumps of hairy, leafy stems up to 5ft tall. Its opposite leaves are distinctive for the way the stem seems to grow through them. The leaves are large and wrinkled, lance-shaped with serrated margins. At the tops of the stems the flower clusters branch to form spreading masses of white flower heads. The plant grows in low, moist places, in prairies, wet woods, marshes and along estuaries, from N.S. to Man., south to Fla. and La.

Joe-pye Weed
Eupatorium maculatum

Joe-pye Weeds are also *Eupatorium* species, but have pink or purple flowers. There are several species in the east, growing in moist places. *Eupatorium maculatum* can be quite a large plant, with stout stems 6ft tall, streaked and spotted with purple, and whorls of 3–5 lance-shaped leaves. In the latter half of summer it bears fuzzy purple flowers in dense, flat-topped clusters terminating the stems. It grows in damp meadows and woods, especially in calcareous soils, from Nf. to B.C., south through the northern U.S., to Md., Ill., and N.M.

Blazing Stars or Gayfeathers, *Liatris* species, are perennial plants, mostly found in dry open places, in open woods, barrens, and prairies in the east and midwest. Each plant has a clump of simple basal leaves and leafy stems bearing long spikes of purple flower heads. They tend to flower in late summer and fall. Some of the showiest are grown in flower gardens, including the Prairie Blazing Star, *L. pycnostachya*, and the Dense Blazing Star, *L. spicata*. They always attract comment for the unusual way the flowers open within the spike, from the top downward. **Rough Blazing Star**, *L. aspera*, is one of the most widespread species, growing in dry places and open woods, especially in sandy soils, from Ont. to N.D., and south to S.C. and Tex.

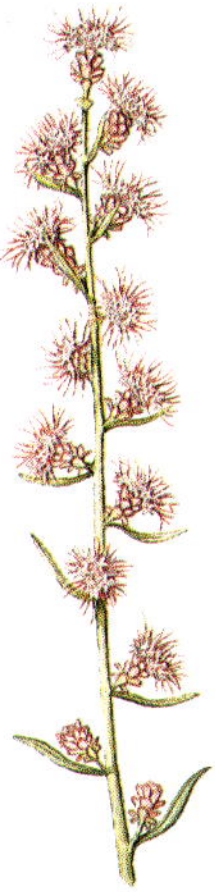

Rough Blazing Star
Liatris aspera

There are almost 100 *Brickellia* species, sometimes called **Brickellbushes**, in western North and South America, mostly in the warmer areas. They are a variable group; many are shrubs, others are annual or perennial herbs. **Large-flowered Brickellbush**, *B. grandiflora*, is one of the most widespread, and one of the few to penetrate into western Canada. It is a perennial herbaceous plant, with erect stems up to 2ft tall, and pointed, heart-shaped leaves. In the latter half of summer the flower heads appear in little nodding clusters on side branches in the leaf axils, and terminating the stems; they are pale yellow or greenish and contain only disk florets, cupped in bracts striped green and yellow. This plant grows in rocky places on slopes and cliffs in the Rocky Mountains from Calif. just into B.C. Further east it occurs in canyons and on hillsides as far as Neb. and N.M.

Large-flowered Brickellbush
Brickellia grandiflora

Sunflower or Daisy family

Canada Thistle
Cirsium arvense

There are over 60 **Thistles** belonging to the genus *Cirsium* in North America. They are spiny plants, with alternate toothed or divided leaves, usually with prickles on their margins. Their flower heads are formed of disk florets cupped in a series of bracts forming an involucre; in many species at least some of the bracts are tipped with spines. Some species have red or purple flowers, others have white or yellow ones. The fruits are achenes, and have several rows of feathery hairs.

Bull Thistle, *Cirsium vulgare*, and Canada Thistle, *Cirsium arvense*, are European plants which have become pestilential weeds in North America. This is because in Europe many insects feed on them, weakening the plants and curtailing their seed production. But these natural controls are missing in North America.

Bull Thistle
Cirsium vulgare

Canada Thistle, *Cirsium arvense*, is found throughout much of North America in fields and waste places. It is an aggressive weed, forming spreading colonies with its far-ranging lateral roots. Its erect stems are branched, up to 5ft tall, with many wavy, lobed, spiny-edged leaves. The pale purple flower heads are solitary or borne in small clusters in the axils of the upper leaves. The flowers are followed by achenes which have dull brownish hairs.

Bull Thistle, *Cirsium vulgare*, is a biennial plant, with a rosette of deeply divided, wavy, spine-tipped leaves in the first year, and a flowering stem in the second. This grows to 5ft tall and has wings adorned with long spines running along its length; its leaves are large, lobed, and spine-tipped, with shorter spines on the upper surface. The large flower heads are solitary or borne in small clusters in the axils of the upper leaves; they have deep, spiny involucres and red-purple florets. The flowers are followed by achenes with white hairs.

Yellow Thistle
Cirsium horridulum

Yellow Thistle, *Cirsium horridulum*, is an American species which grows on roadsides, in fields, on shores, and beside salt-marshes, mostly in the coastal plain from Me. to Fla. and Tex. It is often found in overgrazed pastures. This is usually a biennial plant, with a large rosette of divided, spiny leaves, and an erect stem eventually reaching 4ft in height. The stem is covered with short, white hairs, has similar leaves to those in the rosette, and also has several large flower heads, each one surrounded by smaller, narrow, spiny leaves held erect. The flowers are usually yellow but may be purple, especially on plants growing in the south or further inland.

Musk Thistle
Carduus nutans

Musk Thistle or Nodding Thistle, *Carduus nutans*, is another introduction from Europe, growing on roadsides and in waste places in many parts of the U.S. and southern Canada. This is another biennial thistle, with a rosette of wavy, spiny leaves in the first year, and an erect flowering stem up to 3ft tall in the second. Its stem is winged and the leaves are deeply dissected with spiny tips. The flower heads are nodding, formed of purple disk florets, and surrounded by large, reflexed, spine-tipped bracts. The hairs on its achenes are unbranched, not feathery like those of *Cirsium* species.

Sunflower or Daisy family

Milk Thistle
Silybum marianum

The **Milk Thistle**, *Silybum marianum*, is native to the Mediterranean. It is found scattered as a weed of waste places through much of the U.S. and southern Canada, but is happiest in the south, and common only in Calif. It is an annual or biennial plant, with a rosette of pale green, shining, white-mottled, lobed leaves, with spiny margins. The erect stem grows up to 4ft tall, has smaller clasping leaves, and in early summer it produces large, solitary, nodding flower heads, with red-purple florets. The plant is used in herb medicine to treat liver complaints. It was at one time thought to increase milk flow in nursing mothers.

There are over 20 *Centaurea* species in North America, commonly known as **Knapweeds** or star-thistles, many of them European aliens which have become naturalized. Many are grown for their attractive pink or purple flowers. Their heads are formed entirely of tubular disk florets; in the showiest species the outermost florets are enlarged, and may be dissected into linear segments. A series of dark bracts form the involucre beneath the head; the bracts may have papery edges, or may be spine-tipped. Knapweeds are annual or perennials, often rather tough plants, with alternate or basal leaves.

Spotted Knapweed
Centaurea maculosa

Spotted Knapweed, *Centaurea maculosa*, is a European plant that grows in fields, pastures, and roadsides in eastern areas of the U.S. and Canada, usually on alkaline soils. It is a biennial plant, up to 4ft tall, with wiry, branched stems and dissected linear leaves. Its many flower heads have involucres formed of black-tipped bracts, and the florets are pink-purple, tubular in form, with the outer ones enlarged and divided.

Batchelor's Buttons, *Centaurea cyanea*, has a long history as an agricultural weed in its native Europe, a career curtailed by modern farming methods. However, since it is also a favorite garden plant, it is unlikely to become extinct. Batchelor's Buttons is an annual plant, with an erect, wiry, grooved stem up to 3ft tall, with slender branches, and a cottony texture, especially when young. It has linear leaves and many flower heads with tubular florets, mostly blue but also pink and white, especially in garden varieties. The marginal florets are much enlarged and conspicuous. The involucre of each flower head is bell-shaped and the bracts have fringed, membranous edges. The plant grows in fields, waste places, and on roadsides across southern Canada and in much of the U.S.

Batchelor's Buttons
Centaurea cyanea

Lesser Burdock, *Arctium minus*, and Greater Burdock, *A. lappa*, are European plants, found as weeds in many parts of North America, in waste places and roadsides. Lesser Burdock is the more common. It grows to about 5ft tall, and forms a branched, bushy plant with reddish, often cottony stems, and large, long-stalked, pointed-ovate and rather heart-shaped lower leaves; the leaves become smaller and less heart-shaped higher up the plant. The flower heads have red-purple, tubular florets and hooked bracts making up the involucre. The fruits that follow the flowers are the hooked "burs," which cling to animal fur and to clothing.

Lesser Burdock
Arctium minus

Sunflower or Daisy family

White Lettuce
Prenanthes alba

Chicory
Cichorium intybus

Yellow Salsify
Tragopogon dubius

White Lettuce, *Prenanthes alba*, is one of about 15 *Prenanthes* species in North America, mainly in the east, but also in the midwest and southern Canada. They are perennial plants filled with milky juice; they have erect leafy stems and nodding, bell-like flower heads formed of ray florets. Their leaves are large, often deeply lobed, and alternately arranged. White Lettuce grows in woods from Que. to Man., south to Va. and Mo. It has an erect, purplish, white-bloomed stem up to 5ft tall, with triangular, often lobed lower leaves and lance-shaped upper ones. Its flower heads are usually yellow-white but may be pinkish; they hang in clusters near the top of the stem.

Chicory, *Cichorium intybus*, is a cosmopolitan weed, originally from Europe and Asia, now spread throughout much of the temperate world in waste places, fields, and on roadsides. Its young shoots are eaten in salads or as a vegetable; in Europe its roots are roasted, ground and added to coffee, or used as a coffee substitute. Chicory is a perennial, with a rosette of wavy-toothed leaves, an erect, branched, leafy stem up to 4ft tall, and many bright blue flower heads in the axils of the upper leaves. The heads are formed of strap-shaped florets.

Yellow Salsify, *Tragopogon dubius*, is a European plant, naturalized in much of the U.S. and southern Canada, growing in dry, open places, in waste ground, and on roadsides. It is usually biennial, with elongated leaves, mostly in a basal rosette, and an erect, hollow stem. The plant oozes milky juice if broken. The stem branches a few times to bear solitary terminal flower heads. These are large, formed of pale yellow, strap-shaped florets, with a series of long, slender bracts beneath the head and projecting beyond it. The fruiting heads are spectacular — large balls of achenes, each one with a feathery parachute.

Orange Agoseris
Agoseris aurantiaca

There are about 10 **Mountain Dandelions**, *Agoseris* species, in the Rocky Mountains. They are similar to a true Dandelion, with a rosette of linear, sometimes toothed leaves, and flower heads borne singly on leafless stalks; they exude milky juice. Their flower heads are formed of ray florets and most of the species have yellow flowers. However, **Orange Agoseris**, *A. aurantiaca*, has burnt orange ones which turn purple or deep pink as they age. This plant grows in moist, grassy places in coniferous mountain woods from B.C. to Calif.

Desert Dandelion
Malacothrix glabrata

Desert Dandelion, *Malacothrix glabrata*, is one of about 15 *Malacothrix* species in western North America, many found in dry grassy places, deserts, and sage scrub. They have rosettes of toothed or divided basal leaves; their usually leafless flowering stems may bear a loose cluster of flower heads or only one; and their flower buds commonly nod before they open. Most have yellow flowers, but a few have white ones. Desert Dandelion has narrow, deeply divided leaves, and its flowering stems have few branches, each with two or more flower heads. It grows in sandy plains and washes, in scrub, in deserts and interior valleys, from Ore. to Ida., south to Calif. and across to Ariz., and through Mexico. It flowers in spring, and in wet years may form carpets of yellow flowers in the deserts.

Sunflower or Daisy family

Dandelion
Taraxacum officinale

Dandelion, *Taraxacum officinale*, is a perennial garden weed found throughout the temperate regions of the world. It forms a rosette of wavy-lobed leaves, then in early summer produces several yellow flower heads, each one on a hollow, slightly succulent stalk. Both stalk and leaves exude milky juice if broken. The flower heads are followed by "blowballs" – round balls of parachuted seeds which are blown in the wind. Dandelion leaves, although bitter, make a useful addition to salads; their roots can be roasted and ground to make a good, caffeine-free substitute for coffee, and their flowers can be made into wine.

Cat's-ear
Hypochoeris radicata

Cat's-ear, *Hypochoeris radicata*, may be mistaken for a dandelion but is a hairy plant. It flowers in early summer and its tough, solid flower stems branch to bear several flower heads. There are small, dark bracts on each stem, and each yellow flower head is cupped in an involucre formed of a series of small, bristly, overlapping bracts. The flower heads are greenish or mauve beneath. This is another common weed in North America, found on grassy roadsides, in waste ground, in fields, and pastures.

Fall Dandelion, *Leontodon autumnalis*, resembles Cat's-ear. It has a rosette of deeply lobed leaves, several solid stems branching near the top to bear yellow flower heads, small bracts on the flower stems, and an involucre of overlapping bracts beneath each flower head. The flower heads are streaked with red beneath. This Eurasian plant is a common weed in the northeast, from

N.J. northwards, but is also found scattered in the northwest. It grows in grassy places, on roadsides, in pastures, and on waste ground.

Hawkweeds, *Hieracium* species, are a huge group, with somewhere between 10,000 and 20,000 species, mainly found in the temperate and Arctic regions of the northern hemisphere. They are perennial plants, either with most of their leaves in a basal rosette, or with leafy erect stems. Their flowers are borne in flower heads composed of ray florets, like those of dandelions, but each erect stem is branched and carries several to many heads; most species have yellow flowers. Beneath each head the involucre is formed of bracts in overlapping rows.

Narrow-leaved Hawkweed, *Hieracium umbellatum*, is a species that grows all around the North Pole, across Canada and the northern U.S. in North America. It has leafy stems up to 3ft tall, with many narrow linear, slightly toothed leaves, and a branched cluster of yellow flower heads terminating the stem. It grows in open woods and damp meadows, and on shores.

Mouse-ear Hawkweed, *Hieracium pilosella*, forms spreading tufts of leaves, each rosette producing creeping stems which form new overwintering plants at their tips. The leaves are usually lance-shaped and are densely white-hairy beneath. The solitary, pale lemon-yellow flower heads (quite different from the brassy yellow of most hawkweeds) are borne on leafless, stiffly hairy, erect stems, often only 6in tall. This plant grows as a weed in pastures and fields in the east; it comes from Europe.

Fall Dandelion
Leontodon autumnalis

Narrow-leaved Hawkweed
Hieracium umbellatum

Mouse-ear Hawkweed
Hieracium pilosella

Sunflower or Daisy family

Two-flowered Cynthia
Krigia biflora

Two-flowered Cynthia, *Krigia biflora*, is one of several *Krigia* species native to North America. It is a perennial plant with milky juice. It has a rosette of lance-shaped, often toothed leaves, and several flowering stems with clasping leaves. The uppermost two leaves on each stem are almost opposite, with several forked flower stalks in their axil. The flower heads they bear are solitary, orange-yellow, and formed only of ray florets. This plant is found in woods and meadows, on roadsides and in fields, from Mass. to Man., west to Colo., and south to Ga. and Ariz.

Prickly Sow-thistle, *Sonchus asper*, and Smooth Sow-thistle, *S. oleraceus*, are both common annual weeds of waste places and gardens, originally from Europe. They exude milky juice if broken and have yellow flower heads. Prickly Sow-thistle has very prickly leaves, the lower ones with bases which curl around the stems, and few to several flower heads. Smooth Sow-thistle has weakly spiny leaves, the lower ones clasping but not curling around the stem, and a large branching inflorescence with many flower heads. Young leaves of both plants are edible — in salads or cooked as a potherb — if the spines are removed.

Prickly Sow-thistle
Sonchus asper

Lettuces, *Lactuca* species, are more familiar edible plants. Garden Lettuces are varieties of *Lactuca sativa*, a plant which probably originated in Asia. There are about 10 native American lettuces, annual or perennial plants, with milky juice, alternate leaves, and usually with many flower heads in large, compound inflorescences. **Wild Lettuce**, *Lactuca canadensis*, grows in open woods, in waste places, and fields, from Que. to Sask., south to Fla. and Tex. It is an annual plant, growing up to 10ft tall, with dandelion-like leaves on its stems, and a large, branched inflorescence of small, pale yellow flower heads in late summer. These are followed by parachuted achenes. The young leaves of this plant can be eaten in salads, but they are more bitter than those of Garden Lettuce.

Wild Lettuce
Lactuca canadensis

Florida Lettuce, *Lactuca floridana*, is one of several North American lettuce species with blue flowers, known as blue lettuces. It grows in woods and thickets, and in moist, open places from N.Y. to Kan., south to Fla. and Tex. This is an annual or biennial plant, with toothed, dandelion-like leaves, and a complex inflorescence of pale blue flower heads. The flower heads are followed by clusters of white-haired achenes.

Florida Lettuce
Lactuca floridana

Nipplewort, *Lapsana communis*, is an annual plant with milky juice, and erect, leafy stems up to 5ft tall, the upper half much branched to form a complex inflorescence. The lower leaves of the plant are thin and lobed, with a large terminal lobe and several small lobes or a wing near the base; the leaves on the upper part of the stem are lance-shaped. The many flower heads are small, formed of ray florets, lemon yellow in color, and borne in many clusters. This is not a native plant, but has been introduced from Europe; it grows as a weed in waste places, woods, and fields in much of the U.S. and southern Canada. Its young leaves can be eaten raw in salads or cooked like spinach.

Nipplewort
Lapsana communis

Water Plantain family

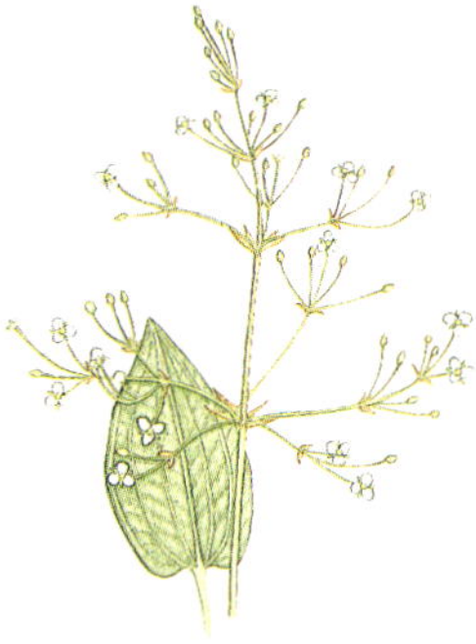

Water Plantain
Alisma plantago-aquatica

Alismataceae A small family with 13 genera and about 90 species of herbs, from the northern hemisphere. They are aquatic or found in wet places.

Family Features Flowers regular, hermaphrodite. Perianth segments 6, in 2 whorls; outer 3 sepal-like, overlapping, persistent; inner 3 petal-like, overlapping, falling; stamens usually 6; ovary superior, of many free carpels. Fruit a cluster of achenes. Leaves basal, long-stalked with open sheathing bases, often with arrow-shaped blades.

There are four **Water Plantains**, *Alisma* species, in North America, including *A. plantago-aquatica*, found across Canada and south in the U.S. to Calif., Wis., and N.Y. It grows in marshes, ponds, slow-moving streams, and ditches, forming a clump of leaves with elliptical or ovate blades. In early summer its 3-ft tall, branched flowering stalk bears many white or pale pink flowers in umbel-like clusters. They are followed by flattened, disk-like fruits borne in rings.

Arrowhead
Sagittaria latifolia

Arrowhead, *Sagittaria latifolia*, gets its other name of Duck Potato from the edible tubers on its rhizomes. The plant grows in marshes and ditches, beside lakes and slow-moving rivers, across southern Canada and to South America. It is a perennial, its leaves emerging from the water to bear narrow, arrow-shaped blades. In summer its 4-ft tall flowering stalks bear whorls of white flowers — male flowers near the top and female flowers beneath. These are followed by heads of winged, flattened achenes.

Agave family

Agavaceae A family of about 19 genera and 500 species, found in warm regions of the world, many in dry areas. Some agaves provide fibers, others food and tequila. Phormiums, yuccas and dracaenas are planted in flower gardens.

Family Features Flowers regular or somewhat irregular, hermaphrodite. Perianth segments petaloid, often fleshy, united into a partial tube; stamens 6, inserted on the tube; ovary superior or inferior with 3 cells. Fruit a berry or capsule. Leaves in basal clump or on the base of the stem, narrow, often prickly-margined, fleshy or fibrous.

Blue Yucca
Yucca baccata

About 40 *Yucca* species, often known as **Spanish Bayonets**, grow in the arid regions of western and southern North America. **Blue Yucca,** *Y. baccata*, has a clump of sword-like, spine-tipped leaves about 3-ft high, with whitish fibers on their edges. In summer its thick, 20-ft tall flowering stalk bears waxy, bell-like flowers, often red-brown on the outside, creamy white on the inside. The flowers are followed by edible fleshy pods. Blue Yucca grows in grassland, deserts, and scrub from Calif. to Colo., across to Tex., and south into Mexico.

There are about 130 **Agaves**, *Agave* species, in North America. *Agave americana* is typical of many, with rosettes of fleshy, spiny leaves 3–6ft tall. Its usually light green or gray-green leaves may be flattened on top, trough-like, or bent backward. A rosette may grow for many years before it flowers, and then dies. The inflorescence grows up to 25ft tall, with many branches bearing umbel-like clusters of yellow flowers. They are followed by oblong capsules with shiny black seeds.

Agave
Agave americana

Lily family

Liliaceae A large family of about 240 genera and 3000 species found throughout the world. Most are herbs. Beautiful garden plants in this family include lilies, tulips, hyacinths, and hostas. Onions, garlic, and leeks also belong to the family. Some members, like Death Camass, are very poisonous; its bulbs may be mistaken for onions, with fatal results.

Family Features Flowers regular or slightly irregular, usually hermaphrodite. Perianth segments usually 6, petal-like, may be free or partly fused into a tube, mostly in 2 distinct but similar whorls; stamens usually 6, opposite the perianth segments; ovary superior, usually with 3 cells. Fruit a capsule or berry. Leaves basal, or else alternate or whorled on erect stems. The plants have rhizomes, corms or bulbs.

Day Lily
Hemerocallis fulva

Day Lilies, *Hemerocallis* species, are old and familiar garden plants. *Hemerocallis fulva* is originally from Japan, but is grown in eastern gardens and also grows wild on roadsides. It forms clumps of arching, bright green, broadly grass-like leaves up to 3ft tall. In summer a well-established clump will send up leafless stems which carry terminal clusters of tawny orange, funnel-shaped flowers.

Desert Lily
Hesperocallis undulata

The **Desert Lily**, *Hesperocallis undulata*, is a related native plant which grows in the southwestern deserts. It forms clumps of sword-like leaves, with wavy-crinkled margins, and in summer produces an erect stem with a raceme of white funnel-shaped, lily-like flowers.

Mariposa Lilies are a group of about 60 western species belonging to the genus *Calochortus*. Each plant forms a single, often large basal leaf, and erect flowering stems grow from the axil of this leaf. These stems may be leafless, or have several reduced leaves. The flowers grow in terminal clusters, and may be erect or nodding, white, yellow, red, purple, or blue, often with complex markings inside the bloom, and often bearded inside. There is a gland at the base of each petal. Many species have showy flowers and are coveted garden plants. The plants produce bulbs, a once important source of food for the Indians.

The **Sego Lily**, *Calochortus nuttallii*, is the State flower of Utah. It grows in dry places, on the plains, in woods and scrub, from Mont. to N.D., south to Ariz. and Neb. The erect, unbranched stems grow up to 18in tall, and their long, narrow leaves often have inrolled margins. The flowers are borne in an umbel-like cluster at the top of the stem; they are white, bearded inside, with complex markings, yellow around the gland and a reddish crescent above the gland.

Sagebrush Mariposa Tulip, *Calochortus macrocarpus*, grows in similar habitats to the Sego Lily, through the Rocky Mountain area from B.C. to Mont., and south to Calif. Its lilac flowers have three broad petals, and three narrow sepals, slightly longer than the petals. The petals are marked with yellow hairs and a crescent of dark red.

Club-haired Mariposa Tulip, *C. clavatus*, is confined to Calif., growing on dry, often rocky slopes, in chaparral and the Coast Ranges. It has yellow flowers, with club-shaped hairs above the glands on the petals.

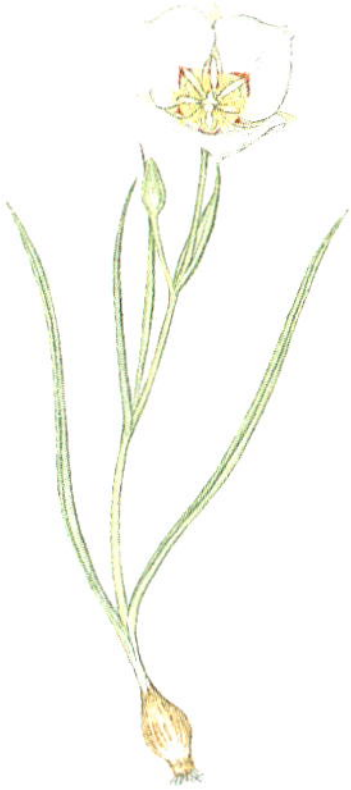

Sego Lily
Calochortus nuttallii

Sagebrush Mariposa Tulip
Calochortus macrocarpus

Club-haired Mariposa Tulip
Calochortus clavatus

Lily family

True **Lilies** belong to the genus *Lilium*, and are a large group of about 90 species, with about 25 in North America. Lilies are temperate region plants, many of them prized ornamentals for gardens. They all form bulbs.

Wood Lily
Lilium philadelphicum

The **Wood Lily**, *Lilium philadelphicum*, is typical of many of our native species. It grows in dry open woods and prairies across southern Canada, south to N.C. in the east, to Ky. and Ariz. in the west. It forms an erect stem 2–3ft tall, with whorls of lance-shaped leaves and 1–5 flowers at the top of the stem. These are funnel-shaped, opening toward the sky, orange-red or yellow in color, with purple spots.

The **Canada Lily**, *Lilium canadense*, grows in wet meadows and along woodland edges, from N.S. to Ont., south to S.C. in the mountains, and to Ala. It has slender stems up to 5ft tall, with whorls of 4–12 lance-shaped leaves, and a cluster of nodding flowers. The flowers are like funnels, with backward-arching petals, yellow or yellow-orange and marked with purple spots.

Canada Lily
Lilium canadense

The Columbia Lily, *L. columbianum* is a western species, often also called the Tiger Lily, and now becoming more uncommon because many plants have been taken to grow in gardens. It has large, orange, purple-spotted flowers nodding at the tops of 4-ft tall stems. In the wild it grows in brush and woodland through the Rocky Mountain area.

There are about 18 **Fritillaries**, *Fritillaria* species, in North America, all from the west. They are delicate plants, which increase slowly with small bulbs.

Checker Lily, *F. lanceolata*, is a widespread species, growing from B.C. to Ida., and south to Calif., in brush and scrub, evergreen forests, and oak woods on the lower slopes of the mountains. It has many bulblets, the largest ones sending up erect, slender stems up to 2ft tall, with several whorls of 3–5 lance-shaped leaves. They flower in spring, with nodding, bowl-shaped flowers hanging from the leaf axils; they vary in color, from purple-brown mottled with yellow, to lemon yellow mottled with brownish-purple. Several similar species have brownish or greenish flowers, but their flowers tend not to be mottled.

Checker Lily
Fritillaria lanceolata

Adder's-tongues or Fawn Lilies, *Erythronium* species, are found throughout much of the U.S. and in southern Canada. There are about 18 species of these beautiful perennial plants in North America, out of a world total of about 25. They are often found in woodland, several in the rich woods of the east, but more in the western mountains. They may have white or yellow flowers; some have funnel-shaped flowers, others have recurved petals. Some have plain leaves, others have leaves mottled with brown.

Yellow Fawn Lily
Erythronium grandiflorum

Yellow Fawn Lily, *Erythronium grandiflorum*, grows in open coniferous woods and on grassy slopes from B.C. to Alta., and south to Calif. It forms colonies of many plants, coming into bloom when the snow melts. Each plant has two elliptical, plain green, basal leaves, and a leafless flowering stalk, with 1–5 nodding, yellow flowers. The flowers have six petals, green-streaked on the outside, and bending backward as they age.

Lily family

Smooth Solomon's Seal
Polygonatum biflorum

The Lily family is a large and varied one, and divided into many subgroups, known as tribes. One of these tribes is the Polygonatae — the Solomon's Seal tribe — a group of plants whose members lack the showiness of some of the other species, but that have a charm of their own. Many are found in the rich woods of the east, growing secretly in shade.

There are several species of **Solomon's Seal**, all belonging to the genus *Polygonatum*. **Smooth Solomon's Seal**, *P. biflorum*, is the commonest, found in rich woods from southern Ont. to Minn., south to Tex. and Fla. It is a perennial plant, with a knotty rhizome, and arching stems in summer growing to 3ft tall, and with many opposite pairs of broad elliptical leaves. In the axil of each leaf there hang dangling, greenish-white, bell-shaped flowers, usually in ones or twos. They are followed by blue-black berries.

False Solomon's Seal
Smilacina racemosa

False Solomon's Seal, *Smilacina racemosa*, has erect stems up to 3ft tall, with broad, elliptical leaves forming a kind of zigzag pattern. In early summer creamy white, fluffy flower clusters appear at the tops of the stems and are followed by reddish berries. This is another perennial plant, with long twisted rhizomes. It grows in rich woods across southern Canada, south in the U.S. to Ga. and Ariz. *Smilacina stellata* is similar, and as widely distributed in moist sandy woods and prairies, but has a much smaller cluster of fluffy flowers.

White Mandarin, *Streptopus amplexifolius*, grows in rich woods across Canada, and south in the U.S. mountains to N.C. and Ariz. It has creeping rhizomes and erect, zigzag stems 2–3ft tall, with broadly ovate, clasping leaves. Solitary greenish-white, bell-like flowers hang on abruptly twisted stalks in the axils of the leaves. A similar species, the Rose Mandarin, *S. roseus*, is found from Nf. to Minn., south in the mountains to N.C., and is also found in the Rocky Mountains from Alas. to Ore. Its rose-pink flowers are borne singly or in pairs, on long dangling stalks in the leaf axils.

White Mandarin
Streptopus amplexifolius

Corn Lily, *Clintonia borealis*, is found in moist woods and woodland bogs, on acid soils from Nf. to Man., south to N.J. and Ind., and then in the mountains to N.C. and Tenn. It has a knotty rhizome which produces 2–5 glossy green, pointed-elliptical leaves in early summer. The leaves have sheathing bases which curl around an erect flowering stalk; the stalk reaches 15in in height and bears a drooping cluster of 3–8 flowers at the tip. Each flower is greenish-yellow and bell-like; they are followed by bluish berries. Wood Lily, *C. umbellulata*, is a similar eastern species; it has greenish-white flowers spotted with purple-brown, and black berries.

Corn Lily
Clintonia borealis

The five **Bellworts**, *Uvularia* species, are found in the east and midwest. They are similar to the Solomon's Seal tribe members and woodland plants like them, but placed in a different tribe. **Wild Oats**, *U. sessilifolia*, grows in woods and thickets from Que. to Minn., south to S.C., Ala., and Ark., in mountains in the south. It is a perennial plant, with a slender rhizome and erect stems up to 1ft tall. The stem is unbranched near the ground, then forks; the upper part of the stem bears stalkless leaves and drooping, creamy yellow, bell-like flowers.

Wild Oats
Uvularia sessilifolia

Lily family

Eastern Camass
Camassia scilloides

The five **Camass Lilies**, *Camassia* species, are all found in North America. **Eastern Camass** or Wild Hyacinth, *C. scilloides*, is the only species that extends into the east, growing in wet open woods and prairies from Wis. to Penn., and south to Tex. and Ga. It has a globe-shaped bulb, from which grow several linear leaves, and an erect flowering stalk up to 2ft tall. The white or violet flowers grow with bracts in a loose, elongated raceme. The similar Western Camass, *C. quamash*, grows in mountain woods and in the interior valleys of the north-western U.S., into southern B.C. The Indians have eaten Camass bulbs for centuries, but the bulbs are similar to those of the Death Cammass, *Zigadenus* species, and a mistake can be fatal.

Death Camass
Zigadenus paniculatus

There are 12 *Zigadenus* species in North America. All are poisonous, but the two most deadly are *Z. venenosus* and *Z. paniculatus*, both known as **Death Camass**, and often responsible for poisoning in livestock. *Zigadenus venenosus* is found in prairies and sagebrush scrub from B.C. to Sask., south to Baja Calif. and Colo. It has grassy, sheathing leaves and an erect, unbranched flowering stalk; this grows up to 2ft tall and has a terminal, pyramidal raceme of whitish flowers. *Zigadenus paniculatus* grows in pine woods and sagebrush scrub from Wash. to Mont., south to Calif. and N.M. Its flowering stalk bears a compound inflorescence with many side stalks and clusters of yellow-white flowers.

Wake-robins are a group of unusual and beautiful plants in the genus *Trillium*, with about 23 species in North America. They are perennial woodland plants. In spring or early summer they form erect stems, each stem bearing a terminal whorl of three leaves, and a single flower in the center of the leaf whorl. The flower has three green sepals and three white, pink or purplish petals. Some species are called birthroots, from their use in Indian herbal medicine to stop bleeding after childbirth.

Purple Trillium
Trillium erectum

Purple Trillium, *Trillium erectum*, was used as a birthroot. It grows in moist, shady woods from Que. to Ont., south to Ga. and Tenn. It has brownish-purple, more or less erect flowers, which smell of decaying flesh; the odor attracts flies, which pollinate the flowers. Toadshade or Red Trillium, *T. sessile*, is one of several species with erect flowers which remain closed; it grows in rich woods in the east and midwest.

Nodding Trillium
Trillium cernuum

Nodding Trillium, *Trillium cernuum*, grows in wet woods from Nf. to Sask., and south to Ga. and Ala., in the mountains in the south. It is one of several white-flowered species in the east; in this one the single white flower hangs on a long stalk below the leaves.

Carrion Flower
Smilax herbacea

Greenbriars, about 15 species in the genus *Smilax*, are sometimes put in a family of their own. They are perennial twining vines, many with woody stems, and they have male and female flowers on separate plants. **Carrion Flower**, *S. herbacea*, is a herbaceous species, with branched green stems that twine through other plants, its stipules transformed into tendrils. It has alternate, pointed, heart-shaped leaves, and dense clusters of yellow-green, foul-scented flowers in the leaf axils. The female flowers are followed by blue-black berries.

Lily family

Nodding Onion
Allium cernuum

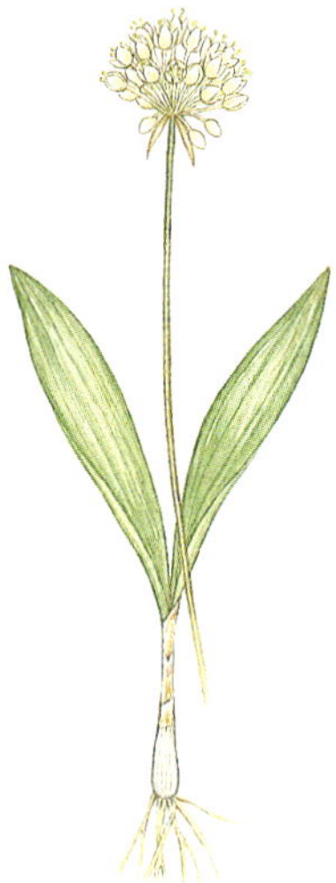

Wild Leek
Allium tricoccum

Onions are a large group of about 700 species in the genus *Allium*, found throughout the northern hemisphere and Africa. They include onions, leeks, and garlic, as well as ornamental alliums grown in flower gardens. There are about 80 in North America; most are native plants and many are edible. Allium bulbs form clumps of linear, often grass-like leaves; mature bulbs also form flowering stems, with flower umbels at first enclosed in a leaf-like or membranous spathe. Some species have bulbils as well as flowers in their spathes.

Nodding Onion, *Allium cernuum*, is found in dry, rocky woods and prairies across Canada and into the U.S., as far as Ore. in the Pacific west, to Mexico and to Ga. in the east. This is one of the best wild species for eating; its scent and flavor are like an onion. It sends up several soft linear leaves in early summer before the flowering stems appear. These grow to 2ft tall, and bear nodding umbels of pink flowers around midsummer.

Wild Leek or Ramp, *Allium tricoccum*, forms colonies in rich woods from N.B. to southern Que., south to Ga. in the mountains, and to Io. in the west. Its strap-like, deep green leaves appear in early spring but die back before mid-summer; as they die the plants come into flower, with 20-in tall stems carrying clusters of creamy-white flowers. Bulbs and leaves are edible, with an onion-like flavor, and are excellent in soups.

Brodiaeas, *Brodiaea* species, and **Triteleias**, *Triteleia* species, are a group of about 40 similar plants with grass-like leaves and erect, leafless stems which terminate in an umbel of usually blue or violet flowers. Most are found in Calif. and Ore. **Harvest Brodiaea**, *Brodiaea elegans*, grows in grassland and open woods, foothills and plains, from Calif. to Ore. It produces grassy leaves that wither before the flowers open. The 15-in tall flower stems bear funnel-shaped, violet flowers in early summer.

White Hyacinth, *Triteleia hyacinthina*, is distinguishable from the others, since it has white flowers. It grows in low, wet meadows, by vernal pools and streams, from B.C. to Ida., south to Calif. It has grassy leaves, and umbels of white, bowl-shaped flowers in summer. Each petal has a green line along its midline.

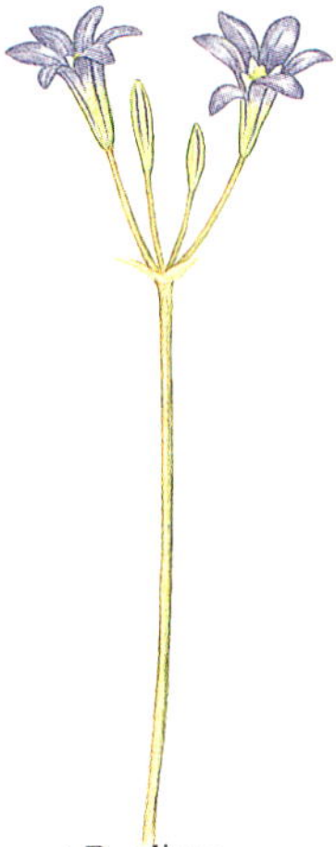

Harvest Brodiaea
Brodiaea elegans

Amaryllis family

Amaryllidaceae About 85 genera and 1100 species, all bulbous plants, most from warm temperate regions. Daffodils and snowdrops are grown in cool gardens, hippeastrums and nerines in the house and greenhouse.

Family Features Flowers solitary or in umbels; usually regular, hermaphrodite. Perianth segments 6, in 2 whorls, sometimes with a corona; stamens 6, in 2 whorls and opposite perianth segments; ovary inferior, with 3 cells. Fruits are usually capsules. Bulbous plants, with a basal clump of linear leaves.

White Hyacinth
Triteleia hyacinthina

Yellow Star Grass, *Hypoxis hirsuta*, grows in dry, open woods from Me. to Man., south to Ga. and Tex. It forms a little clump of hairy, grass-like leaves, no more than 6in tall. However, no grass has star-like, yellow flowers like this; they grow in a small umbel on a slender stalk in early summer.

Yellow Star Grass
Hypoxis hirsuta

Blue Flag
Iris versicolor

Yellow Flag
Iris pseudacorus

Red Iris
Iris fulva

Iris family

Iridaceae A large family with about 60 genera and 800 species of perennial herbaceous plants found throughout the world. Ornamental garden plants include crocuses, irises, and freesias.

Family Features Flowers regular or bilaterally symmetrical, hermaphrodite, usually with 1 or 2 bracts forming a spathe. Perianth segments 6, in 2 whorls of 3 (they may be alike in both whorls or dissimilar); stamens 3, opposite outer perianth segments; ovary inferior with 3 cells. Fruits are capsules. The plants have bulbs, corms, or rhizomes. They form clumps of flattened linear leaves, folded and overlapping at the base, sheathing the bases of the stems.

About 25–30 **Irises**, *Iris* species, grow wild in North America, and others grow in gardens. They have clumps of sword-shaped, overlapping leaves, and separate flowering stems with terminal flower clusters. Iris flowers are showy, with three clawed, outer perianth segments flexed downward (the "falls"), three clawed, usually erect, inner segments (the "standards"), bearded in some species, and a three-cleft style (the "crest"), with one petal-like section arching over each stamen.

Blue Flag, *Iris versicolor*, grows in marshes, wet meadows and on shores from Nf. to Man., south to Va. and Minn. It forms large clumps of erect or arching leaves up to 3ft tall. Around midsummer the flowering stalks bear terminal clusters of violet flowers. The falls are veined with darker blue, and marked with yellow or white at the base.

Yellow Flag, *Iris pseudacorus*, is a European species, its clumps of stiff leaves naturalized beside streams and ponds, in marshes and ditches, from Nf. to Minn., and southward. Its erect flowering stems bear yellow flowers, each with three broad, hanging falls, three smaller, upright standards, and three arching styles, ragged at their tips.

Red Iris, *Iris fulva*, grows in swamps and wet woods from Penn. to Ill., south to Ga. and Mo. It has typical iris leaves and flowers in spring. The orange-brown flowers have three broad, reflexed falls, three narrower reflexed standards, and three arching styles; the flowers look much flatter than those of many irises.

There are over 40 **Blue-eyed Grasses**, *Sisyrinchium* species, in North America. They are small, perennial, grass-like plants, with tufts of overlapping leaves. On separate stems they bear umbels of delicate flowers, each umbel growing from a spathe of two bracts. The perianth segments look like six similar petals.

Pointed Blue-eyed Grass, *Sisyrinchium angustifolium*, forms tufts of grass-like leaves, 20in tall at most. Through much of the summer its erect flowering stems produce terminal umbels of the blue, yellow-eyed flowers which are typical of the group. The plant grows in meadows and open woods in much of southern Canada and the U.S., in mountains in the south.

Pointed Blue-eyed Grass
Sisyrinchium angustifolium

Golden-eyed Grass, *Sisyrinchium californicum*, is found in moist places west of the Cascades, from Calif. to Ore. It forms tufts of 15-in tall, grass-like leaves, and has brown-veined, yellow flowers in early summer.

Golden-eyed Grass
Sisyrinchium californicum

Common Cattail
Typha latifolia

Cattail family

Typhaceae Only one genus, *Typha*, and 10 species, the cattails or bulrushes, found throughout the world. All 10 are aquatic plants, growing in marshes, beside ponds, slow-moving rivers, or ditches. Cattails are perennials, which form erect stems up to 9ft tall, with thick, sword-like leaves. The stiff, unbranched stems bear flowers in terminal cylindrical heads, the greenish female flowers below, and the male flowers above. The male flowers are shed after their pollen has gone, leaving a bare stalk. The brown fruiting head persists into late fall until it breaks up.

Common Cattail, *Typha latifolia*, grows up to 9ft tall, with leaves up to ¾in across. Its male and female flowers form one continuous cylindrical flower spike. Narrow-leaved Cattail, *T. angustifolia*, grows up to 6ft tall, and has ¼-in wide leaves. Its male and female flowers are separated by a section of stem up to 3in long.

Yellow-eyed Grass
Xyris iridifolia

Yellow-eyed Grass family

Xyridaceae A very small family, with 2 genera and about 40 species, from warm regions of the world. About 18 **Yellow-eyed Grasses**, *Xyris* species, are found in the southeastern U.S., in wet places. They are annual or perennial plants, with a clump of straight leaves, and terminal flower spikes on leafless stalks, 3ft tall at most. Each flower spike looks like a cone of woody bracts with protruding yellow flowers. Each flower has three sepals — an outer hooded one, shed as the bud opens, and two lateral, boat-shaped or winged ones which persist. The tubular corolla is three-lobed, and the flower has three or six stamens and a superior ovary.

Spiderwort family

Commelinaceae A family of perennial herbaceous plants, with about 38 genera and 500 species, mainly from tropical and subtropical regions. Dayflowers and spiderworts are grown in flower borders.

Family Features Flowers usually regular, hermaphrodite, solitary or in cymes, in the axils of leaf-like spathes. Perianth segments free, overlapping, in 2 whorls of 3, outer ones sepal-like, inner ones petal-like; stamens usually 6, in 2 whorls of 3, but may be reduced to 3; ovary superior, usually with 3 cells. Fruits are capsules. Leaves have tubular, sheathing, membranous bases. The plants are usually succulent.

Virginia Spiderwort
Tradescantia virginiana

Several **Spiderworts**, *Tradescantia* species, are found in North America, mainly in the south. **Virginia Spiderwort**, *T. virginiana*, grows in moist woods and prairies, from Ga. to Mo., north to Me. and Minn. It forms a clump of erect stems up to 3ft tall, with alternate, linear leaves which hide the stems. The blue flowers are also hidden, by long bracts held at acute angles.

Asiatic Dayflower
Commelina communis

Asiatic Dayflower, *Commelina communis*, is an introduced species which grows in shady, moist, disturbed places. It has sprawling, branching stems, lance-shaped leaves with sheathing bases, and terminal flower clusters in heart-shaped, folded spathes. Each flower has two large blue petals and a smaller whitish one. Similar native species grow in the east and midwest.

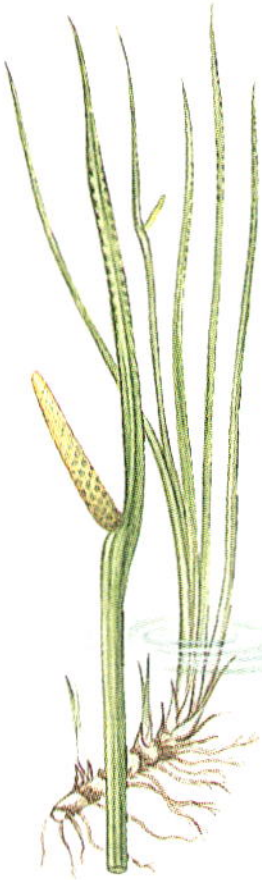

Sweetflag
Acorus calamus

Arrow Arum
Peltandra virginica

Arum family

Araceae A family of herbaceous plants, with about 115 genera and 2000 species found mainly in the tropics, often in jungles. Temperate species are mostly found in wet places. Popular houseplants in this family are grown for their foliage; they include philodendrons and dieffenbachias. Garden species include arums and calla lilies. Many members of the family contain acrid, poisonous sap.

Family Features Flowers very small, often with an offensive scent, borne in a dense spike (a spadix), usually subtended by a leafy spathe. The flowers may be hermaphrodite or unisexual; if unisexual, then male flowers are borne on the upper part of the spadix, females below. Hermaphrodite flowers usually have a perianth but this is absent in unisexual flowers. Stamens 2–8, opposite perianth segments; ovary superior or embedded in spadix, with 1–3 cells. Fruit usually a berry. Leaves usually form a basal clump, growing from the rhizome, and often have sheathing bases.

Sweetflag, *Acorus calamus*, is found in marshes, beside ponds and rivers, from N.S. to Alta., south to Fla. and Colo., across Europe and Asia. It forms colonies of sword-like, wavy-edged leaves up to 5ft tall. The leaves have a scent of tangerines and cinnamon when bruised. The stems look like three-angled leaves and bear flower-spikes about half way up, growing at an angle of about 45°. The spikes bear densely packed, yellowish, hermaphrodite flowers, with an unpleasant scent. Sweetflag rhizomes are used in perfumery and in herb medicine; they may be boiled in syrup to make candy. In medieval times the leaves were strewn on the floors of churches and manor houses for their sweet scent.

Arrow Arum, *Peltandra virginica*, grows in marshes, along shallow rivers and ponds, from Me. to Mich., south to Fla. and Tex., and north into eastern Canada. In early summer the flower spathe develops, like a curled leaf with a wavy margin, curved around the spadix, covering the female flowers, opening to expose the male ones. The flowers are followed by black-brown berries.

Water Arum, *Calla palustris*, grows in swamps and on pond edges, from N.S. to Que., south to Penn. and Minn. From its elongated rhizomes grow long-stalked leaves with ovate blades, 1ft tall at most. Its solitary white spathes open to reveal spadices of yellow flowers. They develop in early summer and are followed by red berries. The whole plant is acrid.

Skunk Cabbage, *Symplocarpus foetidus*, is a perennial plant found in wet meadows and woods, muddy ground and swamps, across much of southern Canada, south to N.C. and Io. It has a thick rhizome and in early spring its purple-brown, green-mottled spathe erupts from the ground, melting the snow around. It protects the knob-like spadix which emits an evil scent. The leaves emerge later in tight rolls, unfurling to become cabbage-like and up to 2ft across.

Jack-in-the-pulpit, *Arisaema triphylla*, grows in moist woods from N.S. to Minn., south to Fla. and La. This perennial plant has two large, divided leaves on long stalks up to 5ft tall. The plant flowers in spring, with a hooded spathe, varying from green to maroon, often streaked with purple. The flowers are followed by scarlet berries.

Water Arum
Calla palustris

Skunk Cabbage
Symplocarpus foetidus

Jack-in-the-pulpit
Arisaema triphylla

Orchid family

Orchidaceae One of the largest plant families, with about 735 genera and 17,000 species known to date. Many are found in temperate regions, but far more grow in tropical jungles, and more are found every year.

Family Features Flowers solitary, or borne in a spike or raceme, hermaphrodite, bilaterally symmetrical. Perianth segments 6, in 2 whorls; often the whorls are unlike, the outer one sepal-like, the inner one petal-like. Often the central sepal becomes the uppermost part of the flower; the sides are formed by 2 lateral sepals and 2 lateral petals, and the central petal hangs down, forming the lip. Stamens 1 or 2, their anthers borne with the stigmas on a structure known as the column. Ovary inferior, usually with 1 cell. The fruit is usually a capsule, with many tiny seeds. Leaves entire, often fleshy, with sheathing bases; often in 2 rows at the base of the stem, or alternate. They may be reduced to scales.

Yellow Lady's-slipper
Cypripedium calceolus

Showy Lady's-slipper
Cypripedium reginae

White Bog Orchid
Habenaria dilatata

About 10 **Lady's-slippers**, *Cypripedium* species, grow in North America, most in damp woods and swamps. Many of these spectacular orchids are now rare. **Yellow Lady's-slipper**, *C. calceolus*, grows across Canada and into the U.S., south to S.C., La., through the Rocky Mountains to N.M., but is not common. In early summer it forms an erect stem up to 2ft tall, with 3–5 elliptical leaves and one or two flowers in the axil of a leafy bract. The flowers have yellow to purple, often wavy sepals, one erect at the top and the two lateral ones joined and pointing downward, two spirally twisted lateral petals, similar in color to the sepals, and a large creamy to bright yellow pouched lip, spotted with magenta inside.

Showy Lady's-slipper, *Cypripedium reginae*, is a rare and beautiful species which grows in mossy woods and bogs from Nf. to N.D., south to Ga. and Mo., in mountains in the south. It forms an erect stem up to 3ft tall, with elliptical, strongly ribbed leaves. From 1–3 flowers are borne at the top of the stem; they have white sepals and lateral petals, and a striking pouch — white, pink or purple in front with pink or purple veins, and deeply furrowed.

About 30 *Habenaria* species are found in North America, mainly in the north. **White Bog Orchid** or Bog Candles, *H. dilatata*, is a perennial plant, with an erect leafy stem 2–3ft tall, and many sheathing leaves. The waxy white, spurred flowers form a long raceme terminating the stem. This orchid grows in wet woods, bogs, and meadows, from Greenland through Canada to Alas., south to Mass., Ind., and Calif.

Bracted Orchid, *Habenaria viridis*, grows in moist woods around the North Pole, south in North America to the northern U.S., through the Appalachians to N.C., and in the Rocky Mountains to Colo. It has many broadly lance-shaped leaves merging into long, linear bracts, and greenish, often purple-tinged flowers in the axils of the bracts.

Ragged Fringed Orchid, *Habenaria lacera*, is one of several fringed orchids in North America. It grows in open swamps and bogs from Nf. to Man., south to S.C., Ala., and Ark. It has an erect stem 2–3ft tall, with lance-shaped leaves and creamy yellow or greenish-yellow flowers. The lip of the flower is divided into three lobes, each one deeply fringed.

Bracted Orchid
Habenaria viridis

Ragged Fringed Orchid
Habenaria lacera

Showy Orchis
Orchis spectabilis

Snake-mouth
Pogonia ophioglossoides

Orchid family

Showy Orchis, *Orchis spectabilis*, has a stout flowering stem up to 1ft tall, growing from a pair of large, glossy, elliptical leaves which sheath its base. It produces several showy flowers at the top of the stem, varying in color from white to pink, sometimes with a pink hood and a white lip. Each flower has a hood formed by the fusion of the sepals and lateral petals, and a long, tongue-shaped, hanging lip with a spur. The flowers grow in the axils of long, leaf-like bracts. This orchid is not very common; it grows in rich woods from N.B. to Neb., and south to Ga. and Ark. The Small Round-leaved Orchis, *O. rotundifolia*, grows throughout Canada, around the Great Lakes, and south to N.Y. It grows in wet woods and on the edges of swamps. It is a smaller plant, with rounded leaves and white or mauve flowers, its lip spotted with red-mauve.

The **Snake-mouth** or Rose Pogonia, *Pogonia ophioglossiodes*, is another bog orchid, growing in open bogs and seepage slopes from Nf. to Minn., south to Fla. and Tex. But in spite of its wide distribution, it is quite rare. It has a slender stem up to 2ft tall, with a single lance-shaped or elliptical leaf part way up. The terminal, solitary, fragrant pink flower grows in the axil of a leaf-like bract. The flower has three similar sepals forming a triangle, two lateral petals arching over the lip, and a spatula-shaped lip, fringed and bearded with short yellow bristles.

The **Giant Helleborine**, *Epipactis gigantea*, grows beside lakes, streams, and springs from B.C. to S.D., south to Calif. and Tex. It is a perennial plant, with short creeping rhizomes from which grow colonies of erect, leafy stems up to 3ft tall. The leaves are large, lance-shaped to broadly ovate. The flowers grow in a few-flowered raceme, each one in the axil of a leaf-like bract, and are quite showy. They have greenish-brown, concave sepals, shorter, purplish lateral petals, and a deeply spoon-shaped, purple lip with a salmon-pink tongue. All parts of the flower are purple-veined.

The **Dragon's Mouth** or Bog-rose, *Arethusa bulbosa*, grows in *Sphagnum* bogs, wet woods and meadows, from Nf. to Minn., south to N.J., and in the mountains to S.C. However, its wide distribution is deceptive, for this is a rare orchid. It flowers in summer, producing a single stalk with 1–3 scale-like bracts and a solitary, scented flower at the tip. This is bright pink, with three erect sepals, two lateral petals arching over the lip, and a showy lip, spotted with deeper pink and with many yellow hairs. As the flower fades and the fruiting capsule develops, the single grass-like leaf appears, maturing with the capsule.

The **Twayblades**, *Listera* species, are a group of about 30 northern orchids found in sub-Arctic and northern temperate regions. They are small perennial plants which have fibrous roots, and slender, erect stems with a pair of broad, opposite leaves near the middle. The small flowers lack spurs, are dull in color, greenish or purplish, and borne in a slender raceme terminating the stem. **Broad-leaved Twayblade**, *Listera convallarioides*, is found in wet woods from Nf. to Alas., south in the U.S. to Mass., Minn., and Calif. It has broadly ovate leaves and up to 20 translucent, yellow-green flowers.

Giant Helleborine
Epipactis gigantea

Dragon's Mouth
Arethusa bulbosa

Broad-leaved Twayblade
Listera convallarioides

Grass-pink
Calopogon pulchellus

Nodding Ladies Tresses
Spiranthes cernua

Western
Rattlesnake Plantain
Goodyera oblongifolia

Orchid family

Grass-pink, *Calopogon pulchellus*, has unusual flowers in which the lip forms the top part of the flower above the other two petals and three sepals. The flowers vary from pink to rose-purple, with a yellow beard on the lip, and grow in a loose raceme of 2–10 blooms at the top of a leafless flower stalk, 6–20in tall. The plant has a rounded corm, which produces a single grass-like leaf and the flowering stalk in early summer. It is found in wet meadows and bogs from Nf. to Ont., around the Great Lakes, south through New England to Fla. and Tex.

Ladies Tresses are a group of about 200 species in the genus *Spiranthes*, with over 20 in North America. They are small orchids, with leafy erect stems and long, spirally twisted racemes of flowers. **Nodding Ladies Tresses**, *S. cernua*, grows in open woods and meadows, fields, and bogs, usually on acid soils, from Nf. to Minn., south to Fla. and Tex. It has grassy leaves, mostly in a basal rosette, and a 3-ft tall flowering stem. Its white flowers arch downward. Most species have whitish flowers, frequently tinged with yellow or pink.

Rattlesnake Plantains belong to the genus *Goodyera*. There are four species in North America, two found over much of the continent, and the others in the east. Their leaves are borne in a basal rosette, and are veined with white so that they resemble snakeskin. **Western Rattlesnake Plantain**, *G. oblongifolia*, grows in woods and forests from B.C. to Que., and around the Great Lakes, south through the Rocky Mountains to Calif. It is the largest of the four, with a stout stem reaching 18in tall, and carrying a spike of whitish flowers. Each flower has a hood formed of the dorsal sepal and attached lateral petals, separate lateral sepals, and a spurless, pouched lip.

The **Fairy Slipper**, *Calypso bulbosa*, produces one rounded leaf in fall; this survives the winter and the flowering season of the following year, withering once flowering is over. The bulb from which it grows sends up another leaf as fall comes again. In spring it produces a stem with one flower. The three sepals and two lateral petals are all linear and pink-purple, arching at the top of the pouched lip. The lip hangs downward and is shaped like a shoe; it is white with pink blotches and bearded with yellow hairs; it has two tiny horns at the toe.

Fairy Slipper
Calypso bulbosa

Coral-roots, *Corallorhiza* species, are saprophytic orchids — yellowish or brownish plants with no roots. Instead they have much branched, fleshy, rounded rhizomes like a piece of coral. There are about 15 species in northern and mountain regions of the northern hemisphere, with several in North America. They are woodland plants, growing where there is ample organic matter in the soil.

Spotted Coralroot, *Corallorhiza maculata*, grows in damp upland forests from Nf. to B.C., south in the Appalachians to N.C., and in the Rocky Mountains to Mexico. In late summer its coral-like rhizomes produce yellowish or purplish flowering stalks 10–20in tall. Each stalk has a few sheaths near the base, the remnant of the leaves, and a raceme of flowers. The sepals and lateral petals are similar in color to the stalks, but the lip is whitish and spotted with purple. This is the largest coral-root.

Spotted Coralroot
Corallorhiza maculata

Glossary

Achene A small, dry, indehiscent fruit with a single seed. Its thin wall distinguishes it from a nutlet.

Alien An introduced plant which has become naturalized.

Alternate An arrangement of leaves on a stem, such that each node bears one leaf on alternate sides of the stem (see Fig. 2).

Annual A plant completing its life cycle within a single year: germinating from seed, flowering, and setting seed itself, then dying.

Anther The portion of a stamen in which the pollen is formed (see Fig. 5).

Axil The place between a lateral branch of a stem, twig or leaf, and the main stem.

Bearded With bristly hairs.

Berry A fleshy fruit, usually containing several seeds. Often used as a more general term for any fleshy fruit.

Biennial A plant which completes its life cycle in two years, developing a root and leaves in its first year, overwintering by means of food stored in the root, then flowering and setting seed in the second year, and dying.

Blade The expanded flat portion of a leaf, in contrast to the stalk.

Bract A specialized leaf with a flower growing in its axil. Bracts may closely resemble leaves, or may differ in size, color or texture, cf. Spathe (see Fig. 1).

Bud An undeveloped flower or shoot, protected by sepals (flower bud) or bud scales (shoot).

Bulb An extremely shortened underground stem with swollen fleshy leaves or leaf bases, in which food is stored. Bulbs may or may not be enclosed in a protective tunic. They are common overwintering and food storage organs in some monocotyledonous plants.

Fig. 1 Parts of a Plant

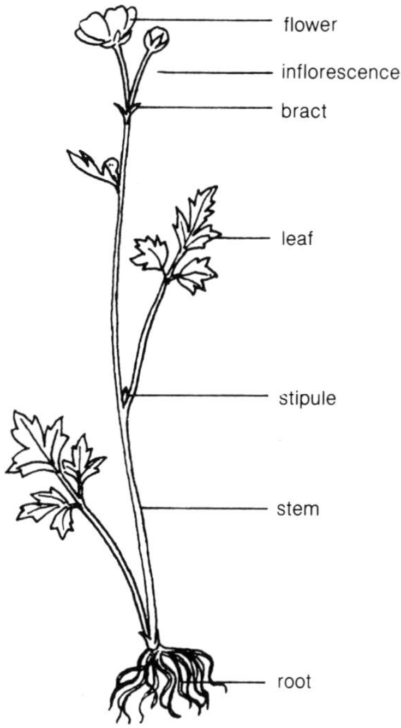

Bulbil A small bulb produced by some plants in the axils of leaves or in the inflorescence.

Calyx The sepals of a flower form the calyx. They are usually green and leaflike, and enclose and protect the flower in bud. They may be joined or free, colored or absent. In many families the calyx persists to enclose the fruit. In a calyx where the sepals are joined, the basal tubular portion is the calyx-tube, and the upper free parts are the calyx-lobes (see Fig. 5).

Capsule A dry fruit formed of several cells, which splits open to release the seeds.

Carpel One of the segments or cells which make up the ovary.

Chaparral A habitat composed of thickets of evergreen, often stiff or spiny shrubs.

Claw The narrow basal section of some petals and sepals.

Compound inflorescence A branched inflorescence composed of several racemes or cymes.

Compound leaf A leaf composed of several leaflets (see Fig. 3).

Corm A short, erect underground stem, swollen with food and frequently acting as an overwintering organ. It is often protected by a scaly tunic. The following year's corm develops on top of the spent one of the previous year.

Corolla The petals of a flower form the corolla. They are often colored and conspicuous, and may bear nectaries, all features designed to attract insects. In some plants they are small, insignificant, or absent (see Fig. 5).

Fig. 2 Leaf Arrangements

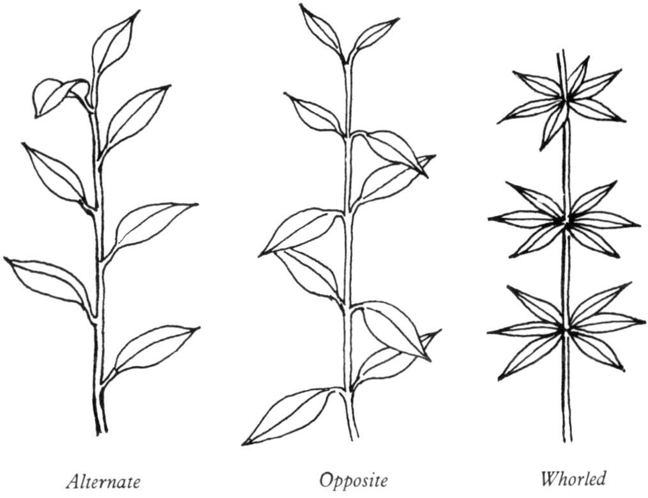

Fig. 3 Leaf Types

Simple Leaves

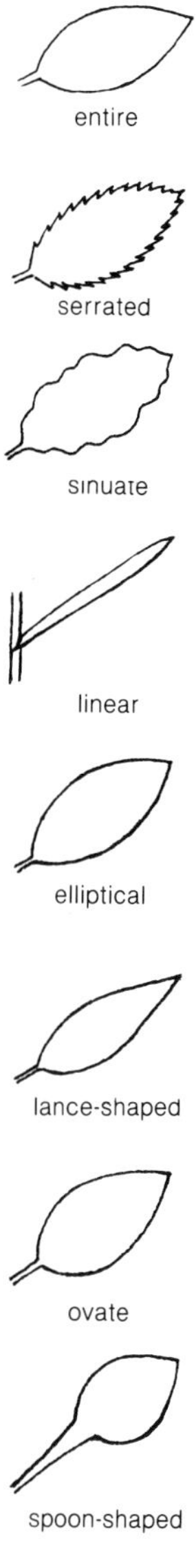

Corona In some plants the flowers have an additional structure between the petals and the stamens (as in the milkweeds). This is called the corona.

Creeping With stems growing along the ground, rooting at the nodes.

Cyme A flat-topped or conical inflorescence, in which the branches develop equally from the center, the central flower opening first in each branch. Each flower is the terminal one when it is formed (see Fig. 4).

Dehiscent Splitting open to release the seeds.

Disk The central portion of the flower head in a member of the Sunflower family. It contains only tubular florets.

Dissected Of a leaf, one cut deeply into segments, and where the segments are themselves deeply cut (see Fig. 3).

Divided Of a leaf, cut into segments, the divisions extending as far as the midrib or the base, cf. Lobed (see Fig. 3).

Elliptical Of a leaf (see Fig. 3).

Entire Of a leaf, with an unbroken margin, not toothed (see Fig. 3).

Evergreen A plant that does not lose its leaves in winter.

Family A unit of biological classification, consisting of a collection of genera sharing particular features, cf. Genus.

Fertile Capable of reproduction; of a stamen, one which produces pollen; of a flower, one which produces viable seed.

Filament The stalk of a stamen (see Fig. 5).

Floret A single flower in the flower head of a member of the Sunflower family. Disk florets are tubular, ray florets are strap-shaped. Flower heads may be composed wholly of disk florets or of ray florets, or may have disk florets in the center (forming the central disk), and ray florets around the margin.

Follicle A dry, dehiscent fruit, opening along one side only.
Free Not joined to other organs.
Fruit A ripened ovary which contains matured seeds, ready for dispersal.
Fused At least partially joined together, united.
Genus (plural genera) A unit of biological classification consisting of a group of species considered to be related through common descent, and indicated by sharing the same first name, cf. Species.
Gland An area on a plant which secretes a liquid, usually an oil or resin. When a plant has many glands, it is described as glandular; when the glands are situated on hairs, it is described as glandular-hairy.
Glochid A barbed hair.
Hair A small, usually slender outgrowth from a plant.
Head A dense flower cluster consisting of many stalkless flowers (see Fig.5).
Herb A non-woody annual, biennial, or perennial plant. If perennial, then dying back to ground level at the end of the season.
Herbaceous Having the texture of a herb; dying back to the ground each year.
Hermaphrodite Containing both male and female organs (stamens and carpels).
Hybrid A plant originating from the cross between two species.
Indehiscent Not opening at maturity to release the seed(s).
Inferior Of an ovary, located beneath the other flower parts (see Fig. 5).
Inflorescence The flower cluster of a plant, including the branches, bracts, and flowers (see Fig.4).
Inserted The point of attachment, e.g. of stamens to the corolla.

heart-shaped

pinnately lobed

palmately lobed

Compound Leaves

pinnate

dissected

palmate

Introduced Not native; having been brought to the country by man within historic times.

Involucre A set of bracts forming a structure like a calyx, beneath an inflorescence. Often used specifically for the structure beneath the condensed, head-like inflorescence of the members of the Sunflower family.

Irregular Bilaterally symmetrical.

Lance-shaped Of a leaf (see Fig. 3).

Latex Milky juice or sap.

Linear Of a leaf (see Fig. 3).

Lobed Of leaves, divided but with the divisions cutting less than halfway to the midrib. The leaves are therefore not divided into leaflets (see Fig. 3).

Membranous Thin and flexible, but usually not green.

Midrib The central vein of a leaf.

Mycorrhiza An association between the roots of certain plants and soil fungi. Orchids cannot survive without their mycorrhizal partners.

Native Endemic; not introduced by man.

Naturalized Well established and growing wild in an area, but coming from another region or part of the world.

Nectary A gland which secretes nectar, usually found on the receptacle or the petals of the corolla.

Node A point on a stem where leaves or roots, or both, arise.

Nodule A small swelling.

Nutlet A small, dry, indehiscent fruit with a relatively thick wall and only one seed.

Opposite Two organs, such as leaves, growing opposite each other at a node (see Fig. 2).

Ovary The part of a flower which contains the ovules (see Fig. 5).

Ovate Of a leaf (see Fig. 3).

Ovule The structure which contains the

Fig. 4 Inflorescence Types

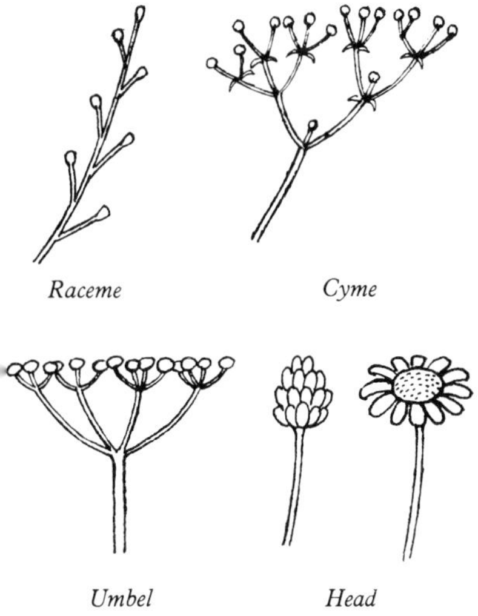

egg. It develops into a seed after fertilization.

Palmate Of leaves, divided into three or more lobes or leaflets, all arising from the same point on the leaf stalk (see Fig. 3).

Pappus The crown of hairs, bristles, or scales on the achene of a member of the Sunflower family.

Parasite A plant which obtains its water and nutrients from another plant to which it becomes attached.

Perennial A plant which lives for several years, usually flowering each year, and (of herbaceous perennials) dying back at the end of the growing season.

Perianth The petals and sepals together.

Perianth Segments The separate "segments" which make up the perianth — they may be like petals or like sepals. This term is often used

Fig. 5 Parts of a Flower

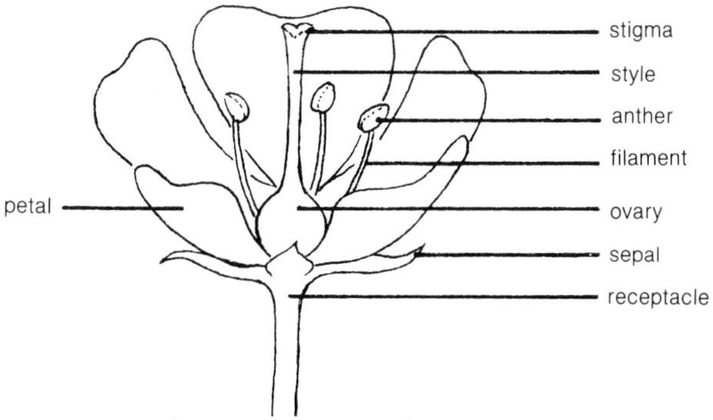

when the all the parts of the perianth are similar, and there is no clear division into sepals and petals.

Persistent Remaining attached to the fruit, especially of sepals or petals.

Petal One segment of the corolla. The petals are often brightly colored and may have nectaries at the base (see Fig. 5).

Pinnate A compound leaf composed of more than three leaflets, arranged in two rows on either side of the central axis or midrib (see Fig. 3).

Pod A dry, dehiscent fruit which opens along both sides. Usually used specifically to describe the fruits of the Pea family.

Pollen Grains The structures which develop inside the anthers, and which contain the male cells. They are carried to the stigma and there develop a pollen tube which grows down the style, carrying the male nucleus with it. When the pollen tube reaches the ovary, the male nucleus fuses with the ovule and the fertilized ovules develop into seeds.

Pollination The carrying of pollen from the anthers to the stigma. It is usually transferred by wind or by insects.

Prickle A sharp outgrowth from a stem or leaf, but irregularly arranged, cf. Spine.

Prostrate Lying flat on the ground.

Raceme An inflorescence with an elongated unbranched central axis, and flowers growing on stalks on each side. The lowermost flowers open first. In theory a raceme can go on elongating indefinitely as the youngest flowers are at the growing tip (see Fig. 4).

Receptacle The flat end of a flower stalk on which the flower parts arise (see Fig.5).

Regular Radially symmetrical.

Rhizome A perennial, underground stem, growing horizontally. Rhizomes may act as an overwintering device, as a food storage organ, or as a method of spreading the plant.

Rosette A basal clump of leaves, appearing to radiate outward from a single spot.

Saprophyte A plant which lacks green coloring and which feeds on dead organic material, often with the help of mycorrhizal fungi.

Scale A thin, membranous bract or leaf.

Seed A ripened ovule.

Sepal One segment of the calyx. The sepals are usually green and leaf-like, and together they enclose and protect the flower bud (see Fig. 5).

Serrated Of a leaf, with a toothed margin where the teeth are pointed.

Simple Of a leaf, with a single, undivided blade.

Sinuate Of a leaf, with a wavy margin (see Fig. 3).

Species A group of similar-looking individual plants which can interbreed

Fig. 6 Flower Types

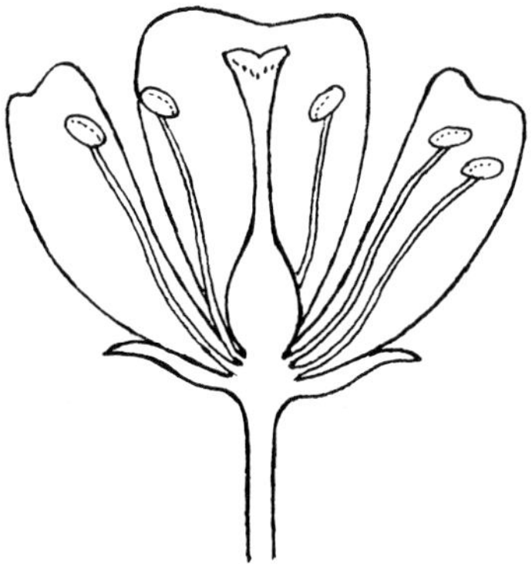

Flower with a superior ovary

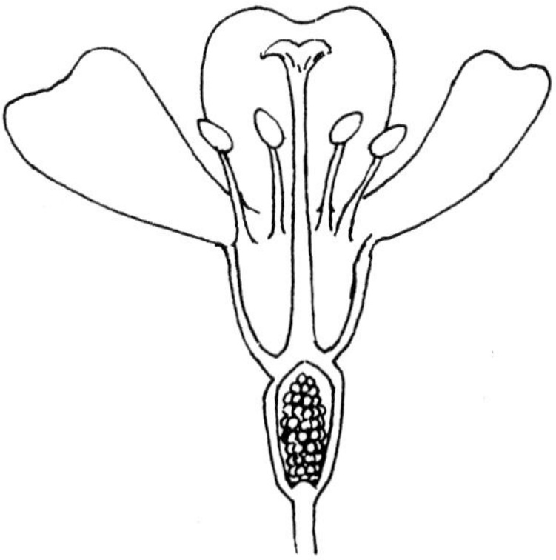

Flower with an inferior ovary

and produce similar-looking offspring true to type.

Spike Strictly, a raceme in which the flowers lack stalks. In a more general use, any spike-like inflorescence.

Spine A stiff, sharp-pointed projection from a plant, often a modified leaf or stipule, cf. Prickle.

Spur A hollow, often slender projection from the base of a sepal or petal, usually containing nectar.

Stamen One of the male reproductive organs of a flower (see Fig. 5).

Sterile Incapable of producing viable pollen (of stamens), or seed (of plants).

Stigma The receptive tip of the style, on which pollen grains must land and adhere for pollination to occur (see Fig. 5).

Stipule An often leaf-like appendage found at the base of the leaf stalk where the stalk is attached to the stem. They usually occur in pairs, one on each side of the stalk (see Fig. 1).

Style The structure at the top of the ovary, connecting it to the stigma where the pollen grains land (see Fig. 5).

Superior Of an ovary, located above the other floral parts and free from them (see Fig. 5).

Tendril A climbing organ, formed from part of a stem or leaf. In the Pea family, where tendrils are common, they are formed from the terminal leaflet of a compound leaf.

Tuber A thickened portion of a root or rhizome, acting as a food storage organ.

Tubercle A rounded swelling.

Tunic The dry, often brown and papery covering around a bulb or corm.

Umbel An umbrella-like inflorescence in which all the flower stalks arise from the same point on the stem (see Fig. 4).

Weed A plant growing where it is not wanted.

Whorl A circle of three or more leaves or flowers growing from a node (see Fig. 2).

Acknowledgments

The author and publisher would like to thank the libraries of the British Museum (Natural History), the Royal Horticultural Society, and the Linnean Society for their help.

Index

(Figures in **bold** type indicate illustrations.)

Acanthus family 154–5
Adder's-tongues (*Erythonium* spp.) 199
Agave family 195
Agaves (*Agave* spp.) **195**
Agoseris, Orange (*Agoseris aurantiaca*) **189**
Agrimony (*Agrimonia gryposepala*) **62**
Alumroot (*Heuchera americana*) **56**
  Midland (*H. richardsonii*) 56
Amaranth family 19
Amaranths (*Amaranthus* spp.) 19
Amaryllis family 205
Anemones (*Anemone* spp.) 37
  Canada (*A. canadensis*) **37**
  Desert (*A. tuberosa*) **38**
  Wood (*A. quinquefolia*) 37
Arnicas (*Arnica* spp.) 179
  European (*A. montana*) 179
  Heartleaf (*A cordifolia*) **179**
Arrowhead (*Sagittaria latifolia*) **194**
Arum, Arrow (*Peltandra virginica*) **210**, 211
  Water (*Calla palustris*) **211**
Arum family 210–11
Aster, Golden (*Chrysopsis villosa*) 170, **171**
Asters, Wild (*Aster* spp.) 172
  New England (*A. novae-angliae*) **172**
  Small White (*A. vimineus*) 172, **173**
  Smooth (*A. laevis*) **172**
Aster, Tansy (*Machaeranthera tanacetifolia*) **169**
Astilbes (*Astilbe* spp.) 56
Avens (*Geum* spp.) 58
  Water (*G. rivale*) **58**
Azalea, Alpine (*Loiseleuria procumbens*) **110**

Baby Blue-eyes (*Nemophila menziesii*) **131**
Baneberries (*Actaea* spp.) 32
  Red (*A. rubra*) **32**
  White (*A. alba*) 32
Barberry family 38
Barrel Cactuses (*Ferocactus* spp.) 29
  Red (*F. acanthodes*) **29**
Batchelor's Buttons (*Centaurea cyanus*) **187**
Beardtongues (*Penstemon* spp.) 146
Bedstraw family 122–3
Bedstraws (*Galium* spp.) 122
  Lady's (*G. verum*) **122**
  Northern (*G. boreale*) **122**
Bee Plant, Rocky Mountain (*Cleome serrulata*) 47
  Yellow (*C. lutea*) **47**
Bee-balm (*Monarda didyma*) **141**
Beeblossom, Scarlet (*Gaura coccinea*) **95**
Bellflower family 158–9
Bellflowers (*Campanula* spp.) 158
  Tall (*C. americana*) **158**
Bellworts (*Uvularia* spp.) 201
Bergamot (*Monarda fistulosa*) 141
Betony, Wood (*Pedicularis canadensis*) **149**
Bindweed, Field (*Convolvulus arvensis*) **128**
  Hedge (*Calystegia sepium*) **128**
Birthwort family 42
Biscuitroot (*Lomatium macrocarpum*) **105**
Bitter Cresses (*Cardamine* spp.) 49
  Pennsylvania (*C. pensylvanica*) 49
Bitter-root (*Lewisia rediviva*) 20
Black-eyed Susan (*Rudbeckia hirta*) **161**
Blanket Flowers (*Gaillardia* spp.) 162
Blazing Star, Giant (*Mentzelia láevicaulis*) 90
Blazing Stars (*Liatris* spp.) 183
  Dense (*L. spicata*) 183
  Prairie (*L. pycnostachya*) 183
  Rough (*L. aspera*) **183**
Bloodroot (*Sanguinaria canadensis*) **45**
Blue Flag (*Iris versicolor*) **206**
Blue Star (*Amsonia tabernaemontana*) **119**
Blue-eyed Grasses (*Sisyrinchium* spp.) 207
  Pointed (*S. angustifolium*) **207**
Blue-eyed Mary (*Collinsia verna*) **147**
Blue-weed (*Echium vulgare*) **133**
Bluebell family 158–9
Bluebell, Virginia (*Mertensia virginica*) **133**
Bluebuttons (*Knautia arvensis*) **157**
Bluets (*Houstonia caerulea*) **123**
Boneset (*Eupatorium perfoliatum*) **182**
Borage family 132–5
Brickellbushes (*Brickellia* spp.) 183
  Large-flowered (*B. grandiflora*) **183**
Brodiaeas (*Brodiaea* spp.) 204
  Harvest (*B. elegans*) **205**
Brooklime, American (*Veronica americana*) **148**
Broomrape family 152
Broomrapes (*Orobanche* spp.) 152
  Spike (*O. multiflora*) **152**
Brown-eyes (*Oenothera clavaeformis*) **97**
Buckbean family 118
Buckbean (*Menyanthes trifoliata*) **118**
Buckwheat family 12–15
Buckwheats (*Eriogonum* spp.) 15
  Flat-crowned (*E. deflexum*) 15

Bugbane, False (*Trautvetteria carolíniensis*) 32, **33**
Bur-marigold (*Bidens cernua*) **163**
Burdock, Greater (*Arctium lappa*) 187
Lesser (*A. minus*) **187**
Burnet, Canadian (*Sanguisorba canadensis*) **59**
Bush Clovers (*Lespedeza* spp.) 68
Slender (*L. virginica*) **68**
Butter-and-eggs (*Linaria vulgaris*) **147**
Buttercup family 30–7
Buttercups (*Ranunculus* spp.) 34–5
Common (*R. acris*) **34**
Cursed (*R. sceleratus*) **34**
Butterfly-weed (*Asclepias tuberosa*) **120**
Butterweeds (*Senecio* spp.) 178

Cactus family 26–9
Cactuses 26–9
Barrel (*Ferocactus* spp.) 29
Claret Cup (*Echinocactus triglochidiatus*) **27**
Fishhook (*Mammillaria* spp.) 28
Foxtail (*Coryphantha vivipara*) 28
Hedgehog (*Echinocereus* spp.) 27
Plains Nipple (*Coryphantha missouriensis*) **28**
Saguaro (*Carnegiea gigantea*) **27**
Simpson's Ball (*Pediocactus simpsonii*) **28**
Camass, Death (*Zigadenus paniculatus* & *venenosus*) **202**
Camass Lilies (*Camassia* spp.) 202
Eastern (*C. scilloides*) **202**
Western (*C. quamash*) 202
Campions (*Silene* spp.) 24
Starry (*S. stellata*) **24**
Cancer-root (*Orobanche uniflora*) **152**
Caper family 47
Cardinal Flower (*Lobelia cardinalis*) **159**
Carrion Flower (*Smilax herbacea*) **203**
Carrot family 100–5
Carrot, Wild (*Daucus carota*) **100**
Catchflys (*Silene* & *Lychnis* spp.) 24
Cat's-ear (*Hypochoeris radicata*) **190**
Catnip (*Nepeta cataria*) **137**
Cattail, Common (*Typha latifolia*) **208**
Narrow-leaved (*T. angustifolia*) 208
Cattail family 208
Celandine (*Chelidonium majus*) **45**
Chamomile (*Anthemis nobilis*) 176
Corn (*A. arvensis*) 176
Stinking (*A. cotula*) 176
Chamomile, Scentless (*Tripleurospermum inodorum*) **176**
Charlock (*Sinapis arvensis*) **51**
Jointed (*Raphanus raphanistrum*) **49**
Checkermallow (*Sidalcea neomexicana*) **85**
White (*S. candida*) 85
Chia (*Salvia columbariae*) 140
Chickweeds (*Stellaria* spp.) 23
Common (*S. media*) **23**
Star (*S. pubera*) **23**
Chickweeds, Mouse-ear (*Cerastium* spp.) 22
Chicory (*Cichorium intybus*) **188**
Chollas (*Opuntia* spp.) 26
Teddy Bear or Jumping (*O. bigelovii*) **26**, 27
Tree (*O. imbricata*) **26**
Cinquefoils (*Potentilla* spp.) 60
Canadian (*P. canadensis*) 60
Common (*P. simplex*) 60
Rough-fruited (*P. recta*) **60**
Sticky (*P. glandulosa*) **60**, 61
Tall (*P. arguta*) **61**
Clarkias (*Clarkia* spp.) 94
Lovely (*C. concinna*) 95
Tongue (*C. rhomboidea*) **95**
Cleavers (*Galium aparine*) **123**
Clematises (*Clematis* spp.) 33
Clovers, Bush (*Lespedeza* spp.) 68
Clovers, Sweet (*Melilotus* spp.) 73
Clovers (*Trifolium* spp.) 72
Bighead (*T. macrocephalum*) **72**
Cow (*T. wormskjoldii*) 73
Hop- (*T. agrarium*) **73**
Red (*T. pratense*) **72**
White (*T. repens*) **72**
Cocklebur (*Xanthium strumarium*) **166**
Cohosh, Blue (*Caulophyllum thalictroides*) **38**
Coltsfoot, Sweet (*Petasites palmatus*) **179**
Columbines (*Aquilegia* spp.) 31
Blue (*A. coerulea*) **31**
Garden (*A. vulgaris*) 31
Wild (*A. canadensis*) **30**, 31
Coral Bells (*Heuchera sanguinea*) 56
Coralroots (*Corallorhiza* spp.) 217
Spotted (*C. maculata*) **217**
Cowberry (*Vaccinium vitis-idaea*) 110, **111**
Cranberry (*Vaccinium macrocarpon*) **110**
Cranesbills (*Geranium* spp.) 76
Carolina (*G. carolinianum*) **76**
Richardson's (*G. richardsonii*) **77**
Spotted (*G. maculatum*) **76**
Cream Cups (*Platystemon californicus*) **46**
Cresses 49, 51, 52
Bitter (*Cardamine* spp.) 49
Garden (*Lepidium sativum*) 51
Rock (*Arabis* spp.) 52
Spring (*Cardamine bulbosa*) **49**
Yellow or Marsh (*Rorippa islandica*) **48**, 49
Crowberry (*Empetrum nigrum*) **111**
Crowberry family 110–11
Crowfoot family 30–7

Crowfoots (*Ranunculus* spp.) 34
Seaside (*R. cymbalaria*) **35**
White Water- (*R. aquatilis*) **35**
Crownbeard, Golden (*Verbesina encelioides*) **163**
Cucumber, Bur- (*Sicyos angulatus*) **89**
Wild (*Echinocystis lobata*) **89**
Cucumber family 89
Cudweeds (*Gnaphalium* spp.) 180
Low (*G. uliginosum*) **180**, 181
Cup Plant (*Silphium perfoliatum*) **167**
Cynthia, Two-flowered (*Krigia biflora*) **192**

Daisy family 160–93
Daisy, Ox-eye (*Chrysanthemum leucanthemum*) **177**
Seaside (*Erigeron glaucus*) **173**
Dandelion (*Taraxacum officinalis*) **190**
Desert (*Malacothrix glabrata*) **189**
Fall (*Leontodon autumnalis*) 190, **191**
Dandelions, Mountain (*Agoseris* spp.) 189
Dayflower, Asiatic (*Commelina communis*) **209**
Deadnettle, Purple (*Lamium purpureum*) 139
White (*L. album*) 139
Deerweed (*Lotus scoparius*) 73
Delphinium, Plains (*Delphinium virescens*) 31
Desert Gold (*Linanthus aureus*) **127**
Desert Trumpet (*Eriogonum inflatum*) **15**
Dill (*Anethum graveolens*) **104**
Docks (*Rumex* spp.) 12
Bitter or Broad-leaved (*R. obtusifolius*) **13**
Curled or Sour (*R. crispus*) **13**
Dodders (*Cuscuta* spp.) **129**
Dogbane (*Apocynum androsaemifolium*) **118**, 119
Dogbane family 118–19
Dogweed, Common (*Dyssodia pentachaeta*) **167**
Downingias (*Downingia* spp.) 159
Toothed (*D. cuspidata*) **159**
Dragon's Mouth (*Arethusa bulbosa*) **215**
Dutchman's Breeches (*Dicentra cucullaria*) **44**
Dutchman's Pipe (*Aristolochia durior*) **42**
Dusty Maiden (*Chaenactis douglasii*) 164, **165**

Easter-bell (*Stellaria holostea*) 23
Elecampane (*Inula helenium*) **180**
Elephant Heads (*Pedicularis groenlandica*) 149
Eriogonum, Flat-crowned (*Eriogonum deflexum*) **15**
Evening Primrose family 92–7
Evening Primroses (*Oenothera* spp.) 96–7
Common (*O. biennis*) **96**
Showy (*O. speciosa*) **96**
Birdcage (*O. deltoides*) **97**
Everlasting, Pearly (*Anaphalis margaritacea*) 180
Eyebright (*Euphrasia americana*) **150**

Fairy Candelabra (*Androsace septentrionalis*) **112**
Fairy Slipper (*Calypso bulbosa*) **217**
Fameflower (*Talinum teretifolium*) **21**
Farewell-to-spring (*Clarkia amoena*) 94, **95**
Featherfoil (*Hottonia inflata*) **115**
Fennel (*Foeniculum vulgare*) **104**
Fiddleneck (*Amsinckia intermedia*) **135**
Figwort family 144–51
Figwort (*Scrophularia lanceolata*) **145**
Filaree (*Erodium cicutarium*) **77**
Fire-on-the-mountain (*Euphorbia heterophylla*) **81**
Fireweed (*Chamaenerion angustifolium*) **92**
Fishhook Cactuses (*Mammillaria* spp.) 28
Tangled (*M. microcarpa*) **28**
Flax family 80
Flax, Wild (*Linum perenne*) **80**
Fleabanes (*Erigeron* spp.) 173
Daisy (*E. annuus*) **173**
Floating Hearts (*Nymphoides aquatica & cordata* **118**
Flower-of-an-hour (*Hibiscus trionum*) **82**
Foamflower (*Tiarella cordifolia*) **55**
Forget-me-not family 132–5
Forget-me-nots (*Myosotis* spp.) 134
Water (*M. scorpioides*) **134**
Forget-me-nots, White (*Cryptantha* spp.) 134–5
Four-o'clock family 16–17
Four-o'clock, Trailing (*Allionia incarnata*) **17**
Four-o'clocks (*Mirabilis* spp.) 17
Colorado (*M. multiflora*) **17**
Foxglove (*Digitalis purpurea*) **148**
Fritillaries (*Fritillaria* spp.) 198
Frostweed (*Helianthemum canadense*) **88**
Fumitory, Common (*Fumaria officinalis*) **44**
Fumitory family 44
Fuchsia, California (*Zauschneria californica*) **94**

Gaillardia, Showy (*Gaillardia pulchella*) **162**
Gallant Soldier (*Galinsoga parviflora*) **165**

Gentian, Autumn or Northern (*Gentianella amarella*) **116**, 117
Gentian family 116–17
Gentians (*Gentiana* spp.) 116
  Closed (*G. andrewsii*) 117
  Downy (*G. puberula*) **116**
  Fringed (*G. crinita*) **116**
Geranium family 76–7
Gerardia, Purple (*Agalinis* or *Gerardia purpurea*) **149**
Gilias (*Gilia* spp.) 126
  Banded (*G. cana*) **126**
  Blue-headed (*G. capitata*) **126**
Gill-over-the-ground (*Glechoma hederacea*) **138**
Ginger, Wild (*Asarum canadense*) **42**
Ginseng, American (*Panax quinquefolius*) **99**
Ginseng family 98–9
Globemallows (*Iliamna* & *Sphaeralcea* spp.) 84
  Mountain (*Iliamna rivularis*) **84**
  Scarlet (*Sphaeralcea coccinea*) **84**
Goatsbeard (*Aruncus dioicus*) **58**, 59
  False (*Astilbe biternata*) **56**, 57
Golden Alexanders (*Zizia* spp.) **104**
Golden-eyed Grass (*Sisyrinchium californicum*) **207**
Goldenrods (*Solidago* spp.) 168
  Canadian (*S. canadensis*) **168**
  Showy (*S. speciosa*) **169**
  Stiff (*S. rigida*) **168**
Goldenweed, Stemless (*Haplopappus acaulis*) **171**
Goldflower, Stemless (*Hymenoxis acaulis*) **162**
Goosefoot family 18
Goosefoots (*Chenopodium* spp.) 18
Gourd family 89
Grass of Parnassus (*Parnassia* spp.) **57**
Grass-pink (*Calopogon pulchellus*) **216**
Greenbriars (*Smilax* spp.) 203
Ground Cherries (*Physalis* spp.) 143
  Clammy (*P. heterophylla*) **143**
Groundnut (*Apios americana*) **69**
Groundsels (*Senecio* spp.) 178
  Common (*S. vulgaris*) **178**
  Threadleaf (*S. douglasii*) **179**
Gumplants (*Grindelia* spp.) 170
Gumweed, Curlycup (*Grindelia squarrosa*) **170**

Harebell (*Campanula rotundifolia*) **158**
Hawkweeds (*Hieracium* spp.) 191
  Narrow-leaved (*H. umbellatum*) **191**
  Mouse-ear (*H. pilosella*) **191**
Heath family 108–11
Heathers, Moss (*Cassiope* spp.) 109
  Mountain (*C. mertensiana*) **109**
Heathers, Mountain (*Phyllodoce* spp.) 109
Heliotrope, Salt (*Heliotropium curassavicum*) **132**
  Wild (*Phacelia distans*) **130**
Helleborine, Giant (*Epipactis gigantea*) 214, **215**
Hemlock (*Conium maculatum*) **102**
  Water (*Cicuta maculata*) **102**
Hemp-nettle (*Galeopsis tetrahit*) **138**
Henbane (*Hyoscyamus niger*) **142**, 143
Henbit (*Lamium amplexicaule*) **139**
Hepatica, Round-leaved (*Hepatica americana*) **37**
  Sharp-leaved (*H. acutiloba*) 37
Herb Robert (*Geranium robertianum*) **77**
Heucheras (*Heuchera* spp.) 56
  Poker (*H. cylindrica*) 56
Hog-peanut (*Amphicarpa bracteata*) **69**
Honeydew (*Horkelia cuneata*) **62**
Honeysuckle family 156
Honeysuckles (*Lonicera* spp.) 156
  Trumpet (*L. sempervirens*) **156**
Hop-clover (*Trifolium agrarium*) 73
Horehound, Cut-leaved Water (*Lycopus americanus*) **141**
  White (*Marrubium vulgare*) **137**
Horkelias (*Horkelia* spp.) 62
Horseweed (*Conyza canadensis*) **171**
Houndstongue (*Cynoglossum officinale*) **132**, 133
Hyacinth, Wild (*Camassia scilloides*) 202
  White (*Triteleia hyacinthina*) **205**
Hyssop, Giant (*Agastache urticifolia*) **136**, 137

Indian Breadroot (*Psoralea esculenta*) 71
Indian Fig (*Opuntia humifusa*) 26
Indian Hemp (*Apocynum cannabinum*) **119**
Indian Paintbrushes (*Castilleja* spp.) 150
Indian Pipe family 107
Indian Pipe (*Monotropa uniflora*) **107**
Indigo, Wild (*Baptisia tinctoria*) **74**
Inside-out Flower, Northern (*Vancouveria hexandra*) **38**
Iris family 206–7
Irises (*Iris* spp.) 206
  Red (*I. fulva*) **206**, 207
Ironweeds (*Vernonia* spp.) 181
  New York (*V. noveboracensis*) **181**
Ivesia, Gordon's (*Ivesia gordonii*) **62**

Jack-in-the-pulpit (*Arisaema triphylla*) **211**
Jack-o'-the-rocks (*Heuchera rubescens*) **56**
Jacob's Ladder (*Polemonium* spp.) 125
  Showy (*P. pulcherrimum*) **124**, 125
Jerusalem Artichoke (*Helianthus tuberosus*) 161

Jimsonweed (*Datura stramonium*) **142**
Joe-pye Weed (*Eupatorium maculatum*) **182**

Kinnikinnick (*Arctostaphylos uva-ursi*) **108**
Knapweeds (*Centaurea* spp.) 186
  Spotted (*C. maculosa*) **186**
Knotweed (*Polygonum aviculare*) **14**

Ladies-tresses (*Spiranthes* spp.) **216**
  Nodding (*S. cernua*) 216
Lady's Thumb (*Polygonum persicaria*) **14**
Lady's-slippers (*Cypripedium* spp.) 212
  Showy (*C. reginae*) **212**, 213
  Yellow (*C. calceolus*) **212**
Lamb's Quarters (*Chenopodium album*) **18**
Larkspurs (*Delphinium* spp.) 30
  Carolina (*D. carolinianum*) **30**
  Spring (*D. tricorne*) 30
Leadplant (*Amorpha canescens*) **70**
Leadwort family 111
Leek, Wild (*Allium tricoccum*) **204**
Lettuces (*Lactuca* spp.) 192
  Florida (*L. floridana*) **193**
  Garden (*L. sativa*) 192
  Wild (*L. canadensis*) **193**
Lettuce, White (*Prenanthes albus*) **188**
Licorice, European (*Glycyrrhiza glabra*) 70
  Wild (*G. lepidota*) **70**
Lilies, Camass (*Camassia* spp.) 202
Lilies, Fawn (*Erythronium* spp.) 199
  Yellow (*E. grandiflorum*) **199**
Lilies (*Lilium* spp.) 198
  Canada (*L. canadense*) **198**
  Columbia (*L. columbianum*) 198
  Wood (*L. philadelphicum*) **198**
Lilies, Mariposa (*Calochortus* spp.) 197
  Sego (*C. nuttallii*) **197**
Lily, Checker (*Fritillaria lanceolata*) **199**
  Corn (*Clintonia borealis*) **201**
  Day (*Hemerocallis fulva*) **196**
  Desert (*Hesperocallis undulata*) **196**
  Wood (*Clintonia umbellulata*) 201
Lily family 196–205
Liverleafs (*Hepatica* spp.) 37
Lizard's Tail family 39
Lizard's Tail (*Saururus cernuus*) **39**
Locoweeds (*Oxytropis* spp.) 65
  Late Yellow (*O. campestris*) **65**
  Purple (*O. lambertii*) **65**
Loosestrife family 91
Loosestrifes (*Lysimachia* spp.) 114
  Fringed (*L. ciliata*) 114
Loosestrifes (*Lythrum* spp.) 91
  Purple (*L. salicaria*) **90**, 91
  Winged (*L. alatum*) **91**
Lopseed family 155
Lopseed (*Phryma leptostachya*) **155**
Lotus, Hill (*Lotus humistratus*) 71
  Spanish (*L. purshianus*) **71**
Lotus Lily or American Lotus (*Nelumbo lutea*) **41**
Louseworts (*Pedicularis* spp.) 149
Lupins (*Lupinus* spp.) 74
  Blue-pod (*L. polyphyllos*) **74**
  Tree (*L. arboreus*) **74**

Madder family 122–3
Madia, Common (*Madia elegans*) **166**
Mallow family 82–5
Mallows 83–5
  Alkali (*Sida hederacea*) **85**
  Checker (*Sidalcea* spp.) 85
  Common (*Malva neglecta*) **82**, 83
  Globe (*Iliamna* & *Sphaeralcea* spp.) 84
  Musk (*Malva moschata*) **83**
  Poppy (*Callirhöe* spp.) 84
  Wheel (*Modiola caroliniana*) **83**
Mandarin, Rose (*Streptopus roseus*) 201
  White (*S. amplexifolius*) 200, **201**
Manzanitas (*Arctostaphylos* spp.) 108
Mariposa Tulips (*Calochortus* spp.) 197
  Club-haired (*C. clavatus*) **197**
  Sagebrush (*C. macrocarpus*) **197**
Marsh Marigold (*Caltha palustris*) **35**
May Apple (*Podophyllum peltatum*) **38**
Mayweed (*Anthemis cotula*) **176**
Meadow Beauty family 98
Meadow Beauties (*Rhexia* spp.) 98
  Common or Virginia (*R. virginica*) **98**
Meadow Rues (*Thalictrum* spp.) 32
  Early (*T. dioicum*) **32**
Medick, Black (*Medicago lupulina*) **73**
Michaelmas Daisies (*Aster* spp.) 172
Milkvetches (*Astragalus* spp.) 64
  Canada (*A. canadensis*) **64**, 65
  Mottled (*A. lentiginosus*) **64**
Milkvine, Fringed (*Sarcostemma cynanchoides*) **121**
Milkweed family 120–1
Milkweeds (*Asclepias* spp.) 120
  Common (*A. syriaca*) **120**, 121
  Showy (*A. speciosa*) **120**, 121
  Whorled (*A. verticillata*) **121**
Milkwort, Sea (*Glaux maritima*) **113**
Miner's Lettuce (*Montia perfoliata*) **20**
Mint family 136–41
Mint, Wild (*Mentha arvensis*) **141**
Miterwort (*Mitella diphylla*) **55**
Moneywort (*Lysimachia nummularia*) **114**, 115
Monkey-flowers (*Mimulus* spp.) 144
  Common (*M. guttatus*) **144**
  Square-stemmed (*M. ringens*) **144**, 145
Monkshoods (*Aconitum* spp.) 31
  Western (*A. columbianum*) **31**

Morning Glory, Common (*Ipomoea purpurea*) **129**
Morning Glory family 128–9
Moschatel (*Adoxa moschatellina*) **155**
Moschatel family 155
Moss Heathers (*Cassiope* spp.) 109
  Mountain (*C. mertensiana*) **109**
Mountain Heathers (*Phyllodoce* spp.) 109
  Cream (*P. glandulifera*) 109
  Pink (*P. empetriformis*) **109**
Mouse-ear Chickweeds (*Cerastium* spp.) 22
  Common (*C. fontanum*) **22**
  Field (*C. arvense*) **22**
Mugwort (*Artemisia vulgaris*) **174**
Mulleins (*Verbascum* spp.) 145
  Common (*V. thapsus*) **145**
Mustard, Black (*Brassica nigra*) 50, **51**
  Hedge (*Sisymbrium officinale*) **50**
  Tansy (*Descurainia pinnata*) **53**
  Tumbling (*Sisymbrium altissimum*) 50
Mustard family 48–53

Nettle, Desert Rock (*Eucnide urens*) **90**
  Spurge (*Cnidoscolus stimulosus*) 81
  Stinging (*Urtica dioica*) **12**
Nettle family 12
Nightshade, Enchanter's (*Circaea alpina*) **94**
Nightshade family 142–3
Nightshades (*Solanum* spp.) 142
  Black (*S. nigrum*) **142**
Nipplewort (*Lapsana communis*) **193**

Obedient Plant (*Physostegia virginiana*) **139**
Onions (*Allium* spp.) 204
  Nodding (*A. cernuum*) **204**
Oraches (*Atriplex* spp.) 18
  Common (*A. patula*) **18**
Orchid, Bracted (*Habenaria viridis*) **213**
  Ragged Fringed (*H. lacera*) **213**
  White Bog (*H. dilatata*) **212**, 213
Orchid family 212–17
Orchis, Showy (*Orchis spectabilis*) **214**
  Small Roundleaved (*O. rotundifolia*) 214
Owl's-clovers (*Orthocarpus* spp.) 151
  Yellow (*O. luteus*) **151**
Ox-eye (*Heliopsis helianthoides*) **160**, 161

Paintbrushes, Indian (*Castilleja* spp.) 150
  Desert (*C. chromosa*) **150**, 151
  Giant Red (*C. miniata*) 151
  Indian (*C. coccinea*) **151**
  Wyoming (*C. linariaefolia*) 150
Parsley family 100–5
Parsnip (*Pastinaca sativa*) **103**
  Cow (*Heracleum lanatum*) **103**
  Water (*Sium suave*) **103**
Partridge-berry (*Mitchella repens*) **123**
Pasque Flower (*Anemone patens*) **36**, 37
Passion Flower family 88
Passion Flower (*Passiflora incarnata*) **88**
Pea & Bean family 64–75
Pea, Beach (*Lathyrus japonicus*) **67**
  Butterfly (*Clitoria mariana*) **69**
  Silver Scurf (*Psoralea argophylla*) **70**
Pearlworts (*Sagina* spp.) 24
  Procumbent (*S. procumbens*) **25**
Peas, Wild (*Lathyrus* spp.) 66
Penstemon, Bush (*Penstemon fruticosus*) **146**
  Southwestern (*P. barbatus*) **146**
Peppergrass (*Lepidium virginicum*) **51**
  Western (*L. montanum*) 51
Periwinkles (*Vinca major* & *minor*) **119**
Peyote (*Lophophora williamsii*) **29**
Phacelia, Common (*Phacelia distans*) 130
  Variable (*P. heterophylla*) **130**
Phlox family 124–7
Phloxes (*Phlox* spp.) 124
  Annual (*P. drummondii*) 124
  Desert Mountain (*P. austromontana*) **124**
  Garden (*P. paniculata*) **124**
Pigweed (*Amaranthus retroflexus*) **19**
Pimpernel, Scarlet (*Anagallis arvensis*) **113**
Pineapple Weed (*Matricaria matricarioides*) **177**
Pinedrops (*Pterospora andromedea*) **107**
Pinesap (*Monotropa hypopitys*) 107
Pink family 22–5
Pink, Fire- (*Silene virginica*) **24**
  Wild (*S. caroliniana*) 24
Pipsissewa (*Chimaphila umbellata*) **106**
Plantain family 153
Plantains (*Plantago* spp.) 153
  Common (*P. major*) **153**
  English (*P. lanceolata*) **153**
Pokeweed family 16
Pokeweed (*Phytolacca americana*) **16**
Popcorn Flower (*Plagiobothrys nothofulvus*) **135**
Poppy, California (*Eschscholtzia californica*) **46**
  Wind (*Stylomecon heterophylla*) **46**
Poppy, Corn or Red (*Papaver rhoeas*) 46
  Fire (*P. californica*) 46, **47**
Poppy family 45–7
Poppy Mallows (*Callirhöe* spp.) 84
Potato-vine, Wild (*Ipomoea pandurata*) 129
Prairie Parsleys (*Lomatium* spp.) 105
Prairie Smoke (*Geum triflorum*) **58**

Prairie Star (*Lithophragma parviflora*) **57**
Prickly Pears (*Opuntia* spp.) 26
  Plains (*O. polyacantha*) **26**
Primrose, Bird's-eye (*Primula mistassinica*) 114
  Parry's (*P. parryi*) 114
Primrose family 112–15
Primulas (*Primula* spp.) 114
Prince's Plumes (*Stanleya* spp.) 53
  Golden (*S. pinnata*) **53**
Puccoon (*Lithospermum* spp.) 132
  Hoary (*L. canescens*) **132**
Pumpkin, Wild (*Cucurbita foetidissima*) **88**, 89
Purple Mat (*Nama demissum*) **131**
Purslane family 20–1
Purslane (*Portulaca oleracea*) **21**
Pussytoes (*Antennaria* spp.) 181
  Plantain-leaved (*A. plantaginifolia*) **181**

Queen of the Prairie (*Filipendula rubra*) **59**

Rabbit Brush (*Chrysothamnus nauseosus*) **169**
Ragweed, Common (*Artemisia artemisifolia*) **165**
  Great (*A. trifida*) 165
Ragworts (*Senecio* spp.) 178
  Golden (*S. aureus*) **178**
Rattleboxes (*Crotalaria* spp.) 75
  Showy (*C. spectabilis*) **75**
Rattlesnake Master (*Eryngium yuccifolium*) **105**
Rattlesnake Plantains (*Goodyera* spp.) 216
  Western (*G. oblongifolia*) **216**
Red Maids (*Calandrinia ciliata*) **21**
River-beauty (*Epilobium latifolium*) **92**
Rock Cresses (*Arabis* spp.) 52
  Hairy (*A. hirsuta*) **52**
  Spreading (*A. divaricarpa*) 52
Rockrose family 88
Rose family 58–63
Rose Pink (*Sabatia angularis*) **117**
Roses (*Rosa* spp.) 63
  Pasture (*R. carolina*) **63**
Rosinweeds (*Silphium* spp.) 167
Rosita (*Centaurium calycosum*) **117**
Ruellia (*Ruellia caroliniensis*) **154**, 155

Sagebrush, Big (*Artemisia tridentata*) **174**
Sage, Wood (*Teucrium canadense*) **136**
Sages (*Salvia* spp.) 140
  Desert or Purple (*S. dorrii*) **140**
St John's-wort, Common (*Hypericum perfoliatum*) **43**
  Marsh (*Triadenum virginicum*) **43**
St John's-wort family 42–3
Salsify, Yellow (*Tragopogon dubius*) **188**
Sand Spurrey (*Spergularia rubra*) **25**
Sand Verbenas (*Abronia* spp.) **16**, 17
  Desert (*A. villosa*) 17
Sarsaparilla, Wild (*Aralia nudicaulis*) **98**, 99
Saxifrage family 54–7
Saxifrages (*Saxifraga* spp.) 54
  Early (*S. virginiensis*) **54**, 55
  Purple (*S. oppositifolia*) **54**
  Spotted (*S. bronchialis*) **54**
Sea Sandwort (*Honkenya peploides*) **25**
Seedbox (*Ludwigia alternifolia*) **93**
Selfheal (*Prunella vulgaris*) **138**
Sennas (*Cassia* spp.) 75
  Wild (*C. hebecarpa* & *C. marilandica*) **75**
Shepherd's Purse (*Capsella bursa-pastoris*) **48**
Shooting Stars (*Dodecatheon* spp.) 112
  Western (*D. pulchellum*) **112**, 113
Silverweed (*Potentilla anserina*) **60**
  Pacific (*P. egedei*) 61
Skunk Cabbage (*Symplocarpus foetidus*) **211**
Skunkweed (*Navarretia squarrosa*) **125**
Sky Rocket (*Ipomopsis aggregata*) **126**
Smartweed family 12–15
Snake-mouth (*Pogonia ophioglossoides*) **214**
Snakeroot, Black (*Sanicula marilandica*) **101**
Snakeweed, Broom (*Gutierrezia sarothrae*) **170**
Snapdragon family 144–51
Snapdragons (*Antirrhinum* spp.) 147
  Common (*A. majus*) **147**
Sneezeweed (*Helenium autumnale*) **164**
Solomon's Seal, False (*Smilacina racemosa*) **200**
Solomon's Seal tribe 200
Solomon's Seals (*Polygonatum* spp.) 200
  Smooth (*P. biflorum*) **200**
Sorrel, Mountain (*Oxyria digyna*) **14**
Sorrels (*Rumex* spp.) 13
  Sheep (Common or Red) (*R. acetosella*) **12**, 13
Sorrels, Wood (*Oxalis* spp.) 78
Sow-thistle, Prickly (*Sonchus asper*) **192**
  Smooth (*S. oleraceus*) 192
Spanish Bayonets (*Yucca* spp.) 195
Speedwells (*Veronica* spp.) 148
  Common (*V. officinalis*) **148**
  Germander (*V. chamaedrys*) 148
  Thyme-leaved (*V. serpyllifolia*) 148
Spiderwort family 209
Spiderworts (*Tradescantia* spp.) 209
  Virginia (*T. virginiana*) **209**
Spikenard (*Aralia racemosa*) **99**

Spikeweed, Common (*Hemizonia pungens*) **167**
Spring Beauty (*Claytonia virginica*) **20**
Spurge family 80–1
Spurges (*Euphorbia* spp.) 80
Cypress (*E. cyparissias*) **80**, 81
Squawroot (*Conopholis americana*) **152**
Squirrelcorn (*Dicentra canadensis*) 45
Starflower (*Lithophragma parviflora*) 57
Starflower (*Trientalis borealis*) **115**
Starworts (*Stellaria* spp.) 23
Long-stalked (*S. longipes*) 23
Stickleaf family 90
Stickleafs (*Mentzelia* spp.) 90
White-stemmed (*M. albicaulis*) **90**
Stickseeds (*Hackelia* spp.) 134
Many-flowered (*H. floribunda*) **134**
Stitchwort, Lesser (*Stellaria graminea*) 23
Storksbills (*Erodium* spp.) 77
Common (*E. cicutarium*) 77
Strawberries, Wild (*Fragaria* spp.) **61**
Sulphur Flower (*Eriogonum umbellatum*) **15**
Sundew family 41
Sundew, Round-leaved (*Drosera rotundifolia*) **41**
Sunflower family 160–93
Sunflower, Woolly (*Eriophyllum lanatum*) **164**
Sunflowers (*Helianthus* spp.) 160
Common (*H. annuus*) **160**
Swamp Candles (*Lysimachia terrestris*) **114**
Sweet Cicely (*Osmorhiza claytoni*) **101**
Sweet Clover, White (*Melilotus alba*) 73
Yellow (*M. officinalis*) **73**
Sweetbriar (*Rosa eglanteria*) **63**
Sweetflag (*Acorus calamus*) **210**

Tansy (*Tanacetum vulgare*) **175**
Tarragon (*Artemisia dracunculus*) 174
Tarweeds (*Hemizonia* & *Madia* spp.) 166
Teasel (*Dipsacus fullonum*) **157**
Teasel family 157
Thimbleweed (*Anemone virginiana*) 37
Thistle, Milk (*Silybum marianum*) **186**
Musk or Nodding (*Carduus nutans*) **185**
Russian (*Salsola iberica*) 18
Thistles (*Cirsium* spp.) 184–5
Bull (*C. vulgare*) **184**
Canada (*C. arvense*) **184**
Yellow (*C. horridulum*) **185**
Thoroughworts (*Eupatorium* spp.) 182
Thrift (*Armeria maritima*) **111**
Tick-trefoils (*Desmodium* spp.) 68
Showy (*D. canadense*) **68**
Tickseed-sunflower (*Bidens aristosa*) 163
Tickseeds (*Coreopsis* spp.) 162
Plains (*C. tinctoria*) **162**
Tiny Trumpet (*Collomia linearis*) **127**
Toadflaxes (*Linaria* spp.) 147
Blue (*L. canadensis*) 147
Toadshade (*Trillium sessile*) 203
Tobaccos (*Nicotiana* spp.) 143
Desert (*N. trigonophylla*) **143**
Touch-me-not family 79
Touch-me-not, Pale (*Impatiens pallida*) **79**
Spotted (*I. capensis*) **79**
Tread-softly (*Cnidoscolus stimulosus*) **81**
Trefoil, Bird's-foot (*Lotus corniculatus*) **71**
Trillium, Nodding (*Trillium cernuum*) **203**
Purple (*T. erectum*) **203**
Red (*T. sessile*) 203
Triteleias (*Triteleia* spp.) 204
Tumbleweed (*Amaranthus albus*) 19
Russian (*Salsola iberica*) 18, **19**
Turtlehead (*Chelone glabra*) **144**, 145
Twayblades (*Listera* spp.) 215
Broad-leaved (*L. convallarioides*) **215**
Twinflower (*Linnaea borealis*) **156**

Valerian family 156–7
Valerians (*Valeriana* spp.) 157
Downy-fruited (*V. acutiloba*) **156**, 157
Velvet-leaf (*Abutilon theophrastii*) **82**
Venus' Comb (*Scandix pecten-veneris*) **101**
Venus' Looking-glass (*Triodanis perfoliata*) **158**, 159
Vervain, Blue (*Verbena hastata*) **154**
European (*V. officinalis*) 154
Vervain family 154
Vetches (*Vicia* spp.) 66
American (*V. americana*) **66**
Common (*V. sativa*) 66
Cow (*V. cracca*) **66**
Vetch, Crown (*Coronilla varia*) **67**
Vetchling (*Lathyrus palustris*) **67**
Vinegar Weed (*Trichostema lanceolatum*) **136**
Violet family 86–7
Violet, Green (*Hybanthus concolor*) **87**
Violets (*Viola* spp.) 86–7
Canada (*V. canadensis*) 87
Common Blue (*V. papilionacea*) **84**
Downy Yellow (*V. pubescens*) **86**, 87
Eastern Dog (*V. conspersa*) 87
Kidney-leaved (*V. renifolia*) **87**
Western Dog (*V. adunca*) **86**
Yellow Prairie (*V. nuttallii*) **87**
Virgin's Bower (*Clematis virginiana*) **33**

Wake-robins (*Trillium* spp.) 202
Wallflower, Garden (*Erysimum* or *Cheiranthus cheiri*) 52
  Western or Plains (*Erysimum asperum*) **52**
Water Horehound, Cut-leaved (*Lycopus americana*) 141
Water Lily family 40–1
Water Lily, Fragrant (*Nymphaea odorata*) **40**
  Yellow (*Nuphar polysepalum*) **40**
Water Pennywort (*Hydrocotyle americana*) **100**
Water Plantain (*Alisma plantago-aquatica*) **194**
Water Plantain family 194
Water Willow (*Decodon verticillatus*) **91**
Watercress (*Nasturtium officinale*) **48**
Waterleaf family 130–1
Waterleafs (*Hydrophyllum* spp.) 131
  Fendler's (*H. fendleri*) 131
  Virginia (*H. virginiana*) **131**
White Forget-me-nots (*Cryptantha* spp.) 134–5
  Common (*C. intermedia*) **135**
Whitlow Grass (*Draba verna*) **52**, 53
Wild Oats (*Uvularia sessilifolia*) **201**
Willowherbs (*Epilobium* spp.) 92
  Parched (*E. paniculatum*) **93**
Windmills (*Allionia incarnata*) **17**
Winecups (*Callirhöe involucrata*) **84**
Wingstem (*Verbesina occidentalis*) 163
Wintercress (*Barbarea vulgaris*) **50**
Wintergreen family 106
Wintergreen (*Gaultheria procumbens*) **108**, 109
Wintergreens (*Pyrola* spp.) 106
  Shortleaf (*P. virens*) **106**
  White (*P. elliptica*) **106**
Wood Sorrel family 78
Wood Sorrels (*Oxalis* spp.) 78
  Upright Yellow (*O. corniculata*) 78
  Violet (*O. violacea*) **78**
  Yellow (*O. europaea*) **78**
Wool Stars (*Eriastrum* spp.) 125
  Sapphire (*E. sapphiricum*) **125**
Wormwood (*Artemisia absinthium*) 174
Woundwort (*Stachys palustris*) **140**

Yarrow (*Achillea millefolium*) **175**
Yellow Cups (*Oenothera brevipes*) **97**
Yellow Flag (*Iris pseudacorus*) **206**
Yellow Rattle (*Rhinanthus crista-galli*) **150**
Yellow Star Grass (*Hypoxis hirsuta*) **205**
Yellow-eyed Grass family 208
Yellow-eyed Grasses (*Xyris* spp.) **208**
Yerba Mansa (*Anemopsis californica*) **39**
Yucca, Blue (*Yucca baccata*) **195**

Zinnia, Plains (*Zinnia grandiflora*) **161**